# The Old World, the New World, and the Creation of the Modern World, 1400–1650

# The Old World, the New World, and the Creation of the Modern World, 1400–1650

## An Interpretive History

Aaron M. Shatzman

**ANTHEM PRESS**
LONDON · NEW YORK · DELHI

Anthem Press
An imprint of Wimbledon Publishing Company
*www.anthempress.com*

This edition first published in UK and USA 2013
by ANTHEM PRESS
75–76 Blackfriars Road, London SE1 8HA, UK
or PO Box 9779, London SW19 7ZG, UK
and
244 Madison Ave #116, New York, NY 10016, USA

*British Library Cataloguing-in-Publication Data*
A catalogue record for this book is available from the British Library.

*Library of Congress Cataloging-in-Publication Data*
Shatzman, Aaron M.
The old world, the new world, and the creation of the modern world,
1400–1650 : an interpretive history / Aaron M. Shatzman.
pages cm
Includes bibliographical references and index.
ISBN 978-0-85728-333-7 (hardback : alk. paper) – ISBN
978-0-85728-328-3 (pbk. : alk. paper)
1. America–Discovery and exploration–Europe. 2.
Europe–Colonies–America. I. Title.
E101.S54 2013
970.01–dc23
2013025577

ISBN-13: 978 0 85728 333 7 (Hbk)
ISBN-10: 0 85728 333 2 (Hbk)

ISBN-13: 978 0 85728 328 3 (Pbk)
ISBN-10: 0 85728 328 6 (Pbk)

Cover image: Theodor de Bry, "Columbus, as he first arrives in India, is received by the
inhabitants and honored with the bestowing of many gifts" (1594). Courtesy of the
University of Houston Digital Library.

This title is also available as an eBook.

*To Karen*


*And for my teachers:*
*Carl N. Degler, John M. Murrin and*
*David M. Potter*

# CONTENTS

# LIST OF FIGURES

# LIST OF ORIGINAL SOURCE MATERIAL

# PREFACE

This book has been a long time in the making. Four decades have passed since my first attempt to write about European colonization in the Americas, in a 34-page essay submitted to Professor Carl N. Degler, who supervised a Winter Quarter reading course in my third year at Stanford. Since he had just completed *Neither Black nor White*, which compared slavery and its consequences in Brazil and the United States, for which he would win the Pulitzer Prize, Degler was very interested in comparative history and familiar with the literature on European colonization in the Americas.

The reading course had allowed me to survey the existing secondary literature in English that examined the era of discovery, exploration, conquest and colonization. I titled my paper "England, France and Spain in America: A Speculative Essay" because I wanted not only to summarize the material I had studied, but also to try to draw some meaning from it and to try to construct an interpretive framework that would organize my discussion of the activities Europeans engaged in as they populated a new world.

Degler read my essay with great care and a critical eye. He made no effort to spare my feelings as he jotted his observations in the manuscript's margins: "not the French," he cautioned; "false alternative," he objected; "you are fudging," he insisted; "*non sequitur*," he pointed out. His summary comments, however, were somewhat kinder than the marginal notations: "A very thoughtful, often original—if sometimes unconvincing—essay. Your compression of many facts into a small compass of argument without losing the train of argument is highly commendable. The section on openness of New World and ideal societies is imaginative."

I had been introduced to the topic of "Comparative Empires" as an undergraduate at Washington University in St. Louis by Professor John M. Murrin. It was he who made history so compelling that I knew I wanted to spend my life trying to understand the past, the history of early America in particular. Murrin ignited my interest not only in English America but also in how the English colonial experience compared with that of the French and the Spanish. During my junior year he insisted that if I wished to study European colonization of the Americas I needed to supplement my mastery of Spanish with at least a reading ability of French. So I enrolled in French 101. He also taught me to think critically. I remember him telling a group of his students that whenever we encountered an idea or a theory, our first response should be to turn it upside down to see if it made as much sense backwards as it did forwards, or if an alternative view might be supported. And he spoke with special admiration, even reverence, about one of his Yale professors, David Potter. Potter had left Yale for Stanford a few years earlier. I wanted to train with the person who had had such a profound influence on my mentor. Thus, although it might seem counter-intuitive to study the history of early America on the West Coast, I headed to Palo Alto.

I sent a copy of my "Speculative Essay" to John Murrin, and we continued to discuss the topic of comparative colonization after he left Washington University to join the history faculty at Princeton. Murrin had just received a contract from Dushkin Publishers to coordinate the first six chapters (Discovery through the American Revolution) of *The Study of American History*, a comprehensive text to be written by a team of scholars. He invited me to participate and together we wrote the first chapter titled "The Americas Become Europe's Frontier." I also authored Chapter Two, "Patterns of Colonial Settlement," and Chapter Five, "The Puritans." The first two chapters were comparative—we devoted as much attention to French and Spanish America as we did to English America. We incorporated some of the ideas from my Stanford essay about the way what Europeans found in the areas they colonized interacted with what they brought with them to the New World to shape the future.

This groundbreaking book offered readers not only a narrative of events but key excerpts from important historians' writings about the subject at hand and a sampling of original source material. Working on this book brought me into direct contact with a wide range of published source material as I searched for original documents that might be included. I recall my great disappointment at not being able to publish more than brief edited versions of the documents we did use, and even more at the way space and budget restrictions forced us to eliminate important material that would have made the book better.

Over the years since *Study* was published, I have continued to refine my ideas about the subject as I have taught it. My Comparative Empires students at both Washington University in the 1980s and at Franklin and Marshall College in the 1990s had to grapple with topics that had occupied historians long before the field of Atlantic history became popular in the last decade. Among the lessons I learned as instructor is that students are eager to read, to think about and to discuss the original documents that historians use to determine what happened in the past, to suggest why events unfolded as they did and to support interpretations that promise to explain the *what*, the *when*, the *how* and the *why*.

My students have been especially interested in looking at graphic evidence and in thinking about the reasons contemporaries were motivated to create visual accounts of events, why they chose to include or exclude specific material and why images are depicted in a certain way. Over the years I have collected a substantial amount of such source material, shared it with my students and learned what is useful or provocative and what fails to generate the response I hoped to elicit when I assigned it as part of a homework project or when I presented it for class discussion. And I have gained from them a pretty clear sense of how much background information (about the people, places, events, etc.) they need to know in order to be able to analyze written or visual evidence without reaching ahistorical conclusions.

I have presented some of the material in this book to members of civic groups and at public lectures. Through the college's Speakers Bureau I frequently appear as a presenter at programs that attract audiences filled with people who are neither historians nor students of history. Three of my formal lectures, "Do Americans Have a National Character?," "The Origins of Slavery and Race Prejudice," and "The Old World and the New World: The Columbian Exchange Revisited," focus on events and themes that are important parts of this book.

Six years ago I hosted Montgomery County Community College's first Fulbright Scholar-in-Residence, Dr. Fernando da Silva Camargo, professor of history at Passo Fundo University in Brazil. Our special and enduring friendship began with conversations about the history of the Americas, about the similarities and differences in our colonial pasts, and about the way we study and teach our respective histories. One spring afternoon Fernando joined me when I delivered a Speakers Bureau lecture to a women's service group at a local library. During my presentation I talked about the impact of open space and the frontier on early settlers and on the development of their plans for the future; and about the way some American historians have argued that the frontier experience had a determining impact on shaping the American national character. This was all new to him, an eminent scholar from a country whose history has been compared with that of the United States in important books. As we drove back to campus Fernando said, "We have nothing like this in Brazilian historiography." During his semester here we spent many hours talking about slavery in the Americas and several memorable days in his campus office reading and translating into English colonial documents relating to slavery from the Portuguese and Spanish empires. It was during his visit that I seriously began to think of expanding my lectures into a book. A few days after Fernando and I delivered a campus lecture about the impact of the European encounter with the Americas on the Old World and on the New World I began to write what is now Chapter Two, an early draft of which he read.

I am also grateful to colleagues at the college who reviewed the manuscript or parts of it. Geographers Sam Wallace and Wayne Brew offered valuable advice on the series of historical maps in Chapter Two. Anthropologist Lynn Swartley O'Brien read the material on the Native American civilizations in Spanish America and helped me to understand more fully the complexity of relationships among the Inca and tributary cultures. African and African American historian Theresa Napson-Williams reviewed my discussion of slavery in the Americas and made helpful suggestions. Her colleagues, historians Stephen Blumm and Lawrence Backlund read the entire manuscript and provided me with many suggestions to improve the narrative. Although I did not incorporate every recommendation, the book is much the better for my colleagues' careful and thoughtful reading.

Among my goals in writing this book has been to use visual evidence in a way that will not merely decorate the text but, far more important, serve as part of the argument itself. All the images in the book are fully identified and attributed, in many cases to open source sites or to the commercial agents of the museums which license their reproduction. But some of the images I wanted the reader to see are so rare, or difficult to acquire, that a special effort to secure them needed to be made, an effort that would have proved fruitless had not a few dedicated individuals offered assistance that deserves special recognition. To: Marianne Hansen, curator/academic liaison for rare books and manuscripts, Bryn Mawr College Library; David Frasier, reference librarian, and Joel Silver associate director and curator of books, Lilly Library (rare books and manuscripts), Indiana University libraries; James Siebold, Cartographic Images; and Megan Butcher, Risë Segal and Janet Murray, reference service librarians at the Library and Archives of Canada; I extend my gratitude for their interest in this project and for contributing significantly to its realization.

I also wish to thank Dr. Scott Ury, head of the Stephen Roth Institute for the Study of Contemporary Antisemitism and Racism at Tel Aviv University, and Professor Sara G. McNeil, Digital History at the University of Houston, for their assistance in obtaining the translation of Juan Ginés de Sepúlveda's Democrates Alter that is reprinted here.

Special thanks to Kathryn Ishler, a member of the information technology staff at the college. Her expertise and her mastery of technology were invaluable as I grappled with the challenges posed by incorporating material from a wide range of sources into the manuscript.

Two men whose names I do not know, and who will never read this book, also deserve words of gratitude—one an attendant in the Museo del Ejercito in Madrid opened a case so I could examine a cedar cross carved from the hull of one of Cortés's ships; the other a guard who unlocked the entrance to the Tinel in Barcelona in order to permit me to stand on the floor of the room where Ferdinand and Isabella received Christopher Columbus to hear his report of his first trip across the Atlantic.

My sincere thanks also to publisher Tej P. S. Sood at Anthem Press for believing in this project, and for providing the resources necessary for my vision for the book to be realized. And to my editor at Anthem, Rob Reddick, I express gratitude for offering sound advice, for helping me complete the process of transforming a manuscript into a monograph and for his impeccable standards of documentation and argument.

To my wife, Karen, who studied history before she studied medicine, and to our children Aliza and Ben, my love and my thanks for reminding me always by being part of my life that, although scholarship is important, there are more important things than writing books.

My objective has been to write a book that introduces the era of European expansion into the wider world from the fifteenth to the seventeenth centuries by providing the reader direct contact with those whose activities are being described. To accomplish this goal I have in many instances allowed the story to be told by the participants.

I have done so because of the incredible richness of the original source material that has survived—well known in many cases to historian specialists—but not widely available to students or those reading about the topic purely because they are interested. Commonly, in history books that offer readers a collection of original documents the sources, often heavily edited, are presented with a brief introductory note, but aside from that are devoid of context. Here the original material is actually part of the narrative.

There is an important reason for devoting nearly a third of the pages to source material: I believe it is far more powerful to let readers learn from eyewitnesses than from a researcher who summarizes the evidence. I could tell you that the Spaniards who accompanied Hernán Cortés into the Valley of Mexico were impressed by the Aztec capital when they entered the city across a causeway. Or I can let you read their breathless account of the experience. I have, wherever practicable in this book, chosen to do the latter. I know that this approach will make the book more difficult to read because the flow of the narrative inevitably will be interrupted. That inconvenience is minor when compared to the potential rewards of reading a first-hand description of an Aztec human sacrificial ceremony, an account of the martyrdom of Jesuit missionaries in Canada or a motivational speech by a Portuguese admiral urging his ship commanders to undertake an assault in the Far East. The book is full of such opportunities.

At the same time, I have tried to write a self-sustaining narrative history that provides readers with all the facts, covers all the important events and addresses all the relevant topics. The book takes a somewhat wider view than what is embraced by the currently "hot" field of Atlantic history. Here you will read not merely about Africa, Europe and the Americas in the age of empire creation, but also about the medieval antecedents to European expansion and the activities of the Portuguese in Asia—critically important if one wishes to understand why and how Europeans ventured across the Atlantic and established outposts in the Americas. Though the body of this book focuses on activities that took place between the years 1400–1650, the narrative begins with a discussion of the background to the era of discovery and colonization before 1400 and in a few instances extends past 1650. Thus, for example, the French experience in Canada is described through the royalization of the colony by King Louis XIV and his minister Jean Baptiste Colbert in 1663. Similarly, the impact of open space on the fate of the New England colonies extends the story of the Puritan experiment into the second half of the seventeenth century.

As the subtitle "An Interpretive History" suggests, I also aim to do more than describe the events and people whose histories comprise the story, supported by source material that makes the narrative richer. The story of European expansion is already pretty well known and there are more than a few excellent books available for anyone who wants to know the who, the how, the when, the why and the what. This book sets out to do more—to address (if not answer) another question: the *so what?*

To get at that question, in this book we will look at issues, events, documents—both written and visual—with an interpretive eye. Why did it matter that the earliest image of

Native Americans to circulate widely in Europe depicted the specific scene that the artist chose to portray? Why does the artist place European ships offshore on the horizon? Why should we be interested in reading accounts from early visitors to the Americas that contradicted inherited wisdom about the climate at certain latitudes? What might have been the consequences of reading such reports on the subsequent attitudes, practices or behavior of Europeans? What was the impact of open space, occupied spaces, the wilderness and the natural resources on the settlers, their settlements and those who sponsored their activities? If Europeans found abundance in the Americas (which they did), did it matter what form that abundance took, or that the natives could resist neither European arms nor germs? Could New Spain have developed as it did in Mexico and Peru had the Spanish settled instead in Virginia? Would English America have developed as it did had the English crown dictated a master plan for all the English colonies, as did the rulers of Spain and France for their colonial empires? What was it about English America that proved so attractive to potential settlers that the population of the English colonies far outpaced that of the French colonies, even though the population of France in 1600 was 20 million while that of England was only 4–5 million? Or, finally, consider a question from the final exam in my course, History 170: Comparative Empires: *In shaping the future which was more important, what Europeans brought with them to the New World or what they found when they got here?*

Addressing these and many other questions is the substance of this book. They are exactly the questions I asked in my Stanford "Speculative Essay" 40 years ago. I am somewhat surprised to report that, in spite of several decades of research and writing about the era of discovery, exploration and settlement by a host of superb scholars since I wrote it, they still remain worth investigating. I would like to think that when Carl Degler found my answers "thoughtful, often original—if sometimes unconvincing" the reason he was not persuaded was because I could not fully explore, much less provide answers to them in only 34 typed pages. I thank Anthem Press for giving me a sufficient number of pages to make my case.

*A. M. S.*
*Blue Bell, PA*
*Summer 2012*

# INTRODUCTION

Eighty years ago the president of the American Historical Association used the forum provided by his address at the group's annual meeting to tell the members that their work was parochial. Herbert Eugene Bolton observed that in studying their own nations' histories scholars had missed the themes that were common to the Americas.

There is need of a broader treatment of American history, to supplement the purely nationalistic presentation to which we are accustomed. European history cannot be learned from books dealing alone with England, or France, or Germany, or Italy, or Russia; nor can American history be adequately presented if confined to Brazil, or Chile, or Mexico, or Canada, or the United States. In my own country the study of thirteen English colonies and the United States in isolation has obscured many of the larger factors in their development, and helped to raise up a nation of chauvinists. Similar distortion has resulted from the teaching and writing of national history in other American countries.

For some three hundred years the whole Western Hemisphere was colonial in status. European peoples occupied the country, transplanted their cultures and adapted themselves to the American scene. Rival nations devised systems for exploiting natives and natural resources, and competed for profit and possession. Some of the contestants were eliminated, leaving at the end of the eighteenth century Spain, Portugal, England, and Russia as the chief colonial powers in America.

By this time most of the European colonies in America had grown up; they now asserted their majority. In the half century between 1776 and 1826, practically all of South America and two-thirds of North America became politically independent of Europe, and a score of nations came into being. Eventually, the entire Western Hemisphere, with minor exceptions, has achieved independent nationality. Since separation from Europe these nations alike have been striving on the one hand for national solidarity, political stability, and economic well being, and on the other hand for a satisfactory adjustment of relations with each other and with the rest of the world.

Our national historians, especially in the United States, are prone to write of these broad phases of American history as though they were applicable to one country alone.

It is my purpose, by a few bold strokes, to suggest that they are but phases common to most portions of the entire Western Hemisphere; that each local story will have clearer meaning when studied in the light of the others; and that much of what has been written of each national history is but a thread out of a larger strand.[1]

Bolton titled his 1932 address "The Epic of Greater America" and it reached a wide audience when published in the organization's journal, the *American Historical Review*, the following year. His was the first call by an influential scholar for historians to use a comparative approach in their work on the Americas. Bolton had taught at the University of Texas for nearly a decade before moving to Stanford in 1909 and finally to the University of California, from which he retired in 1940. All of these schools are located in areas that had been part of Spain's American empire and whose cultural legacy was as much Spanish as it was Anglo-American. During his long and productive career, Bolton's research focused on the Spanish borderlands. Hence it was hardly surprising that he prodded his fellow historians to be attentive to the way the "larger factors"[2] shared by many American nations could be ignored or missed if scholars focused their attention too narrowly.

Bolton noted that all the European colonizing powers confronted the frontier, established universities, imposed feudal or semi-feudal institutions on their colonies, adopted slavery or other forms of forced labor and employed mercantilist economic policies that benefitted the mother country. Bolton's analysis was superficial and his observations were hardly profound, which prompted the eminent Mexican historian Edmundo O'Gorman to write that:

> [T]he larger historical unities and interrelations of the Americas indicated by Professor Bolton appear to me, as unities which may be found in any group of men, simply because they have all been born and raised, they all eat and work. Larger unities no doubt, but unities of Nature and not of human nature, which is the essence of history.[3]

O'Gorman observed that Bolton had ignored fundamental differences among colonial societies. "Does he attach no significance," O'Gorman asked, "to the irreconcilable contrast between one past that is Protestant and another that is Catholic?"[4] Nevertheless, Bolton's call for treating the history of the Americas as a unified subject was influential. Numerous historians followed Bolton's lead.[5] Among the commonalities they identified:

- All European colonizers confronted and subdued Native Americans.
- All sponsors of colonial enterprises saw imperialism as a means to make their own nation rich, great powerful (at the expense of their rivals).
- All were interested in increasing scientific knowledge.
- All shared the European heritage of monarchical government, Christianity and a hierarchical social order.
- All sought economic profit from their colonial ventures.

These scholars have further noted that every European New World colony experienced, as it matured, a split between colonists and Europeans, and specifically between Americans born in America (who resented the special privileges and status enjoyed by the Europeans sent to officiate) and those born in Europe (who viewed those born in the colonies with the disdain one reserves for provincials). They have also pointed out that the economic relationship formed between colony and mother country during the colonial era endured well after independence. All American colonies had served as sources of raw materials and foodstuffs for their mother countries. They continued to do so after they became free nations.

Bolton had studied at the University of Wisconsin with the most prominent American historian of his generation, Frederick Jackson Turner, whose reputation had been established in 1893 when he delivered an address titled "The Significance of the Frontier in American History" at the AHA annual meeting in Chicago. Turner had startled his audience by asserting that the history of the United States was unique, and that the values and the institutions that marked America as great were uniquely American. These were revolutionary ideas. Throughout most of the nineteenth century, even as the nation expanded its borders and exercised ever-increasing influence globally, scholars both in the Americas and in Europe asserted that in large measure American success was the direct consequence of ideas, values and institutions that had been imported from Europe. The most respected (and widely read) scholars, such as Herbert Baxter Adams at the Johns Hopkins University, formulated what they labeled the "germ theory" of American development—the notion that Europeans brought ideological and institutional "seeds" to the American wilderness where, in a fertile environment, they developed and flourished. Baxter's thesis was evident in the title he chose for his most influential publication, *The Germanic Origin of the New England Towns*. American greatness, he argued, had less to do with America and Americans than with Europe and Europeans.

A Wisconsin native and University of Wisconsin graduate, Turner had been one of Adams's students in his American history seminar at Johns Hopkins. After completing his studies, Turner returned home to teach at the university. His seminal Chicago address, scheduled to coincide with the World's Fair celebrating the 400th anniversary of Christopher Columbus's voyage from Europe to America, proved to be nothing short of an intellectual declaration of American independence. Turner argued that the values that define America and Americans, in particular liberty and democracy, owed their origin not to the forests of Germany, but rather to life on the frontier, specifically the American frontier. "American democracy," Turner proclaims, "was born of no theorist's dream; it was not carried in the *Susan Constant* to Virginia, nor in the *Mayflower* to Plymouth. It came out of the American forest, and it gained a new strength each time it touched a new frontier."[6] Perhaps even more important, Turner insists, the character traits we perceive as typically *American* owe their development to the frontier experience. Independence, self-reliance, courage, perseverance, practicality, impatience, even wastefulness and anti-intellectualism—all characteristics that have defined "ideal" Americans—could be traced, Turner asserts, directly to life in the wilderness. Attitudes and behaviors that made sense in a decadent Old World mattered little when one had to overcome the challenges posed by life in the wilderness. What good was book learning or erudition if the task at hand was fording a raging stream in a storm or fighting off an attacking bear? What benefit would be derived from taking the time to erect magnificent stone bridges with carefully carved ornamental decorations which would endure for centuries when the need was to get across a river as soon as possible in order to reach fertile farmland on the prairie or fields of gold in the mountains?

In Turner's view, the frontier was an irresistible force that transformed Europeans into a new breed—*Americans*. In one memorable passage, he asserts:

[T]he frontier is the line of most rapid and effective Americanization. The wilderness masters the colonist. It finds him a European in dress, industries, tools, modes of travel, and thought. It takes him from the railroad car and puts him in the birch canoe. It strips off the garments of civilization and arrays him in the hunting shirt and the moccasin. It puts him in the log cabin of the Cherokee and Iroquois and runs an Indian palisade around him. Before long he has gone to planting Indian corn and plowing with a sharp stick; he shouts the war cry and takes the scalp in orthodox Indian fashion. In short, at the frontier the environment is at first too strong for the man. He must accept the conditions which it furnishes, or perish, and so he fits himself into the Indian clearings and follows the Indian trails ... From the conditions of frontier life came intellectual traits of profound importance. The works of travelers along each frontier from colonial days onward describe certain common traits, and these traits have, while softening down, still persisted as survivals in the place of their origin, even when a higher social organization succeeded. The result is that to the frontier the American intellect owes its striking characteristics. That coarseness and strength combined with acuteness and inquisitiveness, that practical, inventive turn of mind, quick to find expedients, that masterful grasp of material things, lacking in the artistic but powerful to effect great ends, that restless, nervous energy, that dominant individualism, working for good and for evil and withal that buoyancy and exuberance which comes with freedom—these are traits of the frontier, or traits called out elsewhere because of the existence of the frontier.[7]

In spite of the enduring power of Turner's ideas, an alternative approach to understanding America's past has gained traction with some scholars—an approach that harks back to the thesis postulated by nineteenth century historians such as Turner's teacher Herbert Baxter Adams. In 1964, Louis Hartz published *The Founding of New Societies*, in which he and four colleagues argue that in the Americas, South Africa and Australia Europeans used the open space they found to transplant ideas, behaviors, attitudes and practices that then developed unhindered. Without opposition from competing forces, what the Europeans originally brought with them became dominant in a way that never would have been possible in the Old World.

Hartz suggests that what Europeans brought were not entire societies, but rather pieces, or what he labels "fragments" of societies. In the free setting of a colonial environment, the "fragment culture" could develop without having to compromise with the rivals it had left behind. The result, he argues, was that colonial societies were dominated by single philosophies, that these came to be identified with the emerging nations and that alternatives failed to take root.

> When part of a European nation is detached from the whole of it, and hurled outward onto new soil, it loses the stimulus toward change that the whole provides. It lapses into a kind of immobility. Nor does it matter what stage of European history the part embodies, whether it is feudal, as in Latin America and French Canada, bourgeois, as in the United States, Dutch South Africa, and English Canada, or actually radical … as in Australia and British South Africa … When a fragment of Europe becomes the whole of a new nation, it becomes unrecognizable in European terms … When fragmentation … makes it master of a whole region, all sorts of magic inevitably take place. First of all it becomes a universal, sinking beneath the surface of thought to the level of an assumption. Then, almost instantly, it is reborn, transformed into a new nationalism arising out of the necessities of fragmentation itself. Feudalism comes back at us as the French-Canadian Spirit, liberalism as the American Way of Life, radicalism as the Australian Legend.[8]

The current text addresses the competing views of American development offered by Turner and Hartz. Treating the history of the Americas as a whole, as Bolton called for long ago, this book looks at the creation and early development of European outposts in the Americas by focusing both on what the early settlers brought with them (in terms of ideas, institutions, ambitions) and what they found in the areas they settled (in terms of geography, natural resources, indigenous peoples). In some cases, we will discover that what the colonists found allowed them and their sponsors to implement their plans without much interference. We will also find that not every master plan succeeded, that not every venture yielded results that met expectations. If the wilderness was not always an irresistible force that transformed Europeans and their Old World ideas into Americans and their New World ideas, in many cases what they found in America did compel Europeans to modify, sometimes even to abandon their original goals.

No matter where Europeans explored and settled in the Americas they encountered two constants: land and abundance. Sometimes the land was open and sparsely populated. In some areas, indigenous native peoples occupied spaces the Europeans wanted. In no case were Amerindians successfully able to resist domination by the technologically more advanced European invaders or decimation by the diseases they brought with them to the New World. But the interaction of Europeans with particular spaces will be a continuing theme here. So will the kind of abundance that Europeans found in the specific areas they occupied. In some cases the natives themselves were part of the abundance—they often served as a labor force for European masters who had displaced or annihilated their previous Native American masters. Sometimes the abundance was natural resources in the form of fertile land, forests with valuable naval stores and fur-bearing animals, or mineral assets such as gold and silver. How the form of the abundance Europeans found influenced their ability to realize their dreams is another thread that runs through the book.

Examining the impact of abundance and open space on the European colonization of the Americas will help us answer the interpretive question "so what?" as it pertains to the empires themselves and to the individual colonies or social experiments within colonies. But the book also seeks to answer the question as it pertains to discovery itself—what was the consequence of the European encounter with the Americas? Was it only an exchange of commodities, diseases, humans? Or was it more—perhaps significantly more? Can the European encounter with the wider world, and specifically with the Americas, be linked with the transition from the pre-modern to the modern world?

The first chapter covers the origins of European expansion into the wider world by looking at the world order during the Middle Ages and at the forces that motivated Europeans to take their first tentative steps to alter the situation in which they found themselves.

Chapter Two details Christopher Columbus's voyages to the West and Amerigo Vespucci's confirmation that what Columbus had found were not Asian islands, as he believed, but rather a new world. It then moves into an examination of written and visual evidence—including the first image of Native Americans to circulate widely in Europe and a series of maps—that informs a discussion of the significance of the discovery in the transition from the medieval to the modern world.

Chapter Three focuses on the Spanish seaborne empire and the motives that impelled the Spanish to explore, conquer and colonize the New World. It argues that the kinds of resources—both human and natural—that the Spanish found in the areas they colonized allowed them to institute and then to maintain a master plan that they brought with them from the Old World—a master plan designed to address many of the problems that they thought plagued their mother country. It includes vivid source material from Cortés's conquest of the Aztec Empire.

Chapters Four and Five look at Spain's rivals in America, examining French efforts to create a colony in Canada by trying to implement a master plan designed in France and the English settlements along the Atlantic coast, which differed from one another in that each had its own master plan. The natural resources of Canada and English America were not dissimilar. Nor were the types of Native American societies the English and French encountered. These chapters will allow us to consider the way what Europeans brought with them interacted with what they found in determining the future.

Chapter Six provides a summary of the book's argument and offers a few general observations about the impact of the sea and the land on Europeans' New World ventures.

## For Further Reading

Bailyn, Bernard, *Atlantic History: Concept and Contours* (Cambridge, MA, 2005).

Benjamin, Thomas, *The Atlantic World: Europeans, Africans, Indians and Their Shared History, 1400–1900* (Cambridge, 2009).

Breen, T. H., and Timothy D. Hall, *Colonial America in an Atlantic World* (New York, 2004).

Edgerton, Douglas R., Alison Games, Jane G. Landers, Kris Lane and Donald R. Wright, *The Atlantic World: A History* (Wheeling, 2007).

Elliot, J. H., *Do the Americas Have a Common Heritage?* (Providence, 1998).

Faragher, John Mack, (ed.), *Rereading Frederick Jackson Turner: "The Significance of the Frontier in American History" and Other Essays* (New York, 1994).

Hanke, Lewis (ed.), *Do the Americas Have a Common History? A Critique of the Bolton Theory* (New York, 1964).

Hartz, Louis, *The Founding of New Societies: Studies in the History of the United States, Latin America, South Africa, Canada, and Australia* (New York, 1964).

Kupperman, Karen Ordahl, *The Atlantic in World History* (Oxford, 2012).

## Notes

1 Herbert Eugene Bolton, "The Epic of Greater America," *American Historical Review* 38 (1933): 448–9.

2 Ibid.

3 Edmundo O'Gorman, *Do the Americas Have a Common History?*, Points of View 3 (Washington, DC, 1941), 1–10.

4 Ibid.

5 See, for example, William C. Binkley, Arthur P. Whitaker and Silvio Zavala.

6 Frederick Jackson Turner, "The Significance of the Frontier in American History," *American Historical Association Annual Report for 1893* (Washington, DC, 1894), 199–227.

7 Ibid.

8 Louis Hartz, *The Founding of New Societies: Studies in the History of the United States, Latin America, South Africa, Canada, and Australia* (New York, 1964), 3–4.

# Chapter One

# BEGINNINGS: EUROPE AND THE WIDER WORLD

*[F]or that up to his time, neither by writings, nor by the memory of man, was known with any certainty the nature of the land beyond that Cape ... And because the said Lord Infant wished to know the truth of this, since it seemed to him that if he or some other lord did not endeavor to gain that knowledge, no mariners or merchants would ever dare to attempt it—(for it is clear that none of them ever trouble themselves to sail to a place where there is not a sure and certain hope of profit)—and seeing also that no other prince took any pains in this matter, he sent out his own ships against those parts, to have manifest certainty of them all. And to this he was stirred up by his zeal for the service of God and of the King Edward his Lord and brother...*

—Gomes Eannes de Azurara, *Chronicle of the Discovery and Conquest of Guinea* (c. 1453)

## Background

Until the end of World War II, anyone looking at the political and economic condition in which the world's peoples found themselves had to note that Europeans were dominant nearly everywhere. In fact, global history in the following generation was largely the story of how native inhabitants of areas that had long been part of the colonial empire of one or another of the European powers finally regained control over their own destinies. Prior to such recent developments, European hegemony had been an established fact of world history for so long that for several centuries many observers simply took it for granted as a sign of divine will or European racial superiority, or both. But, in fact, Europeans had not always been masters; their global dominance was the result of activities that took place as recently as the nineteenth, and no earlier than the sixteenth, century. Before then, Europeans were anything but dominant, not only in a global context but even in parts of Europe itself.

When Europeans began to consider the possibilities of overseas ventures, the existence of North and South America was not known by Europeans nor any culture familiar to Europeans. Great civilizations were being built in America by Aztec, Inca, Maya and Mississippian Indians—civilizations that in many respects were more "advanced" than

Christendom—but these cultures developed in isolation from the rest of the world and thus for centuries remained unknown to it.

That is not to say, however, that educated Europeans in the late Middle Ages thought that there was no reason to venture out across the Atlantic Ocean. Virtually every informed person knew that the earth was round. In the sixth century BC, the Pythagoreans had said so, Aristotle said so, Plato said so—even in the Book of Isaiah there is a reference to the "circle of the earth." Since three continents were known, Europe, Asia and Africa, and since these were surrounded by water, across the Atlantic from Europe to the west must be Asia. Ancient scholars whom fifteenth-century Europeans considered wholly reliable had even asserted that it might be possible to travel from Europe to the Orient by sailing west. Strabo, a Greek geographer whose work became known in Europe in a published edition of 1469, reported that the authoritative Eratosthenes had said such a voyage was, in theory, capable of being made; and the Roman philosopher Seneca had agreed, predicting that a western world someday would be discovered. The most famous and authoritative of all geographers, Claudius Ptolemy (73–151 AD), whose *Geography* had been published in 1406 in Latin and in many versions after 1475, had grossly overestimated the length of the Eurasian land mass and underestimated the size of the globe. Potential explorers thus were led to believe that they could sail west in the Atlantic and in a reasonable period of time, reach the Orient, where silk, spices and untold wealth might be secured. Christopher Columbus of Genoa was one sailor familiar with such ancient wisdom.

In fact, there *was* a huge land mass across the Atlantic from Europe in almost precisely the location classical geographers had told people to expect to find Asia. That, of course, was America, not Asia. It took Europeans some time to accept the fact that a continental barrier existed that prevented them from sailing due west from home to China, Japan and India, and even longer to value America in its own right. At the outset, the existence of America was an impediment to the realization of those goals that motivated the first European explorers to sail west in the Atlantic. What they were after was a direct sea route to the Far East.

Even if they had known that the path across the Atlantic to Asia was blocked, some Europeans might have sailed there anyway. Numerous myths circulated in medieval Europe that exercised a powerful hold on the imagination and made voyages to the west seem attractive in their own right. From the time of the ancient Greeks, writers had speculated about the existence of a paradise to the west. The setting sun symbolized, for many, not merely that the day ended in the west, but also that the west was where humans went when life itself ended. Some may have thought that the Garden of Eden was there; others located mythical paradises, such as Avalon, where there was eternal beauty, peace, bounty and spring, beyond the horizon where the sun disappeared. Many were convinced that the fabled continent Atlantis, with its advanced civilization and immense wealth, had sunk in the western oceans. Christian lore described not only Irish monks who had set out in small boats and founded their own societies in marvelous and bountiful regions somewhere in the western seas, but also spice islands where Christians had fled to escape Moorish invaders, where they had erected ideal societies. One such island, Antilla, was reputed to be the site of seven perfect Christian cities, and there were men alive in the latter part of the fifteenth century who claimed to have met those who claimed to have been there. Other islands—Mayda, O Brazil, Estotiland and Buss were familiar in name to educated Europeans. As late as the nineteenth century, some maps included references to these places.

No matter how attractive these mythical earthly paradises may have seemed, Europeans were certain that China, Japan and India did exist, and their location, if not their distance from Europe, was known. If other places served as a vague attraction, the wealth of the Orient was a prize many believed lay within the grasp of anyone who could find a sponsor for the necessary voyage, and who had the training in seamanship and the courage to undertake such an endeavor.

In the late Middle Ages, in spite of a body of thought that might serve as a stimulus to expansion overseas, Europeans did not seem to be in any position to act in response to such motivations. Far more powerful, wealthy and "advanced" than Christian Europe was the Empire of the Grand Khan of China. In the thirteenth century, Mongols (Tartars) had gained control of Persia, the Middle East, China, part of Russia and even, for a time, a section of Germany. They controlled the trade routes from China to Europe along which caravans carried the silk and spices Europeans lusted after. The Chinese who produced silk and the islanders of the East Indies who produced spices were never seen by European consumers or even by the merchants based in Italian maritime cities, such as Genoa, Naples, Pisa and especially Venice, who secured their cargoes in Levantine ports, returned to Italy and then distributed the goods throughout Europe. Rather, eastern products passed through many non-Christian hands prior to reaching the Levant, as did the European specie that paid for them. Most Christians were galled to be enriching infidels, but the only alternative was to do without goods they ardently sought.

Buddhism and Islam dominated the heart of Asia, thereby excluding Christianity and cutting any direct contact between Europeans and the native Ming rulers of Cathay who had seized power from the Tartars during the fourteenth century. The East Indies, Hindu in religion and the source of the cinnamon, cloves and pepper needed to season and preserve meat in Europe, were by the fifteenth century coming under the control of Islam, which was simultaneously encroaching on the other center of Hindu strength, India. Other Muslim enemies of Christendom, the nomadic and warlike Ottoman Turks, were about to conquer Byzantium and all of the eastern Mediterranean. In 1453 they took Constantinople, and they continued their conquest until they had seized Egypt, Syria and the Balkans; they were near Vienna by 1529. The Moors, also Muslims, had occupied parts of the Iberian peninsula for years, and displayed no inclination to give it up to Christian rulers. If any group seemed in 1400 to be on the verge of erupting across natural barriers to conquer strange peoples and rule foreign lands it was the Muslims, not the Christians.

Externally weak and contracting in size when compared with other civilizations, Europe's internal life was characterized disorder and decline. Stable rule by a single powerful leader did not exist in Germany, Italy or Spain; instead, local "rulers" exercised power in competition with each other. Ivan III, Prince of Moscow, could not proclaim his independence of the Tartars until 1480. England and France were at war from 1337 to 1453, a period longer even than the conflict's name, the Hundred Years' War. Once peace with France was restored, England promptly unsettled itself in dynastic wars, which lasted until Henry VII came to the throne in 1485. When Louis XI died in 1483 disorders broke out in France. In Italy, while the Renaissance signaled a resurgence of culture and learning, the state and society were marked by treason, murder, plague and the appearance of *condottieri*, or private warriors who could be hired by anyone, and whose loyalties were always subject to change. As if civil disruption were not enough to discourage Europeans by sapping their power, the plague was. The Black Death began in Europe in 1347 and persisted in devastating the population for the next half-century.

With signs of decay all about them, Europeans began seriously to hunt witches. It was reasonable, after all, for people to assume that their troubles were the result of harboring the most wretched of sinners in their midst. There is no doubt that many Europeans responded to the chaos of life by actually seeking to enter pacts with the devil, by performing the "Dance of Death" in cemeteries or by celebrating "Black Masses." Others became flagellants—penitents who inflicted corporeal punishment on themselves to atone for their own and for others' sins.

Even the one institution that served to unite all Europe, the Roman Catholic Church, seemed to be breaking apart. Troubled men ardently called for reform of the church itself. Reformers such as Ockham and Wycliffe in England and Huss in Bohemia argued that clergymen who failed to fulfill their role, who lived both in the world and of it, could be bypassed by the laity who might seek and receive salvation on their own. Pleas for ecclesiastical reform were provoked by scrutinizing the Renaissance popes who had generally proved better and more interested in dealing with the material rather than the spiritual world.

## The Reformation and the Emergence of Nation-States

The future offered no peace for the church. In 1517, the German Martin Luther shattered the unity of Christendom when he formulated the basic principles of Protestantism. Other critics of the worldliness and corruption of the church had preceded Luther, most notably Erasmus of Rotterdam. But unlike Erasmus, Luther broke away from Rome, and his followers, combined with those of John Calvin in Switzerland, whose *Institutes* were published in 1536, were soon so numerous that the vision of a unified Christendom would never again be a reality.

Lutherans and Calvinists were reinforced when Henry VIII, among the strongest kings England had ever known, and who had once written a book attacking Luther, broke with Rome himself. Only the church, which owned nearly a quarter of England, was powerful enough to resist his commands and likely to do so because churchmen owed absolute loyalty to the pope, not to King Henry. In 1529, Henry asked the pope to grant him a divorce from Catherine of Aragon, who had failed to provide him with a male heir. The pope refused. Henry divorced Catherine anyway, married Anne Boleyn (who bore him a daughter, Elizabeth), assumed leadership of the "Church and Clergy of England" and seized the monastic lands. One crucial result of Henry's actions was that in divorcing his Spanish queen and breaking with Rome, he initiated more than a century of sporadic war between England and Catholic Spain. That conflict, both religious and political, became a central part of the larger international struggle between Protestants and Catholics, and would be transported to America where it affected events throughout much of the age of discovery, exploration and colonization.

In a Europe torn by civil and religious turmoil, mythical kingdoms of eternal peace and contentment must have seemed wonderfully alluring. By the middle of the fifteenth century, Europeans had begun to take steps that would ultimately lead them away from a troubled Old World and towards an open and abundant New World. At that time, a number of rulers came to power in Europe, imposed order and peace on their kingdoms, and asserted the power of the monarchy at the expense of the power of the nobility. These "New Monarchs" aroused feelings of nationalism in their subjects and used tax revenue to pay for armies, which guaranteed their sovereignty. One of them, Henry VII of England, was the first of the Tudor dynasty that ruled from 1485 until 1603. In France, Louis XI built a strong army, overawed his nobility and attacked the independent status of many French towns. During the more than 20 years he ruled, the French Estates-General (parliament) met only once. In 1469, Ferdinand of Aragon and Isabella of Castille were wed. While their marriage did not create a Spanish nation, the resulting cooperation of Aragon and Castille did lead in 1492 to the expulsion of the Moors from Spanish soil. More than loyalty to a monarch, it was loyalty to the Roman Church that united the Iberians. The Spanish crown willingly used the church, especially the Inquisition, to compel both unity and loyalty. Finally, in 1438 the seven electors who chose the ruler of the Holy Roman Empire (what is now Germany) selected Charles V, the Archduke of Austria, to be the emperor. He was a Hapsburg and the Hapsburgs retained the emperorship (with one break) from then until 1806. Charles V was the most powerful sovereign of the era, and the Hapsburgs would go on to rule central Europe, the Netherlands, Spain and large parts of Italy and America.

## Motives for Exploration

The New Monarchs not only built unified states with strong central governments which commanded the loyalty of their subjects, they also sought to amass knowledge of the seas and of the ships in which to sail over them. In the fifteenth and sixteenth centuries, rulers had many reasons to expend some of their wealth in financing overseas expeditions. All Christians despised Muslims; and if crusades to the Holy Land were not feasible then surely the infidel could be weakened by small-scale crusades aimed not at the Holy Land but at other Muslim strongholds. Not only might actual attacks be launched by seaborne forces but Christendom could use the seas to obtain the silk and spices it wanted without enriching Muslim merchants and princes in the process. Direct trade by sea with India and China would bypass the Arab intermediaries through whose hands such goods traditionally passed on the way to Europe. European rulers were also acutely aware of the defects that plagued the societies they ruled. If they sent out explorers to lay claim to and hold new territories across the seas, might they not be able to establish more "perfect" societies in areas where they could build from scratch? And were not the chances good that such expeditions would locate some of the islands which myth declared to be the location of paradise, or at least of boundless wealth which could be used to make them rich and powerful—rich and powerful enough to strike definitive blows at Islam? Was it not likely that their agents might encounter "lost" Christian kingdoms whose rulers would join forces with European Christians against their common enemies? And what of religious and national conflict within Europe itself—would not the acquisition of rich overseas territories maximize chances to dominate European affairs for the state that held them and inevitably lead to the predominance of its particular version of Christianity? All these factors motivated European leaders to listen attentively when men appeared at their courts seeking sponsorship for voyages across the oceans and to act favorably upon such requests.

## A Changing Economy

By the middle of the fifteenth century, Europe was in the midst of a commercial revolution, which had begun prior to the era of discovery but was greatly stimulated by the establishment of contacts with the wider world. In the Middle Ages, craftsmen generally produced goods on order and limited their dealings to a particular area, usually a specific town. But as trade areas broadened, it became clear that some could produce certain products better and more efficiently than others. Men with money, or capital, to invest were able to pay people in the country, where town guilds had little control over business, to produce goods for them and then to sell those products anywhere there was a market. Such men revolutionized the European economy and were eager to extend their business from the Europe-centered cloth, mining, printing, shipbuilding and armaments industries into the area of foreign trade. The opening of new markets and sources of supply in the wider world not only greatly stimulated such industries as shipbuilding and arms manufacturing; it also provided entrepreneurs with a field for trade which seemed limitless both in a geographical and an economic sense.

But the costs of financing overseas voyages were staggering. Few had sufficient capital to pay for such exploits; and those who did feared that the risks were too great. Ships might disappear or fleets might find nothing of value once they reached their destination. Thus entrepreneurs devised a method by which individuals with capital to invest could join together in such enterprises, each providing a part of the money necessary to secure ships, crews and trade goods. They would share profits in relation to the amount each had invested. Known as the "joint-stock company," this arrangement made the risks tolerable to financiers and was responsible for numerous enterprises of exploration, trade and settlement by Europeans in areas only recently opened for their activities.

Europeans believed that the world contained a fixed quantity of wealth in the form of precious metals and raw materials. Since this amount of wealth could not be increased, each nation sought to maximize its share both to ensure its own welfare and, equally important, to deprive its rivals of riches which would increase their power. The potential consequences of voyages of discovery and exploration profoundly influenced the hold of such ideas on European policymakers, for they recognized that the wider world contained sources of wealth they might secure for themselves—spices, silk, gemstones, gold and silver, as well as supplies of valuable raw materials and foodstuffs. European leaders reasoned that if they could gain control of territory overseas, its wealth would become their wealth, and their power and prosperity would increase at the expense of their rivals.

## Advances in Mapmaking and Navigation

By the fifteenth century, Europeans had mastered much of the technology necessary to engage in overseas expansion. In fact, without a "post-medieval" sense of geography and astronomy, advances in ship construction and the ability to sail them, and new ways of arming them, even the most efficiently governed medieval European state could not have succeeded overseas. Notions about rich and ideal territories in the western seas were powerful stimulants to programs of exploration, but seamen would have been reluctant to undertake western voyages if their only guide once underway were legendary reports of something that lay somewhere over the western horizon. In 1410, Cardinal Pierre d'Ailly wrote his *Imago Mundi*, a compendium of geographical information gleaned from ancient and medieval sources. The work is important because it supported the theory that Asia could be reached from Europe by sailing westwards across the ocean. It was one of two works that Columbus is known to have studied—a copy of the book published after 1480, preserved in the Biblioteca Colombina in Seville, is filled with his handwritten marginal notations.

The Arabs, believing the Atlantic impossible to sail, had done virtually no original exploring. But they were the Europeans' major source for ancient accounts of the shape of the world. European seamen also relied on portolans, or sea charts, which had been drawn by Italians since the thirteenth century. These were based on the actual experiences of real sailors and indicated the shape of known coastlines, as well as the location of useful ports in the Mediterranean, Black Sea, the part of the Atlantic near Europe and sometimes Africa. In the middle of the fifteenth century, these charts were greatly improved by the ability to ascertain latitude. Once again, it was the Arabs who held such knowledge, which Christian Europeans learned from Portuguese and Italian Jews whose religion did not prohibit dealings with Muslims. Arab astronomers had added to the work of classical scholars by making their own observations of the heavens; by the fifteenth century, Arab seamen navigated by taking bearings on well-known stars. Such methods were communicated to European navigators who then adapted and developed them to solve more difficult problems than Arab navigators (whose sailing was exclusively in well-known waters) ever had to confront. In 1478, a Spanish Jew named Abraham Zacuto used Arab sources to compile tables for use in determining latitude by observing the height of the sun at noon; this idea was then developed by astronomers in the service of the Portuguese king.[1] To make such measurements, fifteenth-century navigators used astrolabes, and a little later quadrants. Thus, by the end of the century European sailors had methods of fixing their latitude and charts on which to plot their courses. Sailors had used compasses to determine direction since the thirteenth century. Europeans could, if they wished, now sail beyond the sight of land and still be reasonably sure of their location. If the Arabs were afraid to sail in the Atlantic, Europeans equipped with knowledge gained from them about geography and astronomy were not.

**Figure 1.1.** Portolan chart signed by Majorcan cartographer Gabriel de Vallseca (1447). Bibliothèque nationale de France in Paris, France.

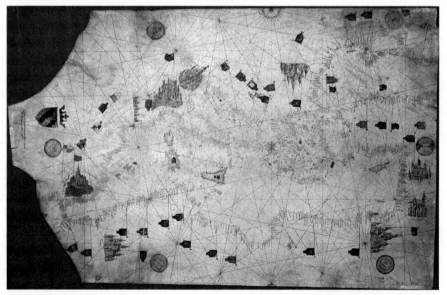

**Figure 1.2.** Portolan chart by Albino de Canepa (1489). The James Ford Bell Library, University of Minnesota.

## The Armed Sailing Ship

Equally as stunning as advances in the ability to navigate on the open seas were fifteenth-century European innovations in the design and construction of ships. In 1400, many European ships were oar driven galleys and those vessels that did rely on the wind commonly had only one mast and a square sail. Such vessels served admirably if the wind came from astern and was steady; though difficult to maneuver they could carry large cargoes. But they were virtually useless in unknown waters, which might hide reefs, rocks and shoals, and which thus required the ability to change course quickly—hence such ships were ill-suited for exploration along strange coasts. The Arabs had developed a different kind of vessel, the *baghla*, which employed two masts, each of which carried a lateen, or triangular sail, which could be adjusted to provide power in almost any kind of wind. The Arabs used these ships to conduct the spice trade across the deep water of the Indian Ocean, and they were superior to any European vessel of the early fifteenth century.

The Portuguese observed such ships in the hands of their enemies the Moors. But rather than build exact copies of them, Portuguese ship designers added a third mast and rearranged the rigging so that their *caravel* handled better and was easier to maneuver (especially when coming about) than the *baghla*. The Portuguese further modified the design in the late fifteenth century by combining square and lateen sails on one vessel. This new ship the *caravela redonda* could sail close to the wind like the *caravel*, but its square sails allowed it to achieve far greater speed than any vessel that employed only triangular sails. In future, all European seagoing vessels would follow this design.

Traditionally, warfare at sea was conducted by professional soldiers who were carried into battle for the purpose by warships. At the bow and stern, "castles" were built, which troops and bowmen might occupy to gain a height advantage over any enemy their vessel encountered. To engage in battle, ships lay alongside each other and battles commonly concluded with one ship's troops boarding the enemy. Europeans had been arming their ships with small artillery pieces fixed fore and aft since the fourteenth century. Such guns were meant to supplement the regular force of soldiers equipped with arquebuses and crossbows. The Portuguese, however, innovated dramatically in the fifteenth century by mounting large guns on deck that alone were sufficient to destroy an enemy vessel. No longer was it necessary to come alongside an enemy and engage him in close combat. Instead, by the middle of the fifteenth century, all a Portuguese warship needed to do was simply stand away from its foe and use its big guns to blow it apart. The rest of Europe was quick to learn the lesson Portugal taught. In future, the enemy's ships, not its men, were the target of naval guns, and for a long time mastery of that principle made European warships supreme on the high seas.

Armed with such technological advantages, and with newly powerful governments to support their endeavors, European seamen began in the fifteenth century to venture further from their home ports. They sailed first to Africa, later to a whole New World, which they claimed, subdued and dominated in the name of Christendom and its sponsoring nations. They used their mastery of the seas to shape the course of world history. Only one part of that story involves the Americas, and even less of it involves the area that was to become the United States. Columbus, after all, was aiming not at the New World when he left Spain in 1492, but at the East Indies. He hoped to find not Amerindians but East Indians. And for quite some time after he stumbled upon it, the land mass he found seemed of dubious value to Europeans. Indeed, the thrust of many, if not most, of the continuing European voyages to the west after 1492 was to find a way to get around or through America and reach what Europeans really wanted—the wealth of the Orient. In an ironic sense then, Columbus's discoveries did serve as a stimulus to continuing exploratory expeditions to the west from Europe. Such voyages were necessary not because Europeans thought America was valuable in its own right and wanted a share of its wealth, but rather because America was an impediment to the realization of other more important goals.

While the search for a western route to the Far East would motivate European voyages to America for years after Columbus's initial discovery, Europeans did not neglect the New World itself. Instead, they rapidly began to explore it in search of wealth and to colonize it. In the process they embarked on an adventure that ultimately changed the world. Indeed, by the end of the era of discovery, exploration and early settlement Europeans had created the "Atlantic World" and thereby established what became the cornerstone of the modern West. This new entity, consisting of western Europe, parts of Africa and America, established contacts with every part of the world and in time came to dominate much of it—socially, economically and politically. The creation of the Atlantic World was the start of an enormous drama and at the outset the Americas was its stage.

## Portugal

King John I sat on the throne of Portugal in 1415. He ruled a small and relatively poor country whose population numbered less than a million. But Portugal had a long coastline among whose inhabitants many made their living from the sea, a commercial class anxious to expand its share of Europe's trade with the Far East and a government that ruled without serious internal opposition. King John had sons who he thought should prove their courage and fitness to rule in actual battle with the Moors. For although the era when Christians mounted large-scale attacks against Islam in the Holy Land had long passed, the spirit of the Crusades persisted in Europe. That spirit was especially strong in states such as Portugal, whose very existence was the result of a long war in which occupying Muslims were expelled and whose southern borders were perilously near areas controlled by the Moors.

King John determined to attack Islam in North Africa, at the fortified town of Ceuta opposite Gibraltar. The assault by sea proved to be a spectacular success. The Portuguese might have destroyed and looted the city and then returned home with their spoils. Instead, they decided to occupy and hold the position, partly because they knew it would serve as a symbol of Christian courage and strength, and thereby encourage further assaults against Islam, and also because Ceuta might prove to be an ideal base for such operations as well as for expeditions whose purpose was exploration of and trade with Africa. In Prince Henry, one of King John's sons, the Portuguese found a leader who was eager to sponsor precisely such expeditions.

Prince Henry had been one of the most admired leaders of the attack against Ceuta. He earned further esteem by leading a second expedition there in 1418 to oppose an attempt by the Moors to recapture the town. The following year, after being named governor of Portugal's southern province, Prince Henry began a settlement at Sagres on the southwest coast. To Sagres Prince Henry invited sailors and scholars—men who wanted to study the sea, ships and navigation. After 1420, he began to send out exploratory expeditions to Africa's west coast.

His motives were numerous. Prince Henry clearly wanted to extend his knowledge of the African coast, and thereby to establish direct trade with the Christians he (and many medieval scholars) thought lived south of the areas occupied by the Moors. Trade would, he hoped, lead to an alliance with Christian princes against the Moors. He was also intent on learning as much as possible about his enemies, and expressed a desire to convert Africans to Christianity. His biographer, Gomes Eannes de Azurara, identified five reasons for Henry's efforts.

In which five reasons appear why the Lord Infant was moved to command the search for the lands of Guinea

*We imagine that we know a matter when we are acquainted with the doer of it and the end for which he did it. And since in former chapters we have set forth the Lord Infant as the chief actor in these things, giving as clear an understanding of him as we could, it is meet that in this present chapter we should know his purpose in doing them. And you should note well that the noble spirit of this Prince, by a sort of natural constraint, was ever urging him both to begin and to carry out very great deeds. For which reason, after the taking of Ceuta he always kept ships well armed against the Infidel, both for war and because he had also a wish to know the land that lay beyond the isles of Canary and that Cape called Bojador, for that up to his time, neither by writings, nor by the memory of man, was known with any certainty the nature of the land beyond that Cape. Some said indeed that Saint Brandan had passed that way; and there was another tale of two galleys rounding the Cape, which never returned. But this doth not appear at all likely to be true, for it is not to be presumed that if the said galleys went there, some other ships would not have endeavoured to learn what voyage they had made. And because the said Lord Infant wished to know the truth of this, since it seemed to him that if he or some other lord did not endeavour to gain that knowledge, no mariners or merchants would ever dare to attempt it—(for it is clear that none of them ever trouble themselves to sail to a place where there is not a sure and certain hope of profit)—and seeing also that no other prince took any pains in this matter, he sent out his own ships against those parts, to have manifest certainty of them all. And to this he was stirred up by his zeal for the service of God and of the King Edward his Lord and brother, who then reigned. And this was the first reason of his action.*

*The second reason was that if there chanced to be in those lands some population of Christians, or some havens, into which it would be possible to sail without peril, many kinds of merchandise might be brought to this realm, which would find a ready market, and reasonably so, because no other people of these parts traded with them, nor yet people of any other that were known; and also the products of this realm might be taken there, which traffic would bring great profit to our countrymen.*

*The third reason was that, as it was said that the power of the Moors in that land of Africa was very much greater than was commonly supposed, and that there were no Christians among them, nor any other race of men; and because every wise man is obliged by natural prudence to wish for a knowledge of the power of his enemy; therefore the said Lord Infant exerted himself to cause this to be fully discovered, and to make it known determinately how far the power of those infidels extended.*

*The fourth reason was because during the one and thirty years that he had warred against the Moors, he had never found a Christian king, nor a lord outside this land, who for the love of our Lord Jesus Christ would aid him in the said war. Therefore he sought to know if there were in those parts any Christian princes; in whom the charity and the love of Christ was so ingrained that they would aid him against those enemies of the faith.*

*The fifth reason was his great desire to make increase in the faith of our Lord Jesus Christ and to bring to him all the souls that should be saved, understanding that all the mystery of the. Incarnation, Death, and Passion of our Lord Jesus Christ was for this sole end—namely the salvation of lost souls—whom the said Lord Infant by his travail and spending would fain bring into the true path. For he perceived that no better offering could be made unto the Lord than this; for if God promised to return one hundred goods for one, we may justly believe that for such great benefits, that is to say for so many souls as were saved by the efforts of this Lord, he will have so many hundreds of guerdons in the kingdom of God, by which his spirit may be glorified after this life in the celestial realm. For I that wrote this history saw so many men and women of those parts turned to the holy faith, that even if the Infant had been a heathen, their prayers would have been enough to have obtained his salvation. And not only did I see the first captives, but their children and grandchildren as true Christians as if the Divine grace breathed in them and imparted to them a clear knowledge of itself.*

*But over and above these five reasons I have a sixth that would seem to be the root from which all the others proceeded: and this is the inclination of the heavenly wheels. For, as I wrote not many days ago in a letter I sent to the Lord King, that although it be written that the wise man shall be Lord of the stars, and that the courses of the planets (according to the true estimate of the holy doctors) cannot cause the good man to stumble; yet it is manifest that they are bodies ordained in the secret counsels of our Lord God and run by a fixed measure, appointed to different ends, which are revealed to men by his grace, through whose influence bodies of the lower order are inclined to certain passions. And if it be a fact, speaking as a Catholic, that the contrary predestinations of the wheels of heaven can be avoided by natural judgment with the aid of a certain divine grace, much more does it stand to reason that those who are predestined to good fortune, by the help of this same grace, will not only follow their course but even add a far greater increase to themselves. But here I wish to tell you how by the constraint of the influence of nature this glorious Prince was inclined to those actions of his. And that was because his ascendant was Aries, which is the house of Mars and exaltation of the sun, and his lord in the XIth house, in company of the sun. And because the said Mars was in Aquarius, which is the house of Saturn, and in the mansion of hope, it signified that this Lord should toil at high and mighty conquests, especially in seeking out things that were hidden from other men and secret, according to the nature of Saturn, in whose house he is. And the fact of his being accompanied by the sun, as I said, and the sun being in the house of Jupiter, signified that all his traffick and his conquests would be loyally carried out, according to the good pleasure of his king and lord.*

Gomes Eannes de Azurara, *Chronicle of the Discovery and Conquest of Guinea*, ed. and trans. by Charles R. Beazley and Edgar Prestage, 2 vols (London, 1896), I: 27–38.[2]

In 1434, one of Prince Henry's captains, Gil Eannes, finally managed to guide a *caravel* around Cape Bojador and thereby establish that the sea to the south was not boiling and that Europeans would not be turned into Africans by the excessive heat, as some had speculated. In 1441, a ship returned from Africa with a cargo of natives who, as heathens and enemies, under Christian practice, might be sold as slaves. The slave trade grew so rapidly after this and offered the prospect of such significant profits that Henry built a fortified trade center on an island off the African coast, obtained a monopoly on the trade from his brother the king, and then confirmed his monopoly with the pope.

Prince Henry also sponsored voyages to the west, into the Atlantic to islands off the African coast—the Canaries, the Azores, the Madeiras and the Cape Verde Islands. These islands were crucial to Portugal since they might serve as bases from which enemies could launch attacks on Portuguese ships making voyages to or from Africa. The Canaries were claimed by the Crown of Castille, and in spite of repeated attempts, Portugal never succeeded in wresting permanent control of them from Spain.

In Madeira, the Portuguese were more successful. Prince Henry sent an expedition there in 1420 and the small settlement thus established soon began a profitable trade in timber, sugar (sent from Sicily) and wine (made of Malvoisie grapes sent from Crete). Henry also sent settlers to the Cape Verde Islands and to the Azores, where he tried to develop a wool industry.

Before his death in 1460, Henry's captains had learned that the coast of Africa to the south of Sierra Leone turned eastward. But Prince Henry did not live to learn that Africa was, in fact, a peninsula around which ships might sail to reach India.

**Figure 1.3.** *The St. Vincent Altarpiece,* painted by Nuno Gonçalves (1450–1470). Many scholars believe that the work includes a portrait of Prince Henry in the third panel (the figure in black hat standing to the right of the saint). Others believe that the kneeling figure in panel five is the prince. The painting includes 60 figures, drawn from every segment of Portuguese society, and provides evidence that Portugal was inclusive rather than exclusive. Some historians have argued that the figure in panel six (*far right*) holding an open book is actually the Grand Rabbi of Lisbon with a copy of the Old Testament in his hands, joining in paying respect to the city's patron saint. Jews and Muslims were protected in the kingdom even after they were driven from Spain. The Portuguese king's decision to expel them in 1496–97 may have been driven by his desire to marry Ferdinand and Isabella's daughter. Museu Nacional de Arte Antiga, Lisbon, Portugal.

In 1475, Portugal and Spain went to war. Portugal lost, but the Treaty of Alcáçovas, concluded in 1479, gave the Portuguese undisputed control over all the Atlantic islands but the Canaries, and a monopoly of trade along the west coast of Africa. King John II came to the Portuguese throne in 1481 and displayed his enthusiasm for exploration almost immediately by constructing a huge fortified warehouse at Elminia on the African coast where slaves, ivory, gold and pepper were traded; by setting up his own school of navigation; and by securing the services of first-rate captains to lead expeditions in his name. In 1487, Bartholomeu Dias rounded the southern tip of Africa, which King John named the Cape of Good Hope. The same year, Pedro da Covilhã left Lisbon for India by the traditional route which took him to Cairo, then to Aden, and finally to Calicut. Before settling in Abyssinia he sent a report to King John from Cairo describing the Malabar Coast of India.

Thus, in 1497, when John decided to send a fleet to India under Vasco da Gama, his planners were prepared not only with Dias's sea route, but also with Covilhã's account of what the expedition would encounter. Da Gama was given four ships and instructed to trade. He was fortunate to encounter in one East African port a Muslim pilot who guided him across the Indian Ocean to Calicut. In spite of fierce opposition from local Arab merchants, who were angered not only by the appearance of a new competitor, but a Christian one at that, da Gama secured a cargo of pepper and cinnamon, returned to Portugal and made a huge profit.

Europeans used such spices as pepper, cinnamon and cloves to flavor and to preserve meat, a necessity since the lack of sufficient feed for cattle during the winter months meant that meat to be eaten in the winter had to be butchered and preserved in the fall. The potential for profit from an all-water route to the spice producing areas of the East was staggering. For even the substantial costs involved in financing a long voyage were far less than those for shipping spices over land and thereby paying profits to the Hindu or Muslim merchants through whose hands the cargo had to pass before it reached ports in the Middle East where Venetian traders bought and sent it on to points all over Europe. What distressed European consumers about this trade was not merely that the many middlemen involved in the process each made a sizable profit, and thereby drove the price of spices upwards dramatically, but that up until the very last stages of the business it was entirely in non-Christian hands. The hated Muslim enemy was being enriched with Christian gold. Hence, one of the animating ideals of the entire Age of Discovery was to secure this trade for European Christians and thereby cut off a major source of revenue to the infidel. Since land routes from the East where spices were produced to Europe where they were consumed were controlled by Muslims and Hindus, the only feasible alternative was a water route. Europeans were quick to perceive that spices shipped by water would surely be cheaper than spices shipped by land. Da Gama made a second voyage to India in 1502 in command of 14 ships. He bombarded Calicut, defeated an Arab fleet sent to oppose him, and thus proved the superiority of Europeans on the seas.

The Portuguese understood that success depended on making use of their naval superiority and they chose a brilliant strategic thinker, Admiral Afonso d'Albuquerque to establish their control of sea routes to the East. D'Albuquerque assumed command in 1509 and the next year his forces captured Goa, a city on an island off the Malabar Coast of India, which would serve as a base for further operations. He then proceeded to establish a string of naval bases in the East. His sole concern was the protection and support of his fleet—d'Albuquerque did not strive for significant territorial gains. In 1511, he led a fleet of 17 ships with 1,200 men in an assault designed to capture Malacca, which controlled the straits that separated the Indian Ocean from the Pacific, the sea route to China. D'Albuquerque's speech to his captains before launching a second attack against the Sultan of Malacca's 20,000 men and 2,000 pieces of artillery, gives us a glimpse of his leadership style and neatly summarizes Portuguese goals.

*Sirs, you will have no difficulty in remembering that when we decided upon attacking this city, it was with the determination of building a fortress within it, for so it appeared to all to be necessary, and after having captured it I was unwilling to let slip the possession of it, yet, because ye all advised me to do so, I left it, and withdrew; but being ready, as you see, to put my hands upon it again once more, I learned that you had already changed your opinion: now this cannot be because the Moors have destroyed the best part of us, but on account of my sins, which merit the failure of accomplishing this undertaking in the way that I had desired. And, inasmuch as my will and determination is, as long as I am Governor of India, neither to fight nor to hazard men on land, except in those parts wherein I must build a fortress to maintain them, as I have already told you before this, I desire you earnestly, of your goodness, although you all have already agreed upon what is to be done, to freely give me again your opinions in writing as to what I ought to do; for inasmuch as I have to give an account of these matters and a justification of my proceedings to the King D. Manuel, our Lord, I am unwilling to be left alone to bear the blame of them; and although there be many reasons which I could allege in favour of our taking this city and building a fortress therein to maintain possession of it, two only will I mention to you, on this occasion, as tending to point out wherefore you ought not to turn back from what you have agreed upon.*

*The first is the great service which we shall perform to Our Lord in casting the Moors out of this country, and quenching the fire of this sect of Mafamede so that it may never burst out again hereafter; and I am so sanguine as to hope for this from our undertaking, that if we can only achieve the task before us, it will result in the Moors resigning India altogether to our rule, for the greater part of them—or perhaps all of them—live upon the trade of this country and are become great and rich, and lords of extensive treasures. It is, too, well worthy of belief that as the King of Malaca, who has already once been discomfited and had proof of our strength, with no hope of obtaining any succour from any other quarter—sixteen days having already elapsed since this took place—makes no endeavour to negotiate with us for the security of his estate, Our Lord is blinding his judgment and hardening his heart, and desires the completion of this affair of Malaca: for when we were committing ourselves to the business of cruising in the Straits [of the Red Sea] where the King of Portugal had often ordered me to go (for it was there that*

*His Highness considered we could cut down the commerce which the Moors of Cairo, of Meca, and of Juda, carry on with these parts), Our Lord for his service thought right to lead us hither, for when Malaca is taken the places on the Straits must be shut up, and they will never more be able to introduce their spiceries into those places.*

*And the other reason is the additional service which we shall render to the King D. Manuel in taking this city, because it is the headquarters of all the spiceries and drugs which the Moors carry every year hence to the Straits without our being able to prevent them from so doing; but if we deprive them of this their ancient market there, there does not remain for them a single port, nor a single situation, so commodious in the whole of these parts, where they can carry on their trade in these things. For after we were in possession of the pepper of Malabar, never more did any reach Cairo, except that which the Moors carried thither from these parts, and forty or fifty ships, which sail hence every year laden with all sorts of spiceries bound to Meca, cannot be stopped without great expense and large fleets, which must necessarily cruise about continually in the offing of Cape Comorim; and the pepper of Malabar, of which they may hope to get some portion because they have the King of Calicut on their side, is in our hands, under the eyes of the Governor of India, from whom the Moors cannot carry off so much with impunity as they hope to do; and I hold it as very certain that if we take this trade of Malaca away out of their hands, Cairo and Me'ca are entirely ruined, and to Venice will no spiceries be conveyed except that which her merchants go and buy in Portugal.*

*But if you are of opinion that, because Malaca is a large city and very populous, it will give us much trouble to maintain our possession of it, no such doubts as these ought to arise, for when once the city is gained, all the rest of the Kingdom is of so little account that the King has not a single place left where he can rally his forces; and if you dread lest by taking the city we be involved in great expenses, and on account of the season of the year there be no place where our men and our Fleet can be recruited, I trust in God's mercy that when Malaca is held in subjection to our dominion by a strong fortress, provided that the Kings of Portugal appoint thereto those who are well experienced as Governors and Managers of the Revenues, the taxes of the land will pay all the expenses which may arise in the administration of the city; and if the merchants who are wont to resort thither—accustomed as they are to live under the tyrannical yoke of the Malays—experience a taste of our just dealing, truthfulness, frankness, and mildness, and come to know of the instructions of the King D. Manuel, our Lord, wherein he commands that all his subjects in these parts be very well treated, I venture to affirm that they will all return and take up their abode in the city again, yea, and build the walls of their houses with gold; and all these matters which here I lay before you may be secured to us by this half-turn of the key, which is that we build a fortress in this city of Malaca and sustain it, and that this land be brought under the dominion of the Portuguese, and the King D. Manuel be styled true king thereof, and therefore I desire you of your kindness to consider seriously the enterprise that ye have in hand, and not to leave it to fall to the ground.*

Afonso d'Albuquerque, *The Commentaries of the Great Afonso Dalboquerque: Second Viceroy of India*, 4 vols (London, 1880), III: 115–19.

**Figure 1.4.** *Admiral Afonso d'Albuquerque* (sixteenth century). Instituto Camões, Portugal.

D'Albuquerque's forces captured Malacca on August 15, 1511. Four years later he established Portuguese control of the Persian Gulf when he took Ormuz. Goa, Malacca and Ormuz served as the centers of strength among the group of bases constructed to ensure Portuguese domination of the seaborne trade routes in the East. Using these bases to resupply their ships with men and provisions, the Portuguese succeeded in gathering for themselves much of the spice trade. By 1514, a Portuguese ship even reached Canton in China. As d'Albuquerque had predicted, any cargoes from the East Indies which arrived in Europe by sea now travelled in Portuguese ships.

Profits from the spice trade were staggering. Historians suggest that merchants could anticipate a gain of from 700 to 1,000 percent on their ventures. One eminent scholar, J. H. Parry, summarized his analysis of the early years of European trading in spices with Asia by noting: "The costs of the trade, and the imposts upon it, were enormous; but so were the profits. It was said that a merchant could ship six cargoes, and lose five, but still make a profit when the sixth was sold."[3]

While all Christendom had to be pleased that control of the spice trade had been wrested from the Muslims, other European states looked on the Portuguese achievement with both admiration and a measure of dismay. An English observer, Sir George Peckham, noted that:

> To this may I adde the great discoueries and conquests which the princes of Portugall haue made round about the West, the South, and the East parts of Africa, and also at Callicut and in the East Indies, and in America, at Brasile and elsewhere in sundry Islands, in fortifying, peopling and planting all along the sayd coastes and Islands, euer as they discouered: which being lightly weyed and considered, doth minister iust cause of yncouragement to our Countreymen ...
>
> I doe greatly doubt least I seeme ouer tedious in the recitall of the particular discoueries and Conquests of the East and West Indies, wherein I was the more bold to vrge the patience of the Reader, to the end it might most manifestly and at large appeare, to all such as are not acquainted with the histories, how the king of Portugall, whose Countrey for popularity and number of people, is scarce comparable to some three shires of England, and the king of Spaine likewise, whose natural Countrey doth not greatly abound with people, both which princes by means of their discoueries within lesse then 90. yeeres past, haue as it appeareth both mightily and marueilously

*enlarged their territories and dominions through their owne industrie by the assistance of the omnipotent, whose aid we shall not need to doubt, seeing the cause and quarrell which we take in hand tendeth to his honour and glory, by the enlargement of the Christian faith.*

Richard Hakluyt, *The Principal Navigations, Voyages, Traffiques and Discoveries of the English Nation*, 16 vols (n.p., n.d.), VIII (America): 30, 33.[4]

And although the French monarch Francis I used a tone of disdainful sarcasm in referring to the Portuguese ruler Manuel I as "*le roi épicier*" (the grocer king), his words failed to conceal his envy. For if Portugal could monopolize the eastern trade by sea, would not the Portuguese become inordinately rich at the expense of the rest of Europe?

## For Further Reading

Boxer, Charles R., *The Portuguese Seaborne Empire: 1415–1825* (New York, 1969).

Cippola, Carlo M., *Guns, Sails, and Empires: Technological Innovation and the Early Phases of European Expansion 1400–1700* (Manhattan, KS, 1988).

Parry, J. H., *The Age of Reconnaissance* (New York, 1963).

_____, *The Establishment of the European Hegemony: 1415–1715* (New York, 1966).

_____, *The Discovery of the Sea* (New York, 1974).

Russell-Wood, A. J. R., *The Portuguese Empire, 1415–1808: A World on the Move* (Baltimore, 1998).

## Notes

1  Zacuto's *Great Book* (1478), written in Hebrew and consisting of 65 astronomical tables, was soon translated into Spanish, Latin (as the *Perpetual Almanac*) and Portuguese. In 1484 King John II of Portugal assembled a group of scholars to find a way to determine latitude using solar observation—they refined Zacuto's work to enable Portuguese navigators to employ the method during their voyages. Forced to leave Spain in 1492 when the Jews were expelled, Zacuto emigrated to Portugal where the monarch appointed him Royal Astronomer. He remained in service to the Portuguese crown until Jews were driven from Portugal by King Manuel I, and settled in Tunisia. Vasco da Gama used Zacuto's tables during his 1497 voyage to India. See J. H. Parry, *The Age of Reconnaissance* (New York, 1963), 110.

2  Available online at http://www.gutenberg.org/ebooks/author/37865 (accessed March 12, 2013).

3  J. H. Parry, *The Age of Reconnaissance* (New York, 1963), 57.

4  Available online at http://www.gutenberg.org/files/25645/25645-h/25645-h.html (accessed June 1, 2013).

# Chapter Two

# EXPANSION: THE OLD WORLD
# AND A NEW WORLD

*And as soon as I arrived in the Indies, in the first island that I found, I took some of them by force, to the intent that they should learn [our speech] and give me information of what there was in those parts. And so it was, that very soon they understood [us] and we them, what by speech or what by signs; and those [Indians] have been of much service. To this day I carry them [with me] who are still of the opinion that I come from Heaven [as appears] from much conversation which they have had with me. And they were the first to proclaim it wherever I arrived; and the others went running from house to house and to the neighboring villages, with loud cries of "Come! come to see the people from Heaven!"*

—Christopher Columbus, letter to Luis de Santangel, Lisbon (1493), 267[1]

*It appears to me, most excellent Lorenzo, that by this voyage most of the philosophers are controverted who say that the torrid zone cannot be inhabited on account of the great heat. I have found the case to be quite the contrary. The air is fresher and more temperate in that region than beyond it, and the inhabitants are more numerous here than they are in the other zones, for reasons which will be given below. Thus, it is certain, that practice is more valuable than theory.*

—Amerigo Vespucci, letter to Lorenzo de' Medici (July 1500)

*I am informed that Signor Galilei transfers mankind from the center of the universe to somewhere on the outskirts. Signor Galilei is therefore an enemy of mankind ... .Is it conceivable that God would trust this most precious fruit of his labor to a minor frolicking star? Would He have sent His Son to such a place? ... I won't have it! I won't be a nobody on an inconsequential star twirling hither and thither. I tread the earth, and the earth is firm beneath my feet, and there is no motion to the earth, and the earth is the center of all things, and I am the center of the earth, and the eye of the creator is upon me. About me revolve ... the lesser lights of the stars and the great light of the sun, created to give light on me that God might see me—Man, God's greatest effort, the center of creation.*

—Words of Old Cardinal to Galileo, Bertolt Brecht, *Galileo* (1952)

## Columbus

In the late fifteenth century while the Portuguese were busy exploring a water route to India around Africa, other Europeans considered reaching the same objective by sailing west. No educated European doubted that theoretically, such a plan was reasonable. For centuries scholars had known that the earth was spherical—as early as the fifth century BC Pythagoras had said so. In the third century BC Eratosthenes, using the techniques of Euclidian geometry, had speculated about the earth's actual circumference. Thus, when Christopher Columbus, a native of Genoa, met with King John II of Portugal in 1484 and sent his brother Bartholomew to visit King Henry VII of England in 1488 to suggest that he lead an expedition to India by sailing west, no one disputed the theoretical basis for such a proposition. His proposals were rejected because his own estimate of the globe's circumference seemed too small, and because the concessions he desired in return for making the voyage seemed too large. He found more receptive potential sponsors when he visited Ferdinand and Isabella in Spain.

Ferdinand of Aragon and Isabella of Castille married (while in their teens) in 1469. Although their marriage did not lead to the creation of one state, it did end conflict between their two kingdoms and allowed a unified attack on the Moors in Granada who in 1492, after ten years of warfare, were finally driven out of the Iberian peninsula. Together, Ferdinand and Isabella sponsored the Spanish Inquisition to purify religion, and expelled all Jews and Muslims from Spain, to purify the population. They also strove to increase the power of the crown at the expense of the nobility and of local communities. Once freed of the Moorish presence on Spanish soil, they were ready to sponsor other activities, especially ones aimed at increasing the wealth and power of their kingdoms.

In April 1492, Columbus concluded an agreement with the Spanish rulers under which they provided him with three ships—the *Niña*, the *Pinta* and the *Santa Maria*, a letter to the "Great Khan" and assurances that he would receive both governmental and commercial privileges in the lands he reached on behalf of the Castilian crown (which formally sponsored the expedition). Columbus first sailed to the Canaries and four weeks later, on October 12, encountered land in almost exactly the location he had expected. Certain that the islands he was exploring were those contemporary geographers asserted lay just off the coast of Cathay in the East Indies, Columbus identified the perplexed natives as Indians and believed Cuba to be Japan. On his return voyage foul weather forced Columbus to put in near Lisbon, and thus the first report of his exploits came to King John II of Portugal and not to the Spanish rulers.

The Portuguese, needless to say, were startled, but did not attempt to keep Columbus from going on to Spain. Rather they asserted that he had not reached India, but instead had bumped into some islands, which, according to the Treaty of Alcáçovas, were rightfully the possessions of the Portuguese crown.

Columbus's description of what he had found was calculated to please his sponsors.

*I know that it will afford you pleasure that I have brought my undertaking to a successful result, I have determined to write you this letter to inform you of everything that has been done and discovered in this voyage of mine.*

*On the thirty-third day after leaving Cadiz I came into the Indian Sea, where I discovered many islands inhabited by numerous people. I took possession of all of them for our most fortunate King by making public proclamation and unfurling his standard, no one making any resistance. To the first of them I have given the name of our blessed Saviour, trusting in whose aid I had reached this and all the rest; but the Indians call it Guanahani. To each of the others also I gave a new name, ordering one to be called Sancta Maria de Concepcion, another Fernandina, another Hysabella, another Johana; and so with all the rest. As soon as we reached the island which I have just said was called Johana, I sailed along its coast some considerable distance towards the West, and found it to be so large, without an apparent end, that I believed it was not an island, but a continent, a province of Cathay. But I saw neither towns nor cities lying on the seaboard, only some villages and country farms, with whose inhabitants I could not get speech, because they fled as soon as they beheld us. I continued on, supposing I should come upon some city, or country-houses. At last, finding that no discoveries rewarded our further progress, and that this course was leading us towards the North, which I was desirous of avoiding, as it was now winter in these regions, and it had always been my intention to proceed Southwards, and the winds also were favorable to such desires, I concluded not to attempt any other adventures; so, turning back, I came again to a certain harbor, which I had remarked. From there I sent two of our men into the country to learn whether there was any king or cities in that land. They journeyed for three days, and found innumerable people and habitations, but small and having no fixed government; on which account they returned. Meanwhile I had learned from some Indians, whom I had seized at this place, that this country was really an island. Consequently I continued along towards the East, as much as 322 miles, always hugging the shore. Where was the very extremity of the island, from there I saw another island to the Eastwards, distant 54 miles from this Johana, which I named Hispana; and proceeded to it, and directed my course for 564 miles East by North as it were, just as I had done at Johana.*

*The island called Johana, as well as the others in its neighborhood, is exceedingly fertile. It has numerous harbors on all sides, very safe and wide, above comparison with any I have ever seen. Through it flow many very broad and health-giving rivers; and there are in it numerous very lofty mountains. All these islands are very beautiful, and of quite different shapes; easy to be traversed, and full of the greatest variety of trees reaching to the stars. I think these never lose their leaves, as I saw them looking as green and lovely as they are wont to be in the month of May in Spain. Some of them were in leaf, and some in fruit; each flourishing in the condition its nature required. The nightingale was singing and various other little birds, when I was rambling among them in the month of November.*

*There are also in the island called Johana seven or eight kinds of palms, which as readily surpass ours in height and beauty as do all the other trees, herbs and fruits. There are also wonderful pine-woods, fields and extensive meadows; birds of various kinds, and honey; and all the different metals, except iron. In the island, which I have said before was called Hispana, there are very lofty and beautiful mountains, great farms, groves and fields, most fertile both for cultivation and for pasturage, and well adapted for constructing buildings. The convenience of the harbors in this island, and the excellence of the rivers, in volume and salubrity, surpass human belief, unless one should see them. In it the trees, pasture-lands and fruits differ much from those of Johana. Besides, this Hispana abounds in various kinds of spices, gold and metals. The inhabitants of both sexes of this and of all the other islands I have seen, or of which I have any knowledge, always go as naked as they came into the world, except that some of the women cover their private parts with leaves or branches, or a veil of cotton, which they prepare themselves for this purpose. They are all, as I said before, unprovided with any sort of iron, and they are destitute of arms, which are entirely unknown to them, and for which they are not adapted; not on account of any bodily deformity, for they are well made, but because they are timid and full of terror. They carry, however, canes dried in the sun in place of weapons, upon whose roots they fix a wooden shaft, dried and sharpened to a point. But they never dare to make use of these; for it has often happened, when I have sent two or three of my men to some of their villages to speak with the inhabitants, that a crowd of Indians has sallied forth; but when they saw our men approaching, they speedily took to flight, parents abandoning their children, and children their parents. This happened not because any loss or injury had been inflicted upon any of them. On the contrary I gave whatever I had, cloth and many other things, to whomsoever I approached, or with whom I could get speech, without any return being made to me; but they are by nature fearful and timid. But when they see that they are safe, and all fear is banished, they are very guileless and honest, and very liberal of all they have. No one refuses the asker anything that he possesses; on the contrary they themselves invite us to ask for it. They manifest the greatest affection towards all of us, exchanging valuable things for trifles, content with the very least thing or nothing at all. But I forbade giving them a very trifling thing and of no value, such as bits of plates, dishes, or glass; also nails and straps; although it seemed to them, if they could get such, that they had acquired the most beautiful jewels in the world. For it chanced that a sailor received for a single strap as much weight of gold as three gold solidi; and so others for other things of less price, especially for new blancas, and for some gold coins, for which they gave whatever the seller asked; for instance, an ounce and a half or two ounces of gold, or thirty or forty pounds of cotton, with which they were already familiar. So too for pieces of hoops, jugs, jars and pots they bartered cotton and gold like beasts. This I forbade, because it was plainly unjust; and I gave them many beautiful and pleasing things, which I had brought with me, for no return whatever, in order to win their affection, and that they might be- come Christians and inclined to love our Kino; and Queen and Princes and all the people of Spain; and that they might be eager to search for and gather and give to us what they abound in and we greatly need.*

*They do not practice idolatry; on the contrary, they believe that all strength, all power, in short all blessings, are from Heaven, and that I have come down from there with these ships and sailors; and in this spirit was I received everywhere, after they had got over their fear. They are neither lazy nor awkward; but, on the contrary, are of an excellent and acute understanding. Those who have sailed these seas give excellent accounts of everything; but they have never seen men wearing clothes, or ships like ours.*

*As soon as I had come into this sea, I took by force some Indians from the first island, in order that they might learn from us, and at the same time tell us what they knew about affairs in these regions. This succeeded admirably; for in a short time we understood them and they us both by gesture and signs and words; and they were of great service to us. They are coming now with me, and have always believed that I have come from Heaven, notwithstanding the long time they have been, and still remain, with us. They were the first who told this wherever we went, one calling to another, with a loud voice,* Come, Come, you will see Men from Heaven. *Whereupon both women and men, children and adults, young and old, laying aside the fear they had felt a little before, flocked eagerly to see us, a great crowd thronging about our steps, some bringing food, and others drink, with greatest love and incredible good will.*

*In each island are many boats made of solid wood; though narrow, yet in length and shape similar to our two-bankers, but swifter in motion, and managed by oars only. Some of them are large, some small, and some of medium size; but most are larger than a two-banker rowed by 18 oars. With these they sail to all the islands, which are innumerable; engaging in traffic and commerce with each other. I saw some of these biremes, or boats, which carried 70 or 80 rowers. In all these islands there is no difference in the appearance of the inhabitants, and none in their customs and language, so that all understand one another. This is a circumstance most favorable for what I believe our most serene King especially desires, that is, their conversion to the holy faith of Christ; for which, indeed, so far as I could understand, they are very ready and prone.*

*I have told already how I sailed in a straight course along the island of Johana from West to East 322 miles. From this voyage and the extent of my journeyings I can say that this Johana is larger than England and Scotland together. For beyond the aforesaid 322 miles, in that portion which looks toward the West, there are two more provinces, which I did not visit. One of them the Indians call Anan, and its inhabitants are born with tails. These provinces extend 180 miles, as I learned from the Indians, whom I am bringing with me, and who are well acquainted with all these islands.*

*The distance around Hispana is greater than all Spain from Colonia to Fontarabia; as is readily proved, because its fourth side, which I myself traversed in a straight course from West to East, stretches 540 miles. This island is to be coveted, and not to be despised when acquired. As I have already taken possession of all the others, as I have said, for our most invincible King, and the rule over them is entirely committed to the said King, so in this one I have taken special possession of a certain large town, in a most convenient spot, well suited for all profit and commerce, to which I have given the name of the Nativity of our Lord; and there I ordered a fort to be built forthwith, which ought to be finished now. In it I left as many men as seemed necessary, with all kinds of arms, and provisions sufficient for more than a year; also a caravel and men to build others, skilled not only in this trade but in others. I secured for them the good will and remarkable friendship of the King of the island; for these people are very affectionate and kind; so much so that the aforesaid King took a pride in my being called his brother. Although they should change their minds, and wish to harm those who have remained in the fort, they cannot; because they are without arms, go naked and are too timid; so that, in truth, those who hold the aforesaid fort can lay waste the whole of that island, without any danger to themselves, provided they do not violate the rules and instructions I have given them.*

*In all these islands, as I understand, every man is satisfied with only one wife, except the princes or kings, who are permitted to have 20. The women appear to work more than the men; but I could not well understand whether they have private property, or not; for I saw that what every one had was shared with the others, especially meals, provisions and such things. I found among them no monsters, as very many expected; but men of great deference and kind; nor are they black like the Ethiopians; but they have long, straight hair. They do not dwell where the rays of the Sun have most power, although the Sun's heat is very great there, as this region is twenty-six degrees distant from the equinoctial line. From the summits of the mountains there comes great cold, but the Indians mitigate it by being inured to the weather, and by the help of very hot food, which they consume frequently and in immoderate quantities.*

*I saw no monsters, neither did I hear accounts of any such except in an island called Charis, the second as one crosses over from Spain to India, which is inhabited by a certain race regarded by their neighbors as very ferocious. They eat human flesh, and make use of several kinds of boats by which they cross over to all the Indian islands, and plunder and carry off whatever they can. But they differ in no respect from the others except in wearing their hair long after the fashion of women. They make use of bows and arrows made of reeds, having pointed shafts fastened to the thicker portion, as we have before described. For this reason they are considered to be ferocious, and the other Indians consequently are terribly afraid of them; but I consider them of no more account than the others. They have intercourse with certain women who dwell alone upon the island of Mateurin, the first as one crosses from Spain to India. These women follow none of the usual occupations of their sex; but they use bows and arrows like those of their husbands, which I have described, and protect themselves with plates of copper, which is found in the greatest abundance among them.*

*I was informed that there is another island larger than the aforesaid Hispana, whose inhabitants have no hair; and that there is a greater abundance of gold in it than in any of the others. Some of the inhabitants of these islands and of the others I have seen I am bringing over with me to bear testimony to what I have reported. Finally, to sum up in a few words the chief results and advantages of our departure and speedy return, I make this promise to our most invincible Sovereigns, that, if I am supported by some little assistance from them, I will give them as much gold as they have need of, and in addition spices, cotton and mastic, which is found only in Chios, and as much aloes-wood, and as many heathen slaves as their majesties may choose to demand; besides these, rhubarb and other kinds of drugs, which I think the men I left in the fort before alluded to, have already discovered, or will do so; as I have myself delayed nowhere longer than the winds compelled me, except while I was providing for the construction of a fort in the city of Nativity, and for making all things safe.*

*Although these matters are very wonderful and unheard of, they would have been much more so, if ships to a reasonable amount had been furnished me. But what has been accomplished is great and wonderful, and not at all proportionate to my deserts, but to the sacred Christian faith, and to the piety and religion of our Sovereigns. For what the mind of man could not compass the spirit of God has granted to mortals. For God is wont to listen to his servants who love his precepts, even in impossibilities, as has happened to me in the present instance, who have accomplished what human strength has hitherto never attained. For if anyone has written or told anything about these islands, all have done so either obscurely or by guesswork, so that it has almost seemed to be fabulous.*

*Therefore let King and Queen and Princes, and their most fortunate realms, and all other Christian provinces, let us all return thanks to our Lord and Saviour Jesus Christ, who has bestowed so great a victory and reward upon us; let there be processions and solemn sacrifices prepared; let the churches be decked with festal boughs; let Christ rejoice upon Earth as he rejoices in Heaven, as he foresees that so many souls of so many people heretofore lost are to be saved; and let us be glad not only for the exaltation of our faith, but also for the increase of temporal prosperity, in which not only Spain but all Christendom is about to share.*

*As these things have been accomplished so have they been briefly narrated. Farewell.*

*CHRISTOPHER COLOM,*

*Admiral of the Ocean Fleet.*

*Lisbon, March 14th.*

Christopher Columbus, *The first letter of Christopher Columbus to the noble lord Raphael Sanchez announcing the discovery of America; reproduced in facsimile from the copy of the Latin version of 1493 now in the Boston public library; with a new translation,* trans. by Henry W. Haynes (Boston, 1891), 5–16.[2]

The letter was circulated widely in Europe, with eleven editions being published in 1493, and an additional six between 1494 and 1497.

Ferdinand and Isabella reacted to Columbus's report by outfitting a second fleet he could use to explore further, and in September 1493 he left Cadiz at the head of seventeen Spanish ships. In the Indies Columbus tried to establish a colony, but his brothers, in whose hands he left the settlers while he continued to explore could not govern effectively, and in 1496 Columbus returned to Spain. He led a third expedition in 1498 and a fourth in 1502. But by then the Spanish rulers realized that although Columbus was a gifted navigator, he was an inept administrator. In 1500, they sent Francisco de Bobadilla to the area as governor and thereby revoked Columbus's political privileges. Columbus and his brothers returned to Spain in chains.

Among the consequences of Columbus's first voyage was a serious diplomatic dispute between Portugal and Spain. The route Portuguese sailors used when navigating around Africa took them far out to sea to the south and west before it turned east. The Portuguese claimed, with some justification, that the areas Columbus had explored and settled actually fell within the area confirmed to Portugal by the Treaty of Alcáçovas. To resolve the conflict, Spain and Portugal turned to the papacy, which traditionally had settled issues over which Christian nations disagreed, and which exercised authority over the relations of Christians with non-Christians. In 1493, Pope Alexander VI issued a series of four papal bulls which not only confirmed Spanish title to the areas Columbus had reached, but also seemed to support any future Spanish claim to sovereignty over areas in the Far East which her ships might reach by sailing west. Alexander's seeming favoritism toward Spain was attributed to the fact that he was Spanish, and Portugal was hardly satisfied. In 1494, therefore, Spanish and Portuguese envoys concluded the Treaty of Tordesillas, under the terms of which a line was drawn bisecting the Atlantic. Portugal would be sovereign in areas to the east and Spain in areas to the west of the line. What the Spanish did not realize was that the line touched the South American coast and left in Portuguese control a large segment of the continent, which included what would become Brazil.

As the turn of the century approached, other seamen explored the Atlantic. The Spanish sent out Alonso de Ojeda and Juan de la Cosa who explored the area around the Venezuela coast in 1499. In 1499–1500, Peralonso Niño secured a cargo of pearls in the same area. Portuguese finally touched South America in 1500 when Pedro Álvares Cabral, sailing to India after da Gama and following his general route, headed initially south and west and encountered the Brazilian coast, where he noted the presence of brazilwood, crucial to the dyeing industry. In 1496, King Henry VII of England licensed John Cabot, an Italian who resided in Bristol, to sail to the west in search of the Chinese mainland. Cabot sailed far north of the route the Portuguese and Spanish had taken, and in three voyages made before 1498 he "discovered" what is now Newfoundland, Nova Scotia and New England. But he found no rich cargo to load for sale in Europe, certainly no spices, and he died during his last trip. The best-remembered of Columbus's followers was a Florentine, Amerigo Vespucci, who sailed first for Spain, then for Portugal and finally ended his career as Pilot Major of Spain. In fact, Vespucci was the archetype of a new kind of mariner—the professional explorer. Like mercenary soldiers, such seamen largely disregarded national loyalties, and would willingly serve whatever country offered the best terms. Portugal, Spain, England and later France eagerly employed ships' captains who had mastered the techniques of navigation and whose voyages would permit them to lay claim to and exploit distant lands and peoples.

Vespucci claimed to have made four trips to the west, but only two are generally considered authentic. The first he made in 1499 in a Spanish vessel. In 1501, now employed by Portugal, Vespucci followed Cabral's route to Brazil and then proceeded south down the coastline for at least two thousand miles. After this voyage, it was clear to everyone that Columbus had indeed found a continent, but not Asia, and Vespucci described it in stunning detail in letters, which were frequently published after 1503. His July 1500 letter to Lorenzo de' Medici, which includes the first European descriptions of toucans and anacondas, and concludes with disparaging comments about his Portuguese-sponsored competitor Vasco de Gama (who is not identified by name), is particularly informative.

*MOST EXCELLENT AND DEAR LORD,*—*It is a long time since I have written to your Excellency, and for no other reason than that nothing has occurred to me worthy of being commemorated. This present letter will inform you that about a month ago I arrived from the Indies, by way of the great ocean, brought by the grace of God safely to this city of Seville. I think your Excellency will be gratified to learn the results of my voyage, and the most surprising things which have been presented to my observation. If I am somewhat tedious, let my letter be read in your more idle hours, as fruit is eaten after the cloth is removed from the table.*

*You will please to note that, commissioned by his highness the King of Spain, I set out with two small ships, the 18th of May, 1499, on a voyage of discovery to the southwest, by way of the Fortunate Isles, which are now called the Canaries. After having provided ourselves there with all things necessary, first offering our prayers to God, we set sail from an island which is called Gomera, and, turning our prows southwardly, sailed twenty-four days with a fresh wind, without seeing any land. At the end of that time we came within sight of land, and found that we had sailed about thirteen hundred leagues, and were at that distance from the city of Cadiz, in a southwesterly direction. When we saw the land we gave thanks to God, and then launched our boats and, with sixteen men, went to the shore, which we found thickly covered with trees, astonishing both on account of their size and their verdure, for they never lose their foliage. The sweet odors which they exhaled (for they were all aromatic) highly delighted us, and we were rejoiced in regaling our senses.*

*We rowed along the shore in the boats to see if we could find any suitable place for landing; but, after toiling from morning till night, we found no way of passage, the land being low and densely covered with trees. We concluded, therefore, to return to the ships and make an attempt to land at some other spot.*

*One very remarkable circumstance we observed in these seas, which was that, at fifteen leagues distance from the land, we found the water fresh, like that of a river, and we filled all our empty casks with it. Sailing in a southerly direction, still along the coast, we saw two larger rivers issuing from the land; and I think that these two rivers, by reason of their magnitude, caused the freshness of the water in the sea adjoining. Seeing that the coast was invariably low, we determined to enter one of these rivers with the boats, and did so, after furnishing them with provisions for four days, and twenty men well armed. We entered the river and rowed up it nearly two days, making a distance of about eighteen leagues; but we found the low land still continuing and so thickly covered with trees that a bird could scarcely fly through them.*

*We saw signs that the inland parts of the country were inhabited; nevertheless, as our vessels were anchored in a dangerous place, in case an adverse wind should arise, at the end of two days we concluded to return. Here we saw an immense number of birds, including parrots in great variety, some crimson in color, others green and lemon, others entirely green, and others again that were black and flesh-colored [these last were probably toucans]. And oh! the songs of other species of birds, so sweet and so melodious, as we heard them among the trees, that we often lingered, listening to their charming music. The trees, too, were so beautiful and smelled so sweetly that we almost imagined ourselves in a terrestrial paradise; yet none of those trees, or the fruit of them, were similar to anything in our part of the world.*

*On our way back we saw many people of various descriptions fishing in the river. Having arrived at our ships, we raised anchor and set sail in a southerly direction, standing off to sea about forty leagues. While sailing on this course, we encountered a current running from southeast to northwest, so strong and furious that we were put into great fear and were exposed to imminent peril. This current was so strong that the Strait of Gibraltar and that of the Faro of Messina appeared to us like mere stagnant water in comparison with it. We could scarcely make headway against it, though we had the wind fresh and fair; so, seeing that we made no progress, or but very little, we determined to turn our prows to the northwest.*

*As, if I remember aright, your Excellency understands something of cosmography, I intend to describe to you our progress in our navigation by the latitude and longitude. We sailed so far to the south that we entered the torrid zone and penetrated the circle of Cancer … Having passed the equinoctial line and sailed six degrees to the south of it, we lost sight of the north star altogether, and even the stars of Ursa Major—or, to speak better, the guardians which revolve about the firmament—were scarcely seen. Very desirous of being the author who should designate the other polar star of the firmament, I lost, many a time, my night's sleep, while contemplating the movement of the stars about the southern pole. I desired to ascertain which had the least motion, and which might be nearest to the firmament; but I was not able to accomplish it with such poor instruments as I used, which were the quadrant and astrolabe. I could not distinguish a star which had less than ten degrees of motion; so that I was not satisfied, within myself, to name any particular one for the pole of the meridian, on account of the large revolution which they all made around the firmament.*

*While I was arriving at this conclusion, I recollected a verse of our poet Dante, which may be found in the first chapter of his "Purgatory," where he imagines he is leaving this hemisphere to repair to the other and attempting to describe the antarctic pole, and says:*

*"To the right hand I turned, and fixed my mind*
*On the other pole attentive, where I saw*
*Four stars ne'er seen before, save by the ken*
*Of our first parents. Heaven of their rays*
*Seemed joyous. O! thou northern site, bereft*
*Indeed, and widowed, since of these deprived!"*

*It seems to me that the poet wished to describe in these verses, by the four stars, the pole of the other firmament, and I have little doubt, even now, that what he says may be true. I observed four stars in the figure of an almond which had but little motion; and if God gives me life and health I hope to go again into that hemisphere and not to return without observing the pole. In conclusion I would remark that we extended our navigation so far south that our difference in latitude from the city of Cadiz was sixty degrees and a half, because, at that city, the pole is elevated thirty-five degrees and a half, and we had passed six degrees beyond the equinoctial line. Let this suffice as to our latitude. You must observe that this our navigation was in the months of July, August, and September, when, as you know, the sun is longest above the horizon in our hemisphere and describes the greatest arch in the day and the least in the night.*

*On the contrary, while we were at the equinoctial line, or near it, the difference between the day and night was not perceptible. They were of equal length, or very nearly so...*

*It appears to me, most excellent Lorenzo, that by this voyage most of the philosophers are controverted who say that the torrid zone cannot be inhabited on account of the great heat. I have found the case to be quite the contrary. The air is fresher and more temperate in that region than beyond it, and the inhabitants are more numerous here than they are in the other zones, for reasons which will be given below. Thus, it is certain, that practice is more valuable than theory.*

*Thus far I have related the navigation I accomplished in the South and West. It now remains for me to inform you of the appearance of the country we discovered, the nature of the inhabitants and their customs, the animals we saw, and of many other things worthy of remembrance which fell under my observation. After we turned our course to the north, the first land we found inhabited was an island at ten degrees distant from the equinoctial line [island of Trinidad]. When we arrived at it we saw on the sea-shore a great many people, who stood looking at us with astonishment.*

*We anchored within about a mile of land, fitted out the boats, and twenty-two men, well armed, made for the land. The people, when they saw us landing and perceived that we were different from themselves (because they have no beards and wear no clothing of any description, being also of a different color—brown, while we were white), began to be afraid of us and all ran into the woods. With great exertion, by means of signs, we reassured them and found that they were a race called cannibals, the greater part, or all of whom, live on human flesh. Your Excellency may be assured of this fact. They do not eat one another, but, navigating with certain barks which they call canoes, they bring their prey from the neighboring islands or countries inhabited by those who are their enemies, or of a different tribe from their own. They never eat any women, unless they consider them as outcasts. These things we verified in many places where we found similar people. We often saw the bones and heads of those who had been eaten, and they who had made the repast admitted the fact and said that their enemies stood in greater fear of them on that account.*

*Still, they are a people of gentle disposition and fine stature, of great activity and much courage. They go entirely naked, and the arms which they carry are rare bows, arrows, and spears, with which they are excellent marksmen. In fine, we held much intercourse with them, and they took us to one of their villages, about two leagues inland, and gave us our breakfast. They gave whatever was asked of them, though I think more through fear than affection; and after having been with them all one day we returned to the ships, sailing along the coasts, and finding another large village of the same tribe. We landed in the boats and found they were waiting for us, all loaded with provisions, and they gave us enough to make a very good breakfast, according to their ideas.*

*Seeing they were such kind people and treated us so well, we did not take anything from them, but made sail until we arrived at a body of water which is called the Gulf of Paria. We anchored off the mouth of a great river, which causes the gulf to be fresh, and saw a large village close to the sea. We were surprised at the great number of people to be seen there, though they were without weapons and peaceably disposed. We went ashore with the boats, and they received us with great friendship and took us to their houses, where they had made good preparations for a feast. Here they gave us three sorts of wine to drink; not the juice of the grape, but made of fruits, like beer, and they were excellent. Here, also, we ate many fresh acorns, a most royal fruit, and also others, all different from ours, and all of aromatic flavor.*

*What was more, they gave us some small pearls and eleven large ones, telling us that if we would wait some days they would go and fish for them and bring us many of the kind. We did not wish to be detained, so, with many parrots of different colors, and in good friendship, we parted from them. From these people it was we learned that those of the before-mentioned island were cannibals and ate human flesh. We issued from the gulf and sailed along the coast, seeing continually great numbers of people; and when we were so disposed we treated with them, and they gave us everything we desired. They all go as naked as they were born, without being ashamed, and if all were related concerning the little shame they have it would be bordering on impropriety, therefore it is better to suppress it.*

*After having sailed about four hundred leagues, continually along the coast, we concluded that this land was a continent, which might be bounded by the eastern parts of Asia, this being the commencement of the western parts of the continent, because it happened that we saw divers animals, such as lions, stags, goats, wild hogs, rabbits, and other land animals which are not found in islands, but only on the main-land. Going inland one day with twenty men, we saw a serpent all of twenty-four feet in length and as large in girth as myself. We were very much afraid, and the sight of it caused us to return immediately to the sea. Oftimes, indeed, I saw many ferocious animals and enormous serpents. When we had navigated four hundred leagues along the coast, we began to find people who did not wish for our friendship, but stood waiting for us with their bows and arrows. When we went ashore they disputed our landing in such a manner that we were obliged to fight them, and at the end of the battle they found they had the worst of it, for, as they were naked, we always made great slaughter. Many times not more than sixteen of us fought with no less than two thousand, in the end defeating them, killing many, and plundering their houses.*

*One day we saw a great crowd of savages, all posted in battle array, to prevent our landing. We fitted out twenty-six men, well armed, and covered the boats on account of the arrows which were shot at us and which always wounded some before we landed. After they had hindered us as long as they could, we leaped on shore and fought a hard battle with them. The reason why they had so much courage and made such great exertion against us was that they did not know what kind of a weapon the sword was, or how it cuts! So great was the multitude of people who charged upon us, discharging at us such a cloud of arrows that we could not withstand the assault, and, nearly abandoning the hope of life, we turned our backs and ran for the boats. While thus disheartened and flying, one of our sailors, a Portuguese, who had remained to guard the boats, seeing the danger we were in, leaped on shore and with a loud voice called out to us: "Face to the enemy, sons, and God will give you the victory!" Throwing himself upon his knees, he made a prayer, then rushed furiously upon the savages, and we all joined him, wounded as we were. On that they turned their backs and began to flee; and finally we routed them, killing more than a hundred and fifty. We burned their houses also—at least one hundred and eighty in number. Then, as we were badly wounded and weary, we went into a harbor to recruit, where we stayed twenty days, solely that the physician might cure us. All escaped save one, who was wounded in the left breast and died.*

*After we were cured we recommenced our navigation; and through the same cause we were often obliged to fight with a great many people, and always had the victory over them. Thus continuing our voyage, we came to an island fifteen leagues distant from the main-land. As at our arrival we saw no collection of people, eleven of us landed. Finding a path inland, we walked nearly two leagues and came to a village of about twelve houses, in which were seven women who were so large that there was not one among them who was not a span and a half taller than myself. When they saw us they were very much frightened, and the principal one among them, who seemed certainly a discreet woman, led us by signs into a house and had refreshments prepared for us. They were such large women that we were about determining to carry off two of the younger ones as a present to our king; but while we were debating this subject, thirty-six men entered the hut where we were drinking. They were of such great stature that each one was taller when upon his knees than I when standing erect. In fact, they were giants; each of the women appeared a Penthesilia, and the men Antei. When they came in, some of our number were so frightened that they did not consider themselves safe, for they were armed with very large bows and arrows, besides immense clubs made in the form of swords. Seeing that we were small of stature they began to converse with us, in order to learn who we were and from what parts we came. We gave them fair words, and answered them, by signs, that we were men of peace and intent only upon seeing the world. Finally, we held it our wisest course to part from them without questioning in our turn; so we returned by the same path in which we had come—they accompanying us quite to the sea-shore, till we went aboard the ships.*

*Nearly half the trees on this island are of dye-woods, as good as any from the East. Going from this island to another in the vicinity, at ten leagues distance, we found a very large village, the houses of which were built over the sea, like those of Venice, with much ingenuity. While we were struck with admiration at this circumstance, we determined to go to see them; and as we went into their houses the people owning them attempted to prevent us. They found out at last the sharpness of our swords, and thought it best to let us enter. Then we found these houses filled with the finest cotton, and the beams of their dwellings are made of dye-woods. In all the parts where we landed we found a great quantity of cotton, and the country filled with cotton-trees. All the vessels of the world, in fact, might be laden in these parts with cotton and dye-wood.*

*We sailed three hundred leagues farther along this coast, constantly finding savage but brave people, and very often fighting with and vanquishing them. We found seven different languages among them, each of which was not understood by those who spoke the others. It is said that there are not more than seventy-seven languages in the world; but I say that there are* more *than a thousand, as there are more than forty which I have heard myself. After having sailed seven hundred leagues or more our ships became leaky, so that we could hardly keep them free, with two pumps going. The men also were much fatigued, and the provisions growing short. We were then within a hundred and twenty leagues of the island called Hispaniola, discovered by the Admiral Columbus six [eight] years before. So we determined to proceed to it and, as it was inhabited by Christians, to repair our ships there, allow our men a little repose, and recruit our stock of provisions; because, from this island to Castile there are three hundred leagues of ocean, without any land intervening. In seven days we arrived at this island, where we stayed two months, refitted our ships, and obtained a supply of provisions.*

*We afterwards sailed through a shoal of islands, more than a thousand in number. We sailed in this sea nearly two hundred leagues, directly north, until our people had become worn with fatigue, through having been already nearly a year at sea. Their allowance per diem was only six ounces of bread for eating, and three small measures of water for drinking. Whereupon we concluded to take some prisoners as slaves, and loading the ships with them to return at once to Spain. Going, therefore, to certain islands, we possessed ourselves by force of two hundred and thirty-two, and then steered our course for Castile. In sixty-seven days we crossed the ocean, arriving at the Azores, thence sailed by way of the Canary Islands and the Madeiras to Cadiz.*

*We were absent thirteen months on this voyage, exposing ourselves to awful dangers, discovering a very large country of Asia, and a great many islands, the largest of them all inhabited. According to the calculations I have made with the compass, we have sailed about five thousand leagues … We discovered immense regions, saw a vast number of people, all naked, and speaking various languages, numerous wild animals, various kinds of birds, and an infinite quantity of trees, all aromatic. We brought home pearls in their growing state, and gold in the grain; we brought two stones, one of emerald color, the other of amethyst, which was very hard, at least half a span long, and three fingers thick. The sovereigns esteem them most highly and have preserved them among their jewels. We brought home also a piece of crystal, which some jewelers say is beryl, and, according to what the Indians told us, they had a great quantity of the same. We brought fourteen flesh-colored pearls, with which the queen was highly delighted. We brought many other stones which appeared beautiful to us; but of all these we did not bring a large number, as we were continually busied in our investigations and did not tarry long in any place.*

*When we arrived at Cadiz we sold many slaves, two hundred then remaining to us, the others having died at sea. After deducting the expense of transportation we gained only about five hundred ducats, which, having to be divided into fifty-five parts, made the share of each very small. However, we contented ourselves with life, and rendered thanks to God that during the whole voyage, out of fifty-seven Christian men, which was our number, only two had died, they having been killed by Indians. I have had two quartan agues since my return; but I hope, by the favor of God, to be well soon, as they do not continue long now and are without chills. I have passed over many things worthy of being remembered, in order not to be more tedious than necessary, all of which are reserved for the pen, and in the memory.*

*They are fitting out three ships for me here, that I may go on a new voyage of discovery, and I think they will be ready by the middle of September. May it please our Lord to give me health and a good voyage, as I hope again to bring very great news and discover the island of Trapobana, which is between the Indian Ocean and the Sea of Ganges. Afterwards I intend to return to my country and seek repose in the days of my old age … I have resolved, most excellent*

*Lorenzo, that as I have thus given you an account by letter of what has occurred to me, to send you two plans and descriptions of the world, made and arranged by my own hand and skill. There will be a map on a plain surface, and the other a view of the world in a spherical form, which I intend to send you by sea, in care of one Francesco Lotti, a Florentine, who is here. I think you will be pleased with them, particularly the globe, as I made one, not long since, for these sovereigns, and they esteem it highly. I could have wished to come with them personally; but my new departure for making other discoveries will not permit me that great pleasure …*

*I suppose your excellency has heard the news brought by the fleet which the King of Portugal sent two years ago to make discoveries on the coast of Guinea. I do not call such a voyage as that one of discovery, but only a visit to discovered lands; because, as you will see by the map, their navigation was continually within sight of land, and they sailed round the whole southern part of the continent of Africa, which is proceeding by a way spoken of by all cosmographical authors. It is true that the navigation has been very profitable, which is a matter of great consideration here in this kingdom, where inordinate covetousness reigns.*

*I understand they passed from the Red Sea and extended their voyage into the Persian Gulf, to a city called Calicut, which is situated between the Persian Gulf and the river Indus. More lately, the King of Portugal has received from sea twelve ships very richly laden, and he has sent them again to those parts, where they will certainly do a profitable business, if they arrive in safety.*

*May our Lord preserve and increase the exalted state of your excellency, as I desire.*
*Amerigo Vespucci.*
July 18th, 1500.

Amerigo Vespucci, "Letter to Lorenzo de' Medici," in Frederick A. Ober,
*Amerigo Vespucci* (New York and London, 1907), 110–25.[3]

One mapmaker and scholar, Martin Waldseemuller, suggested that Vespucci's feats had earned him the honor of giving his name to the continent, hence America, a feminized version of Amerigo. Doubtless Vespucci was pleased, but his joy was shared only by the Portuguese who realized that the new continent effectively blocked a western water route to the East Indies. Other European nations would be forced to overcome a continental barrier before they could challenge Portugal for the trade of Asia.

In 1513, Vasco Nuñez de Balboa, a Spanish adventurer who lived in the West Indies, travelled to the mainland in search of gold and saw the Pacific Ocean. Reports that only a tiny strip of land separated the Atlantic from the Pacific at Panama bolstered the hopes of everyone anxious to find a western route to the East. Ferdinand Magellan, a Portuguese who had spent time in the East Indies, suggested to the Spanish rulers that he could accomplish that goal. Portugal, of course, was not eager to sponsor an expedition which, if successful, would open a way to the East for Spain and which might prove that some of the most valuable sources of spices in the East lay in the Spanish zone of control as defined by the Tordesillas line (which, the Spanish stressed, should circle the globe rather than be limited to the Atlantic, as the Portuguese asserted). The Spanish rulers were eager to accept Magellan's proposal to discover rich trading sources inside the Spanish demarcation by sailing a Spanish route. In 1519, he left Seville with five ships. His voyage, through the straits that bear his name, across the immense Pacific to the Philippines (where Magellan was killed while taking part in a local war in 1521), was one of the greatest feats of this era of discovery. The expedition continued from the Philippines along the coast of Borneo to the Moluccas where a cargo of cloves was secured. The single ship that returned to Spain, under the command of Sebastián del Cano, a Spaniard, had circumnavigated the globe in three years. The Portuguese were outraged that Spain had dared send traders into an area ostensibly closed to the Spanish, and war in the East Indies was averted only when the Spanish king, at war with France and greatly in need of cash, determined to sell his rights to the area. He did so in 1529, for 350,000 ducats, and a new line of demarcation was drawn, well to the east of the spice islands.

## The Significance of European Voyages of Discovery

The impact of Europeans' late-fifteenth-century encounter with the Americas traditionally has been portrayed by describing how both Europe and America were changed. Scholars have filled thousands of pages in examining what historian Alfred Crosby has labeled "The Columbian Exchange," focusing on what Europeans brought to the New World and what the New World sent back to Europe.[4] The narrative includes the horses, manufactured goods, political systems and diseases that were introduced into the Americas by the agents of European expansion. The story continues with the foodstuffs, raw materials, gold, silver and diseases, such as syphilis, the Americas sent back to the Old World. It is a tale full of heroes, villains, saints and sinners—of triumph and disaster. It includes what is probably the greatest demographic catastrophe in history (the annihilation by conquest and disease—particularly smallpox—of Amerindians) and the "solution" to the labor problem in Spanish and Portuguese America of introducing slaves from Africa. The story is especially vivid because nearly every component can be measured or quantified—the amount of silver mined at Potosí, the rate at which the number of cattle increased in the Valley of Mexico as the number of natives decreased, the effect of the potato on the diet of Europeans, the number of slaves shipped from Angola.

The discovery of America clearly revolutionized the European economy. America gave Europe more than fish, fur, tobacco, naval stores and foodstuffs such as sugar and rice; it also gave Europe enormous quantities of gold and silver. So much bullion, in fact, flooded from America into Europe that the production of goods could not keep pace. The result was that until 1650 Europe experienced continuous inflation, with prices doubling in the half century before 1600, and tripling between 1500 and 1650. Generally it was the merchants who benefitted from this "price revolution," since they controlled goods whose value in money was steadily increasing, and their status in society rose accordingly.

But compelling as the traditional narrative is, it is incomplete. For the European "discovery" of a new world had a profound psychological impact on Europeans that, though impossible to quantify, was just as important in shaping the future as were the components of the traditional story. The European encounter with the Americas—a new world—fundamentally reshaped the way Europeans thought about themselves and about their place in the universe and, therefore, played a critically important role in the birth of the modern world. To establish that relationship we must examine evidence that gets at ideas, attitudes and emotions. Such evidence defies our ability to measure or quantify. The case it makes, however, is persuasive.

### The Impact of Discovery: Europeans Confront Native Americans

Though Columbus maintained throughout his life that he had sailed to Asia, once Europeans began to meet natives it was clear that the peoples who inhabited the Indies and the American coastal areas were strikingly different from those described by medieval travelers to China. Nor were the Native American settlements anything like the rich cities described in the accounts of merchants such as Marco Polo. The very existence of the Amerindians posed a problem for Europeans. Were they humans? If so, how could their existence be reconciled with the story of creation related in the Bible? Was the Bible wrong? Was it incomplete? If these creatures were descendants of Adam and Eve, how did they get to the Americas?

One who grappled with the question was the Jesuit José de Acosta, who wrote his *Natural and Moral History of the Indies* in 1587 after spending fifteen years in Spanish America. The work had a great impact throughout Europe, and was translated into many languages, including English (1604). His success in reconciling the existence of the indigenous population with the biblical story of creation is worth reading:

By what meanes the first men might come to the Indies, the which was not willingly, nor of set purpose.

*Now it is time to make answer to such as say there are no Antipodes, and that this region where we live cannot bee inhabited. The huge greatnes of the Ocean did so amaze S. Augustine as he could not conceive how mankind could passe to this new-found world. But seeing on the one side wee know for certaine, that many yeeres agoe there were men inhabiting in these parts, so likewise we cannot deny but the scripture doth teach us cleerely, that all men are come from the first man, without doubt we shall be forced to beleeve and confesse, that men have passed hither from Europe, Asia, or Affricke, yet must wee discover by what meanes they could passe. It is not likely that there was an other Noes Arke by the which men might be transported into the Indies, and much lesse any Angell to carie the first man to this new world, holding him by the haire of the head, like to the Prophet* Abacuc: *for we intreat not of the mightie power of God, but only of that which is conformable unto reason, & the order and disposition of humane things. Wherefore these two things ought to be held for wonderfull and worthie of admiration, yea, to bee numbred among the secrets of God. The one is; how man could passe so huge a passage by Sea and Lande. The other is; that there beeing such multitudes of people, they have yet beene unknowne so many ages. For this cause I demaund, by what resolution, force or industrie, the Indians could passe so large a Sea, and who might be the Inventer of so strange a passage? Truely I have often times considered thereof with my selfe, as many others have done, but never could I finde any thing to satisfie mee. Yet will I say what I have conceived, and what comes presently into my minde, seeing that testimonies faile mee, whom I might follow, suffering myselfe to be guided by the rule of reason, (although it be very subtill.) It is most certaine, that the first men came to this land of* Peru *by one of these two meanes, either by land or by sea. If they came by sea, it was casually, and by chance, or willingly, & of purpose. I understand by chance, being cast by force of some storme or tempest, as it happens in tempestuous times. I meane done of purpose, when they prepared fleetes to discover new lands. Besides these two meanes I see it is not possible to find out any other, if wee will follow the course of humane things, and not devise fabulous and poeticall fictions; for no man may thinke to finde another Eagle as that of* Ganimede, *or a flying Horse like unto* Perseus, *that should carie the Indians through the aire; or that peradventure those first men have used fishes, as Mirtnaids, or the fish called a Nicholas, to passe them thither. But laying aside these imaginations and fopperies, let us examine these two meanes, the which will bee both pleasant and profitable …*

Notwithstanding all that hath bene said, it is more likely that the first inhabitants of the Indies, came by land.

*I conclude then, that it is likely the first that came to the* Indies *was by shipwracke and tempest of wether, but heereupon groweth a difficultie which troubleth me much. For, suppose wee grant that the first men came from farre Countries, and that the nations which we now see are issued from them, and multiplied, yet can I not conjecture by what meanes brute beastes (whereof there is great aboundance) could come there, not being likely, they should have bin imbarked and carried by sea. The reason that inforceth us to yeeld, that the first men of the* Indies *are come from Europe or Asia, is the testimonie of the holy scripture, which teacheth us plainely, that all men came from* Adam. *We can therefore give no other beginning to those at the* Indies, *seeing the holy scripture saieth, that Gen. all beasts and creatures of the earth perished, but such as were reserved in the Arke of* Noe, *for the multiplication and maintenance of their kinde; so as we must necessarily referre the multiplication of all beastes to those which came out of the Arke of* Noe, *on the mountaines of* Ararat, *where it staied. And by this meanes, we must seeke out both for men and beastes the way whereby they might passe from the old world to this new.*

José de Acosta, *Natural and Moral History of the Indies,*
trans. by E. G. (London, 1604), 50–52, 64.[5]

What is important here is not that European scholars proved able to accommodate the discovery of a new land into their existing theories or beliefs, but that their encounter with the Americas prompted them to question inherited knowledge, which they felt compelled to align with what they actually observed. They were forced to reconcile their beliefs with evidence that could be seen and touched, and which, therefore, could not be denied.

Some anticipated that in the New World Europeans would encounter the monstrous races described in travel accounts by writers like Marco Polo and Sir John Mandeville. Mandeville's narrative (thought to be authentic by his contemporaries but now believed to be fraudulent), first published in French in 1356, described humans with dog's faces, and was reprinted at least three times in the early sixteenth century. Columbus reported that Indian informants described residents of Cuba who had tails. A woodcut produced in Strasbourg in 1525 by Lorenz Fries depicts American Indians as dog-headed cannibals, butchering humans. As late as the end of the sixteenth century Levinus Hulsius published an image of headless natives with facial features in their torsos (blemmyae) that was based on a description of the inhabitants of Guayana attributed to the English courtier and colonizer Sir Walter Raleigh. The image below, from the end of the fifteenth century, illustrated the "Second poem on India" by the Italian poet and bishop Giuliano Dati, which was based on Columbus's account of his discoveries. The second figure from the left is a blemmye, the figures on the far right are sciapods, creatures with feet so large that they provide shade from the sun when raised.

The first image of Native Americans that circulated widely in Europe—a woodcut printed in Augsburg—dates from the turn of the sixteenth century (1500–1504). It must have aroused intense interest because it depicted creatures that had never been seen

**Figure 2.1.** Illustration from Giuliano Dati, "Second Poem on India." The Bernardo Mendel Collection, Indiana University, Bloomington.

**Figure 2.2.** Engraving (after the woodcut) by Johann Froschauer for an edition of Amerigo Vespucci's *Mundus Novus*, published in Augsburg in 1505. *Mundus Novus* is an account of a purported third voyage (actually Vespucci's second in 1501–1502) to the New World, specifically to the eastern coast of Brazil.

in Christendom and, given the myths about monstrous races, fantastic islands or lost ancient civilizations that pervaded Europe from antiquity through the Renaissance, it seemed to provide answers to questions that had been posed for ages. At the same time, however, the images in the Augsburg woodcut raised a host of new, and deeply troubling issues European viewers could not ignore. The woodcut's impact surely was equivalent to what would occur today were a spacecraft to return from a distant galaxy with photos of extraterrestrials.

Publication of the original woodcut coincided with Vespucci's two voyages of exploration, the second of which in 1501 established beyond doubt that Columbus had bumped into a new continent. Thus Europeans who looked at the images of the American natives depicted here could not avoid wondering where these people came from. If their very existence provoked questions (and for some observers, doubt), then what did Europeans think when they considered the scene so carefully depicted by the artist? Here we observe noble, even god-like creatures who strike poses that evoke images familiar to Europeans who knew and admired the classical age. The natives stand erect. Their musculature is impressive. They are dignified and handsome. The curly-haired young boy in the center looks like a classical Greek or Roman statue as he gestures toward another child (a sibling?) who reaches for a woman (his mother?) who sits nursing an infant as she gently touches the child with her left hand. Look at that woman and that baby. They comprise an image known to every European—an iconic Madonna and Child. These are perfect creatures, ideal humans.

The figures in the woodcut, and later etching, appear virtually without clothing. In his important book *O Strange New World* (1952), the scholar Howard Mumford Jones wonders what Europeans, especially the Germans, must have thought when they learned that in the New World the inhabitants wore little clothing. Northern Europe's climate was often brutally harsh and in order to keep warm people covered themselves in heavy constricting clothing. What must it have meant that in the New World people could live without the need for such protection from the elements? What an idyllic, perfect place this must have seemed. And if heavy clothing was unnecessary, what was it about this place and these people that led them to live almost naked without shame? In the Garden of Eden Adam and Eve were without sin, hence without shame, hence without the need to cover their bodies. In the Garden of Eden, the weather was never harsh and humans needed no coats or hats. Was the New World the Garden of Eden and were its naked inhabitants God's original innocent and uncorrupted creations?

But look more closely at the images. Above the Dionysus-like cherubic little boy who is gesturing toward the Madonna and Child we see human body parts smoking over a fire. To the left one figure gnaws on a human arm as another grasps a dismembered thigh. This clearly is not Eden.

What were Europeans to make of these images? What must they have thought when they saw godlike creatures (in heroic poses) performing satanic acts? Here we have the perfect example of what Howard Mumford Jones labeled "image" and "anti-image." Virtually all the sources cited by Jones convey a monolithic message. Images and texts typically describe either the good (image) or the bad (anti-image). Both visual artists and writers generally portrayed either a benign or bucolic landscape filled with docile attractive humans and animals or savage natives engaged in demonic activities in a frightening environment that might include strange and fearsome beasts. What is striking about this print is that it simultaneously portrays both the good and the bad without any hint of self-contradiction. Here we see the origin of European ambivalence toward Native Americans—were the natives innocent and noble or were they corrupt and savage? Were they candidates for conversion or for eradication? Or were they, in the European mind, as in the Augsburg woodcut, both?

Before we leave this picture of Amerindians to consider other images, look toward the horizon where two European ships lie offshore. Why are they included in this portrayal of an American scene?

Their presence is hardly accidental. Indeed, it is of critical importance because those ships establish for the viewer that the scene illustrated by the artist represents the reality of life in America. By placing Europeans, in the image the artist demonstrates that the picture is based on direct observation by Europeans who personally witnessed what the viewer is seeing. This artistic device was well known in northern Europe during the Renaissance. Perhaps the best example is Jan van Eyck's *Arnolfini Wedding*, painted in

**Figure 2.3.** Jan van Eyck, *Arnolfini Wedding* (1434). National Gallery, London/Art Resource, New York.

**Figure 2.4.** *Arnolfini Wedding*, detail. Art Resource, New York.

1434, in which the artist inserts an image of himself painting the work into a circular mirror placed on a wall between the bride and groom.

By painting himself into the scene Van Eyck establishes that the wedding did, in fact, take place and that he personally witnessed the ceremony.

Surely the creator of the Augsburg woodcut placed two European ships just offshore in order to establish the veracity of the scene he portrayed. What he is telling the viewer is that no matter how shocking the images, this was the reality Europeans encountered in America. Given the inherently contradictory message about the nature of the natives (at once godlike and demonic), it was essential that the accuracy of the representation be proved. The artist chose to accomplish that goal by including European eyewitnesses in the image.

The picture of Native Americans presented in the Augsburg woodcut proved compelling. Given the European appetite for news from the New World, and especially for visual evidence of the discoveries, the sheet as published must have enjoyed wide circulation. The audience for the image was expanded significantly by the unabashed way the figures in the woodcut were copied and then redistributed by others. Look at the image of Native Americans that illustrated the cover of *De Novo Mondo*, published in Antwerp by Jan van Doesborch about 1520. The male's pose, clothing and spear are identical to those

**Figure 2.5.** Cover illustration from Jan van Doesborch, *De Novo Mondo: A Facsimile of an Unique Broadsheet Containing an Early Account of the Inhabitants of South America: Together with a Short Version of Heinrich Sprenger's Voyage to the Indies* (*c.* 1520), ed. and trans. by M. E. Kronenberg (The Hague, 1927). Special Collections Library, Bryn Mawr College.

of the figures in the Augsburg woodcut. The female with her children are direct copies of the Madonna and Child group in the woodcut. Similarly, the image of a human head and limb roasting over an open fire come directly from the earlier Augsburg work.

These images reinforced written accounts that described the inhabitants of the New World in terms that ranged from expressions of admiration to horror. The original Augsburg woodcut was published with a German text beneath the image that read, in part: "The people are thus naked, handsome, brown, their heads, necks, arms, private parts (and the) feet of men and women are a little covered with feathers. The men also have many precious stones in their faces and breasts. Nor does any one possess any thing, but all things are in common. And the men have as wives those who please them, being they mothers, sisters, or friends, wherein they make no distinction. They also fight with each other and eat each other, even the slain and hang the same flesh in the smoke. They become a hundred and fifty years old. And have no government."[6] What were Europeans to think of such people and of the place they lived?

### The Impact of Discovery: Creation of the Modern World

If early images from the era of exploration and discovery led Europeans to ask questions about the accuracy of what they had been told about the world and its inhabitants, and especially about the biblical story of creation, imagine the impact on their collective psyche when cartographers produced maps of a world that traditional authorities had asserted did not exist. Inherited wisdom held that God created the universe and placed the Earth at its center. Of all the creatures God created to inhabit Earth, man was supreme. Indeed, not only had God created humans in His own image, but He sent His son to die a human death to redeem mankind. It is not surprising, therefore, that European world maps (*mappamundi*) perfectly mirrored that narrative.

Consider the well-known thirteenth-century *Psalter Map*.

The Earth is depicted as a sphere (as noted earlier, all educated Europeans knew that the Earth was round). Jerusalem is at the very center. Above are Jesus and two angels. At the bottom of the map are dragons. Just below Jesus is the Garden of Eden, the earthly paradise. To the right is the Red Sea (colored red and divided to permit passage by the Hebrew slaves from Egypt to the Holy Land). A fish swims in the Sea of Galilee, Noah's Ark sits on a mountain, and a number of biblical cities are identified. The map was not drawn from personal experience or from travelers' reports. Instead, it was created based on a preconceived sense of the world's shape and designed quite intentionally to bolster that view. This is the world God created and over which He watches. This is a world in which humans know their place and in which their field of action is clearly defined (and restricted). The map offers a comforting, reassuring image because it reinforces what all authoritative sources (Bible, pope, bishop, priest, monarch) asserted was true. In this world one could trust in certainties and sleep contentedly knowing that God was watching over existence and eternity.

Two centuries later, in 1410, Cardinal Pierre d'Ailly included a world map in his *Imago Mundi*—a map of critical importance because we know that Columbus studied the text. Here we have a perfectly circular Earth with Europe to the left, Asia to the right and Africa below Europe. The Southern hemisphere is largely blank. The Mediterranean Sea is prominent, as are the tropic and latitude lines.

D'Ailly's text incorporates two theories that we now know are errors, but which had a profound impact on Columbus's proposal to sail to Asia from Europe by a route to the west. D'Ailly accepted the fourth-century BC Greek geographer Erastothenes' estimate of the size (circumference) of the world, which he seriously underestimated. D'Ailly also incorporated Ptolemy's second-century AD estimate of the extent of the land mass of Asia, which he significantly overestimated. Combining a smaller Earth with a larger Asia, it was perfectly reasonable to assume that one could sail west from Europe and reach the East Indies before food and water supplies were exhausted. Moreover, D'Ailly's latitude lines placed China due west from Europe—a direct voyage that ought to be relatively simple once a pilot found a supporting wind.

The last great surviving pre-Columbian world map dates from 1489, and was drawn by the cartographer Henricus Martellus. It is detailed and sophisticated, with the coastlines of Europe and Africa, especially those on the Mediterranean Sea, depicted with great accuracy.

**Figure 2.6.** *The Psalter Map* (*c.* 1225–50). British Library (Add.MS 28681, fol 9r).

**Figure 2.7.** Pierre d'Ailly, *Imago Mundi* (1410). Cartographic Images.

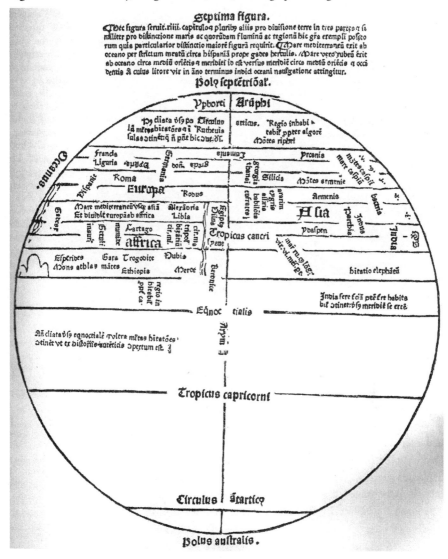

The Martellus map documents with precision the extent of European (Portuguese) voyages along the African coast. We see exactly where Bartholomew Dias's voyage around the southern tip of Africa ended—at that point the cartographer stops identifying specific locations along the coast. We also see clearly what was not known by Europeans. The massive Asian continent is virtually without specifically identified locations. Instead, we see rivers and mountains that seem to appear as much for decoration as they do to

**Figure 2.8.** Henricus Martellus, *Insularium* (*c.* 1490). British Museum.

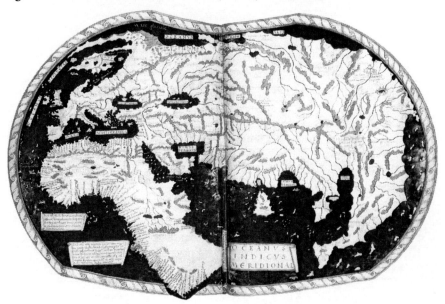

serve as a guide for travelers or for students of geography. The east coast of Asia shows a bloated peninsula-like land mass that may be Japan or China. It is clear that Martellus had no recent first-hand evidence to use as he drew Asia—his images are based on travelers' accounts, fables and second- or third-hand reports by seamen who had met and spoken with other seamen in Mediterranean or African ports.

What we have then are a series of historical documents that provide a consistent view of the world and its place in the universe. Though hundreds of years separate the Martellus map from the *Psalter Map*, there really is no fundamental difference in the two. All that has happened in the intervening centuries, as Europe gradually moved from the Middle Ages into the Renaissance, is that Europeans succeeded in filling in the details of God's design. The Earth of the last decade of the fifteenth century, in spite of advances in technology, heightened interest in the wisdom of classical scholars and efforts by Europeans to venture into the wider world, was no different from the Earth of the thirteenth century. Martellus' map is merely a more accurate and detailed version of the *Psalter*.

In fact, Martellus depicted a world that would have been understood not only in the thirteenth century, but far earlier. For all its detail, the Martellus map is essentially what scholars label a T-O map, a circle that circumscribes the three continents—Europe, Asia and Africa. A good example is Isidore of Seville's world map, drawn in the seventh century.

T-O maps depicted not only the geographical shape of the world, but also reinforced the eternity and the immutability of God's creation. This is the world as created. This is

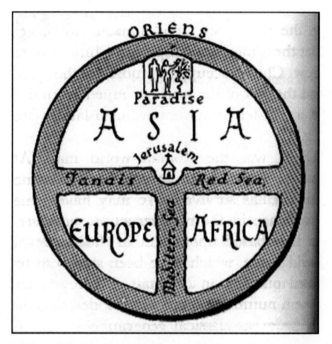

**Figure 2.9.** Isidore of Seville, *Etymologiarum sive Originum libri XX* (seventh century). Cartographic Images.

> Concerning the earth we are told that it is named from its roundness (orbis) which is like a wheel; whence the small wheel is called "orbiculus." For the Ocean flows round it on all sides and encircles its boundaries.
>
> The ancients did not divide these three parts of the world equally, for Asia stretches right from the south, through the east to the north, but Europe stretches from the north to the west and thence Africa from the west to the south. From this it is quite evident that the two parts, Europe and Africa, occupy half of the world and that Asia alone occupies the other half. The former were made into two parts because the Great Sea (called the Mediterranean) enters from the Ocean between them and cuts them apart …

the world described in the Bible. This is the world as portrayed by every authoritative scholar, geographer and cleric. This is the world as it is, as it was and as it always will be. This is where God placed man and its boundaries describe the limit of man's activities. This is a world that does not change. To alter it would be to defy God and God's agents on Earth, just as opposition to the rulers of church and state placed by God in positions of authority would be seen as opposing God's plan. In this world, individuals occupied defined positions in society, which were parts of that master plan. In this world, to seek change could be interpreted as opposing God's will. In this world humans were born into roles they were expected to occupy for life—roles their ancestors had filled and which their descendants would fill. This was an unchanging world of certainties, of eternal truths.

**Figure 2.10.** Juan Vespucci, *Planisphere* (1526). Hispanic Society of America, New York.

**Figure 2.11.** Map by Diego Ribero (1529). Biblioteca Apostolica Vaticana.

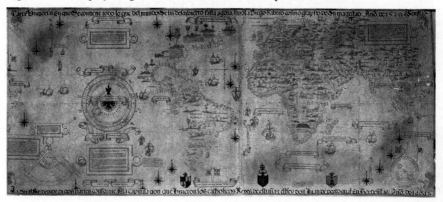

Then, suddenly, in half a human lifetime, everything changed. After Vespucci's two voyages at the turn of the sixteenth century it was clear that Columbus had bumped not into Asian islands but rather into a new continent that was not supposed to be there and into new peoples whose existence challenged the biblical story of creation. The pace at which Europeans gained detailed knowledge of the extent of this New World, and of its shape, is stunning. Look at two world maps, one Spanish and the other Portuguese, from 1526 and 1529, drawn by Juan Vespucci and Diego Ribero.

The facsimile copy of the Ribero map below was drawn in 1893.

These beautiful maps, based on actual observation by Europeans, represent the beginning of the modern age. They are a kind of Declaration of Independence from a world whose boundaries were fixed at creation and whose outlines were determined not by observation, research or experience, but rather by tradition, precedent, theory or the dictate of authority.

The implications, of course, were staggering. Could the Bible be wrong? Could the church hierarchy be wrong? Clearly, Ptolemy was wrong and if he had made serious

**Figure 2.12.** Diego Ribero, *Second Borgian map by Diego Ribero* (Seville, 1529). Library and Archives Canada (NMC 15174).

errors, what ancient authority in any field could be trusted? We know that scholars like Acosta grappled with such questions. During his voyage to the Indies he travelled through what he labeled the "Torrid Zone," where humans, according to classical authorities, were not supposed to be able to survive the intense heat. When that proved not to be the case Acosta wrote: "What could I do then but laugh at Aristotle's *Meterology* and his philosophy? For in that place and that season, where everything, by his rules, should have been scorched by the heat, I and my companions were cold."[7] Vespucci had reached the same conclusion two decades earlier when he told Lorenzo di Medici that "by this voyage most of the philosophers are controverted who say that the torrid zone cannot be inhabited on account of the great heat. I have found the case to be quite the contrary. The air is fresher and more temperate in that region than beyond it, and the inhabitants are more numerous here than they are in the other zones, for reasons that will be given below. Thus, it is certain, that practice is more valuable than theory."[8]

If the physical contours of the Earth itself could change, was anything immune from change? Was the inherited social order maintained by both church and state a reflection of a divinely ordained scheme, or was it a way to ensure that the powerful would retain their privileged positions?

And what were the implications for humans' view of themselves and of their ability to influence, if not control, their own fates? It was humans, after all, using technology they created, who had mastered nature and changed the world. Must not this have profoundly altered humans' sense of their own power? Must not the recognition that the world they inherited was not immutable, but could be transformed by human actions, have had both a liberating and an empowering effect? Were not humans now free to think they might act to control the future as opposed to accepting the status quo? Was not their field of activity now expanded? If humans could venture into the unknown, forbidding sea and reshape their world, who was to say they needed to limit their field of activity at all? Might not men now dream about, and actually aspire to leaving Earth itself to master the universe? Was there anything humans could not do?

In the world of the *Psalter Map*, humans passively (and contentedly) accepted their social/economic status and their fate as part of a divinely ordained master plan. If a couple had failed to produce offspring they might accept it as God's will and look to the Bible and consider the story of Abraham and Sarah. In the post-Columbian world, they would seek the help not of a priest, but rather of a human reproduction specialist whose approach could range from *in vitro* fertilization to the administration of any number of pharmaceutical products created by researchers to promote fertilization.

Perhaps the most significant consequence of the European discovery of the New World was simply that it introduced the concept of change not merely as a possibility, but as a positive good. This is, in fact, America's great gift to the world. Once the era of discovery was replaced by actual European colonization, the implications of this idea were fully realized. People came to America precisely to change their lives, or to change the circumstances under which they lived their lives. In America, change is precisely what attracted immigrants and what new settlers anticipated. This was, and still is, revolutionary.

Of course, change is, by definition, threatening to individuals, groups and institutions with vested interests and inherited positions of power and wealth. To the extent the New World (by its mere existence) caused humans to question established ways of acting or thinking it represented a threat to powerful interests. It also undermined the traditional view of the Earth as the center of the universe. Listen to the words of a cardinal, a prince of the Catholic Church, to the astronomer Galileo Galilei as written by Berthold Brecht in his play *Galileo* (1952):

> I am informed that Signor Galilei transfers mankind from the center of the universe to somewhere on the outskirts. Signor Galilei is therefore an enemy of mankind ... Is it conceivable that God would trust this most precious fruit of his labor to a minor frolicking star? Would He have sent His Son to such a place? ... I won't have it! I won't be a nobody on an inconsequential star twirling hither and thither. The earth is the center of all things, and I am the center of the earth, and the eye of the Creator is on me. About me revolve ... the lesser lights of the stars and the great light of the sun, created to give light on me that God might see me—Man, God's greatest effort, the center of creation.[9]

The universe Brecht's cardinal describes is the universe of the *Psalter* and of the other pre-Columbian maps. That universe was destroyed by the European discovery of the Americas and by the science of which it was a part and which it stimulated. As important as were the gold, silver, horses, viruses and crops, which constituted the components of the Columbian Exchange, it is the psychological, intellectual and emotional impact of discovery that proved transformative.

## For Further Reading

Crosby, Alfred W., *The Columbian Exchange: Biological and Cultural Consequences of 1492* (Westport, CT, 1972).
_____, *The Columbian Voyages, the Columbian Exchange, and Their Historians* (Washington, DC, 1987).
Elliott, J. H., *The Old World and the New, 1492–1650* (Cambridge, 1970).
Grafton, Anthony, *New Worlds, Ancient Texts: The Power of Tradition and the Shock of Discovery* (Cambridge, MA, 1992).
Greenblatt, Stephen, *Marvelous Possessions: The Wonder of the New World* (Chicago, 1991).
Mumford Jones, Howard, *O Strange New World: American Culture: The Formative Years* (New York, 1964).
Seed, Patricia, *Ceremonies of Possession in Europe's Conquest of the New World, 1492–1640* (Cambridge, 2006).

## Notes

1 Available online at http://www.gutenberg.org/files/18571/18571-h/18571-h.htm (accessed June 1, 2013).

2 Available online at http://archive.org/details/firstletterofchr00colu (accessed March 12, 2013).

3 Available online at http://www.gutenberg.org/files/19997/19997-h/19997-h.htm (accessed March 12, 2013).

4 Alfred W. Crosby, *The Columbian Exchange: Biological and Cultural Consequences of 1492* (Westport, CT, 1972).

5 Available online at http://olivercowdery.com/texts/1604Acos.htm (accessed March 12, 2013).

6 See http://commons.wikimedia.org/wiki/File:Cannibalism_in_the_New_World,_from_Vespucci. jpg (accessed March 12, 2013).

7 José de Acosta, quoted in Anthony Grafton, with April Shelford and Nancy Siraisi, *New Worlds, Ancient Texts: The Power of Tradition and the Shock of Discovery* (Cambridge, MA, 1995), 1.

8 Amerigo Vespucci, "Letter to Lorenzo de' Medici," in Frederick A. Ober, *Amerigo Vespucci* (New York and London, 1907), 114. Online at http://archive.org/details/firstletterofchr00colu (accessed March 12, 2013).

9 Bertolt Brecht, *Galileo*, trans. by Charles Laughton, ed. by Eric Bentley (New York, 1966), 72–3.

# Chapter Three

# SPAIN ASCENDANT: CONQUEST AND COLONIZATION

*The man rules over the woman, the adult over the child, the father over his children. That is to say, the most powerful and most perfect rule over the weakest and most imperfect. This same relationship exists among men, there being some who by nature are masters and others who by nature are slaves. Those who surpass the rest in prudence and intelligence, although not in physical strength, are by nature the masters. On the other hand, those who are dim-witted and mentally lazy, although they may be physically strong enough to fulfill all the necessary tasks, are by nature slaves. It is just and useful that it be this way. We even see it sanctioned in divine law itself, for it is written in the Book of Proverbs: "He who is stupid will serve the wise man." And so it is with the barbarous and inhumane peoples [the Indians] who have no civil life and peaceful customs. It will always be just and in conformity with natural law that such people submit to the rule of more cultured and humane princes and nations. Thanks to their virtues and the practical wisdom of their laws, the latter can destroy barbarism and educate these [inferior] people to a more humane and virtuous life. And if the latter reject such rule, it can be imposed upon them by force of arms. Such a war will be just according to natural law ...*

—Juan Ginés de Sepúlveda, *On the Reasons for the Just War among the Indians* (1547)

*And Montezuma thereupon sent [and] charged the noblemen ... to go to meet [Cortés] ... They gave them golden banners, precious feather streamers, and golden necklaces.*

*And when they had given them these, they appeared to smile; they were greatly contented, gladdened. As if they were monkeys they seized upon the gold. It was as is their hearts were satisfied, brightened, calmed. For in truth they thirsted mightily for gold; they stuffed themselves with it; they starved for it; they lusted for it like pigs.*

*And they went about lifting on high the golden banners; they went moving them back and forth; they went taking them to themselves. It was as if they babbled. What they said was gibberish.*

—Fray Bernardo de Sahagún, *General History of the Things of New Spain* (Florentine Codex) (1540–1585)

## Settlement and Colonization of the New World

Once Europeans realized that Columbus's discovery was, in fact, an entire continent with perhaps massive untapped resources, they proceeded to consider the establishment of permanent settlements there. At minimum, leaders reasoned, they should stake out and secure with settlements areas that might prove valuable as points of embarkation for further discoveries, among which a western sea passage through America was the most ardently desired. The early explorers had already brought back not only small quantities of gold and pearls but numerous reports from the natives of vast stores of precious stones and metals that were merely waiting to be "discovered" and exploited.

Some Europeans had other plans for America. The Old World was cluttered with visible evidence of the errors of previous generations—with foul and confused cities, with certain groups of people whose existence corrupted the "purity" of national populations, with institutions or persons who could cite privileges gained during previous centuries to resist or thwart absolute rule by their monarchs. In the Old World, every new idea found an opposition based on "traditional wisdom" whose exponents exercised sufficient power or influence to prevent its fair trial. To men with new ideas, or old ideas never given a chance, America offered a magnificent opportunity. For America represented open space, a place where innovative social, religious, and political theoreticians might bring to realization programs for which the Old World simply had no room, or which if attempted would arouse debilitating or fatal opposition from other more established groups.

At the outset, the only obstacle to the free use of America by such men could come from indigenous native peoples. But Europeans did not come to America prepared to fail. Their technology (especially their firearms) was superior to anything Native Americans might use to resist. Their knowledge of science armed Europeans with a sense of mastery that, in turn, bolstered their self-confidence. Their Christianity made them certain of the rectitude and morality of their purpose, and reinforced their conviction that they were "superior" to the "heathens" they encountered. That sense of superiority extended to their own institutions of society and government and made them believe that those institutions could be transported across an ocean and successfully function in that New World. Indeed, Europeans came to America convinced in most cases that the institutions they intended to erect there would, once established, prove of far greater benefit to the natives than those which had evolved in response to Native American needs on Native American land.

### Spain in America

Spaniards were the first Europeans since the Vikings to settle in America, and the first to realize that in the relative freedom of the American continent they might create communities free of the defects that plagued society in the Old World. Ferdinand and Isabella completed the reconquest of Spain from the Moors the year Columbus embarked on his first voyage to the New World. The monarchs were full of the crusading spirit, eager to cleanse Spanish society of all aliens (Moors) and heretics (Jews), and determined to rule Spain absolutely. The problem in all this was that while they could initiate strong measures to expel non-Spanish and non-Catholic people, support the Inquisition to purify religion and sponsor efforts to extend the wealth and influence of their kingdoms, they could not totally eradicate their own history. Even if there were no Moors left on Spanish soil there surely were Moorish buildings; and if there were no visible Jews there surely were secret Jews. Their desire to rule absolutely was also confounded by the presence in Spain of numerous entities—local rulers and towns—which, during the long struggle with the Moors, had been granted special privileges or exemptions by Spanish rulers in return for their services against the enemy. The Moors had been eliminated but a degree of local autonomy had not.

Thus, precisely when Spaniards began to build settlements in the West Indies, the Spanish monarchs were especially sensitive to the problems that plagued rulers who granted too much power to local leaders or institutions, and who permitted alien and, hence, potentially disloyal groups to live in areas they ruled. In the New World, the Spanish rulers saw clearly the opportunity they had been given—they could assert their prerogatives without much interference and thereby create a pure society, a society free of the defects they perceived in Spanish society.

Since Isabella had officially sponsored Columbus's voyage of discovery, the land he claimed devolved not on Spain, but on the ruler of Castille. In Aragon, royal decisions required approval by the Cortés, the assembly. Royal power in Castille, however, was not limited in this manner. Spanish America came to be ruled by an absolute monarch whose vision of an ideal society did not include a place for assemblies. From the outset the Spanish rulers determined that one-fifth of all gold produced in America be set aside for the crown, thereby ensuring their independence of the nobility in financial matters. Similarly, the crown decreed that Jews, Moors, gypsies and (after the Reformation), Protestants could not settle in Spanish America. Any foreigners who sought to come were carefully examined to ensure that they were good Catholics. In America, the Spanish crown would be supreme and unchallenged. Religion would be pure and serve to unite the colonies with the mother country. One Spanish missionary, Vasco de Quiroga, established actual Indian communities in New Spain that were modeled on Thomas More's *Utopia*. What matters about such social experiments is not so much that ultimately they failed to succeed, but rather that the open space of America was the only place they could be attempted.

## Model Cities

Spanish efforts to use America to realize goals unattainable in the Old World can be examined through the microcosm of urban development. Renaissance Europeans viewed cities as symbols of the societies that created them. Beautiful well-designed communities not only added to the quality of life but served as visual statements about the high regard their citizens had for an ordered society. But in Spain, as throughout Europe, no single planner had designed its cities. In fact, cities in the Old World had developed slowly and haphazardly. While there was virtually nothing rulers could do to alter Europe's cities, in the New World community planners could develop ideas without the need to take into account pre-existing structures. In the uncluttered landscape of America, a single preconceived master plan could be used, and as early as 1514 the Spanish crown sent an agent to the New World with instructions for the building of Panama City. Before the end of the century, laws were promulgated that rigidly governed the layout of all towns in Spanish America. The result was that Spanish towns in the New World were built according to an "ideal" pattern devised in Spain, which included a central plaza surrounded by major ecclesiastical and municipal buildings and special sections set aside for specific trades. Indeed, the crown was so intent on controlling urban growth that frequently towns were established by royal order well before the surrounding area was settled to the degree that it could support a town. King Philip II's instructions, *Royal Ordinances Concerning the Laying Out of New Towns*, issued in 1573, were quite specific.

> *Having made the chosen discovery of the province, district, and land which is to be settled, and the sites of the places where the new towns are to be made, and the agreement in regard to them having preceded, those who go to execute this shall perform it in the following manner: On arriving at the place where the town is to be laid out (which we order to be one of those vacant and which by our ordinance may be taken without doing hurt to the indians and natives, or with their free consent), the plan of the place shall be determined, and its plazas, streets, and building lots laid out exactly, beginning with the main plaza. From thence the streets, gates, and principal roads, shall be laid out, always leaving a certain proportion of open space, so that although the town should continue to grow, it may always grow in the same manner. Having arranged the site and place that shall have been chosen for settlement, the foundation shall be made in the following manner.*
>
> *Having chosen the place where the town is to be made, which as abovesaid must be located in an elevated place, where are to be found health, strength, fertility, and abundance of land for farming and pasturage, fuel and wood for building, materials, fresh water, a native people, commodiousness, supplies, entrance and departure open to the north wind. If the site lies along the coast, let consideration be had to the port and that the sea be not situated to the south or to the west. If possible, let there be no lagoons or marshes nearby in which are found venomous animals and corruption of air and water.*
>
> *The main plaza whence a beginning is to be made, if the town is situated on the seacoast, should be made at the landing place of the port. If the town lies inland, the main plaza should be in the middle of the town. The plaza shall be of an oblong form, which shall have at the least a length equal to one and a half times the width, inasmuch as this size is the best for fiestas in which horses are used and for any other fiestas that shall be held.*
>
> *The size of the plaza shall be proportioned to the number of the inhabitants, having consideration to the fact that in indian towns, inasmuch as they are new, the population will*

continue to increase, and it is the purpose, that it shall increase. Consequently, the choice of a plaza shall be made with reference to the growth that the town may have. It shall be not less than two hundred feet wide and three hundred feet long, nor larger than eight hundred feet long and thirty two feet [sic] wide. A moderate and good proportion is six hundred feet long and four hundred feet wide.

From the plaza shall run four main streets, one from the middle of each side of the plaza; and two streets at each corner of the plaza. The four corners of the plaza shall face the four principal winds. For the streets running thus from the plaza, they will not be exposed to the four principal winds which cause much inconvenience.

The whole plaza round about, and the four streets running from the four sides shall have arcades, for these are of considerable convenience to the merchants who generally gather there. The eight streets running from the plaza at the four corners shall open on the plaza without any arcades and shall be so laid out that they may have sidewalks even with the street and plaza.

The streets in cold places shall be wide and in hot places narrow; but for purposes of defense, where horses are to be had, they are better wide.

The streets shall run from the main plaza in such wise that although the town increase considerably in size, no inconvenience may arise which may cause what may be rebuilt to become ugly or be prejudicial to its defense and commodiousness.

Here and there in the town smaller plazas shall be laid out, in good pro- portion, where are to be built the temples of the cathedral, the parish churches and the monasteries, such that everything may be distributed in good proportions for the instruction of religion.

As for the temple of the cathedral, if the town is situated on the coast, it shall be built in part so that it may be seen on leaving the sea, and in a place where its building may serve as a means of defense for the port itself.

For the temple of the cathedral, the parish church, or monastery, building lots shall be assigned, next after the plaza and streets and they shall be so completely isolated that no building shall be added there except one appertaining to its commodiousness and ornamentation.

After that a site and location shall be assigned for the royal council and cabildo house and for the custom house and arsenal near the temple and port itself so that in times of need the one may aid the other. The hospital for the poor and those sick of non-contagious diseases shall be built near the temple and its cloister; and that for those sick with contagious diseases shall be built in such a place that no harmful wind passing through it, may cause harm to the rest of the town. If the latter be built in an elevated place, so much the better.

The site and building lots for slaughter houses, fisheries, tanneries, and other things productive of filth shall be so placed that the filth can be easily disposed of.

It will be of considerable convenience if those towns which are laid out away from the port and inland be built if possible on the shores of a navigable river; and the attempt should be made to have the shore where it is reached by the cold north wind; and that all the trades that give rise to filth be placed on the side of the river and sea below the town.

The temple in inland towns shall not be placed on the plaza but distant from it and in such a place that it may be separated from any building which approaches it and which has no connection *with it; and so that it may be seen from all parts. In order that it may be better embellished and have more authority, it must, if possible, be built somewhat elevated above the ground in order that steps will lead to its entrance. Nearby close to the main plaza shall be built the royal houses and the council and cabildo house, and the customs house so that they shall not cause any embarrassment to the temple but lend it authority. The hospital of the poor who shall be sick with non-contagious diseases, shall be built facing the cold north wind and so arranged that it may enjoy the south wind.*

*The same arrangement shall be observed in all inland places which have no shore provided that considerable care be given to providing the other conveniences which are required and which are necessary.*

*Building lots shall not be assigned to individual persons in the plaza where are placed the buildings of the church and royal houses and the public land of the city. Shops and houses shall be built for merchants and these shall be the first to be built and for this all the settlers of the town shall contribute, and a moderate tax shall be imposed on goods so that these buildings may be built.*

*The other building lots shall be distributed by lot to the settlers, those lots next to the main plaza being thus distributed and the lots which are left shall be held by us for assignment to those who shall later become settlers, or for the use which we may wish to make of them. And so that this may be done better, the town which is to be laid out should always be shown on a plan.*

*Having made the plan of the town and the assignment of building lots, each of the settlers shall set up his tent on his plot if he should have one. For this purpose the captains shall persuade them to carry tents. Those who do not possess tents shall build their huts of such materials that can be obtained easily, where they may have shelter. As soon as possible all settlers shall make some sort of a palisade or ditch about the plaza so that they may receive no harm from the indian natives.*

*A commons shall be assigned to the town of such size that although the town continues to grow, there may always be sufficient space for the people to go for recreation and for the cattle to be pastured without any danger.*

*Adjoining the commons there shall be assigned pastures for the work animals and for the horses as well as for the cattle belonging to the slaughterhouses and for the usual number of cattle which the settlers must have to some goodly number according to ordinance, and so that they may also be used as the common property of the council. The rest of the land shall be assigned as farm lands, of which lots shall be cast in proportion to the amount, so that there shall be as many farms as there are building lots in the town. And should there be irrigated lands, lots shall be cast for them, and they shall be distributed in the same proportion to the first settlers according to their lots. The rest shall remain for ourselves so that we may assign it to those who may become settlers.*

*The settlers shall immediately plant all the seeds they take with them and all that they can obtain on the farm lands after their distribution. For this purpose, it is advisable that they go well provided; and in the pastures especially all the cattle that they take with them and all that they can collect so that the cattle may begin to breed and multiply immediately.*

*The settlers having planted their seeds and made arrangements for the cattle to a goodly number, and with good diligence (from which they may hope to obtain abundance of food), shall commence with great care and activity to establish their houses and to build them with good foundations and walls. For that purpose they shall go provided with molds or planks for buildings them, and all the other tools for building quickly and at small cost.*

*They shall arrange the building lots and edifices placed thereon in such a manner that the rooms of the latter may enjoy the air of the south and north as these are the best. The buildings of the houses of the whole town generally shall be so arranged that they shall serve as a defense and fort against those who may try to disturb or invade the town. Each house in particular shall be so built that they may keep therein their horses and work animals, and shall have yards and corrals as large as possible for health and cleanliness.*

*They shall try so far as possible to have the buildings all of one form for the sake of the beauty of the town.*

*The faithful executors and architects and persons who may be deputed therefor by the governor shall be most careful in the performance of the above. They shall hurry the labor and building so that the town may be completed in a short time.*

*Should the natives care to place themselves under the defense of the town, they must be made to understand that it is desired to build a town there not in order to do them any harm nor to take their possessions from them, but to maintain friendship with them and to teach them to live in a civilized manner, to teach them to know God, and to teach them His law, under which they shall be saved. This shall be imparted to them by the religious, ecclesiastical persons, and persons deputed therefor by the governor and by means of good interpreters. By means of all good methods possible, the attempt shall be made to have the town laid out with their goodwill and consent. However, should they not consent after having been summoned by various means on different occasions, the settlers shall lay out their town, but without taking anything that may belong in particular to the indians and without doing them other hurt than what may be necessary for the defense of the settlers and so that the town should [not] be molested.*

*Until the new town shall have been completed, the settlers shall try as much as possible to avoid communication and intercourse with the indians and shall not go to their towns and shall not amuse themselves nor give themselves up to sensual pleasures in the land. Neither shall the indians enter the precincts of the town until after it has been built and placd in a condition of defense, and the houses so built that when the indians see them they shall wonder and understand that the Spaniards settle there for good and not for the moment only; and so that they may fear them so much that they will not offend them and hall respect them so much as to desire their friendship. When they begin to build the town, the goveror shall assign some one person to take care of the sowing and cultivation of the land with wheat and vegetables of which the settlers may immediately make use for their maintenance. He shall also see that the cattle are put out to pasture where they shall be safe and where they shall cause no hurt to the cultivated land nor to anything belonging to the indians; and so that also the town may be served, aided, and sustained by the aforesaid cattle and their young.*

Zelia Nuttall, "Royal Ordinances Concerning the Laying out of new Towns," *Hispanic American Historical Review* 4, no. 4 (November 1921): 249–54; and 5, no. 2 (May 1922): 249–54. Reproduced courtesy of Duke University Press.

Once Columbus's rights in the West Indies were revoked, Spanish leaders set out to order their possessions in the New World. The small supply of gold in the Indies was quickly dissipated and early settlers turned to sheep and cattle grazing to secure a livelihood. But what was economically beneficial for the Europeans proved disastrous to the indigenous population; with astounding speed, the animals imported by the Spanish destroyed the arable land of the Carib natives. And the Indians proved horribly susceptible to European diseases. They died off with shocking speed.

Some commentators, especially resident churchmen, asserted that the settlers simply worked the Indians to death. The crown, anxious to persuade Iberians to remain in the Indies in order both to secure the area for Spain and to Christianize the natives, decided to grant to settlers rights to the labor of and tribute from Indians in a village or a group of villages. Such a grant was labeled an *encomienda*. In return, the grantee or *encomendero* had to pledge that he would render military service, and defend and Christianize the Indians entrusted to him. A grant of *encomienda* was not considered perpetual—commonly it extended for the life of the original *encomendero*, or for several "*vidas*" (literally, lives or generations).

The Indians whose labor and wealth was disposed of were, in the official view, legally free. Since they were all subjects of the Spanish crown they could not be enslaved—a principle announced by Queen Isabella herself in 1498 when she responded to a report that Columbus had permitted Spaniards to return to Spain from Hispaniola with slaves by saying, "What power of mine does the admiral hold to give my vassals to anyone?"[1] The Queen did acknowledge in 1503 that natives who committed abominations such as cannibalism might be punished by enslavement. This standard, combined with the medieval Christian practice of enslaving pagans (typically Moors) captured in a "just war" and who refused to convert, led to expeditions designed specifically to capture Indians who were sold into slavery in areas where labor was needed. Such practices ultimately led the crown in 1542 to declare that no Indian could be enslaved since all of them were "vassals of the crown of Castile."

*Encomienda* promised to solve the labor problem the Spanish encountered. Since many of the societies they conquered had incorporated forced labor and tribute into their social orders, the Spaniards in many cases simply substituted themselves for the overlords they replaced. In theory *encomienda* simultaneously met the labor needs of the Spaniards while ensuring that the natives would remain free and would be protected. Doubtless, there is truth in the assertion that many Indians were brutally overworked under *encomienda*. Since the *encomenderos* were acutely aware that their privileges were not perpetual, they strove to extract the maximum benefits from "their" Indians in the minimum amount of time.

But the key problem for the Indians was not overwork, but European diseases to which they had no immunity. The population of Hispaniola, a million in 1492, had plummeted to about 14,000 by 1509. Aware of abuses in the system the crown consistently sought to limit the power of the *encomenderos*, or to abolish *encomienda* completely. To address problems associated with *encomienda*, in 1512–13 the crown promulgated the Laws of Burgos, which attacked *encomienda* abuses. While sanctioning the existence of *encomiendas* in the Indies, the laws limited their size and directed that the natives be well treated, Christianized and carefully protected from slavery. Such a policy was entirely consistent with royal goals. The Indians were free subjects of the crown—only the Spanish monarch could distribute grants of *encomienda*. Spain's rulers clearly perceived that if the *encomendero* class gained too much power, it might be able to threaten absolute rule.

*We order and command that all the chiefs and Indians dwelling on the Island of Espanola, now or in the future, shall be brought from their present dwelling places to the villages and communities of the Spaniards who reside, now or in the future, on the said Island; and in order that they be brought of their own volition and suffer no harm from the removal, we hereby command Don Diego Columbus, our Admiral, Viceroy, and Governor of the said Island, and our appellate judges and officers of it, to have them brought in the manner that seems best, with the least possible harm to the said chiefs and Indians, to this end encouraging them and urging them with praise; and we charge and command them most earnestly to do this with much care, fidelity, and diligence, with greater regard for the good treatment and conservation of the said Indians than for any other respect, desire, or interest, particular or general.*

*Also, we order and command that the citizen to whom the said Indians are given in encomienda shall, upon the land that is assigned to him, be obliged to erect a structure to be used for a church, on a site selected by you, the said Admiral, judges, and officers, or by the visitor appointed by you; and in this said church he shall place an image of Our Lady and a bell with which to call the Indians to prayer; and the person who has them in encomienda shall be obliged to have them called by the bell at nightfall and go with them to the said church, and have them cross themselves and bless themselves, and together recite the* Ave Maria, *the* Pater Noster, *the* Credo, *and the* Salve Regina, *in such wise that all of them shall hear the said person, and the said person hear them, so that he may know who is performing well and who ill, and correct the one who is wrong; and since the period we command to be allowed them for rest before nightfall is principally for the purpose of having them rested at the hour of evening prayer, in case any Indian should fail to come to the said church at the said time, we command that on the day following he shall not be allowed to rest during the said period; but he shall still be urged to go to prayers the next night; and we also command that each morning, before they go to work, they shall be obliged to go to the said church and pray as they do in the evening; but they shall not be obliged on that account, to rise earlier than is customary, that is, at full daylight. …*

*Also, we order and command the prelates and priests who, now and in the future, collect the tithes from the estates where the said Indians are, to maintain priests continually in the said churches of the said estates, to say masses on Sundays and obligatory feast days; and [we order and command] also that the said priests shall have charge of confessing those who know how to confess, and of teaching those who do not. Thus Our Lord will be served, and, if the contrary is done, He has been and will be disserved.*

*Also, we order and command that at the mines where there are a sufficient number of Indians churches shall be built, in convenient places proved by you, our said Admiral, judges, and officers, or by the person by you, so that all the Indians who are at the mines may hear Mass on the said feast days; and we command the settlers and Spaniards who bring the said Indians to extract gold, to observe with them the same procedure that is followed on the estates, as prescribed above, under the same penalties applied in the same manner.*

*Also, we order and command that whoever has fifty Indians or more in encomienda shall be obliged to have a boy (the one he considers most able) taught to read and write, and the things of our Faith, so that he may later teach the said Indians, because the Indians will more readily accept what he says than what the Spaniards and settlers tell them; and if the said person has a hundred Indians or more he shall have two boys taught as prescribed; and if the person who has Indians does not have them taught as ordered, we command that the visitor who in our name has charge shall have them taught at the cost of such person. And because the King, my Lord and Father, and I have been informed that several persons are employing Indian boys as pages, we order and command that the person who does so shall be obliged to teach them to read and write, and all the other things that have been prescribed above; and if he fails to do so the boys shall be taken from him and given to another ...*

*Also, we order and command that, after the Indians have been brought to the estates, all the founding [of gold] that henceforth is done on the said Island shall be done in the manner prescribed below: that is, the said persons who have Indians in encomienda shall extract gold with them for five months in the year and, at the end of these five months, the said Indians shall rest forty days, and the day they cease their labor of extracting gold shall be noted on a certificate, which shall be given to the miners who go to the mines; and upon the day thus designated all the Indians shall be released in the district where the founding is to be done, so that all the Indians of each district shall go to their houses on the same day to rest during the said forty days; and in all the said forty days no one shall employ any Indians in extracting gold, unless it is a slave, on pain that for every Indian that any person brings to the mines in the said period of forty days shall pay half a gold peso, applied in the aforesaid manner; and we command that in the said forty days you, the said officers, shall be obliged to finish the founding. And we command that the Indians who thus leave the mines shall not, during the said forty days, be ordered to do anything whatever, save to plant the hillocks necessary for their subsistence that season; and the persons who have the said Indians in encomienda shall be obliged, during these forty days of rest, to indoctrinate them in the things of our Faith more than on other days, because they will have the opportunity and means to do so.*

*Also, since we have been informed that if the Indians are not allowed to perform their customary dances [areytos] they will receive great harm, we order and command that they shall not be prevented from performing their dances on Sundays and feast days, and also on work days, if they do not on that account neglect their usual work stint.*

*Also, since the most important consideration for the good treatment and increase of the Indians is their subsistence, we order and command that all persons who have Indians shall be obliged to maintain those who are on their estates and there to keep continually a sufficiency*

*of bread and yams and peppers, and, at least on Sundays and feast days, to give them dishes of*
*cooked meat, as is prescribed in the article that says that on feast days when they go to Mass they*
*shall be given better pots of meat than on other days ...*

*Also, we order and command that no person or persons shall dare to beat any Indian with*
*sticks, or whip him, or call him dog, or address him by any name other than his proper name*
*alone; and if an Indian should deserve to be punished for something he has done, the said person*
*having him in charge shall bring him to the visitor for punishment, on pain that the person who*
*violates this article shall pay, for every time he beats or whips an Indian or Indians, five pesos*
*gold; and if he should call an Indian dog, or address him by any name other than his own, he*
*shall pay one gold peso, to be distributed in the manner stated ...*

*Also, we order and command that in each community of the said Island there shall*
*be two visitors' in charge of inspecting the whole community, together with its mines and*
*estates, its shepherds and swineherds, and they shall ascertain how the Indians are being*
*taught in the things of our Faith, and how their persons are being treated, and how they are*
*being maintained, and how they or the persons who have them in charge are obeying and*
*fulfilling these our ordinances, and all the other things that each of them is obliged to do;*
*and we command them to have particular care in all this, and we charge their consciences*
*with it ...*

The Laws of Burgos, trans. and ed. L. B. Simpson (San Francisco, 1960), 16–17, 20–21,
24–5, 32, 35. Reproduced courtesy of the Greenwood Publishing Group.

In spite of the noble intentions of the Crown, the Laws proved ineffective, especially since some Spaniards soon located new and staggeringly rich areas on the mainland, whose native population, if the wealth were to be exploited, would require the control *encomienda* provided.

The Spanish crown had good reasons to attack *encomienda*. But other opponents of the institution appeared during the early years of Spanish settlement in America. The most vocal, and surely the most effective critic of the institution was Bartolomé de las Casas. A Dominican friar who became bishop of Chiapas in Mexico, Las Casas had begun his career in the New World as a participant in the cruel exploitation of the natives in the West Indies. In his numerous published works, the most famous of which was his *History of the Indies*, he condemned Spanish activities in America, arguing that Spain did have a right to its presence in the Indies but had abused the privilege in subjecting the natives to labor so harsh and cruel that many died at the hands of men who were on their soil ostensibly to "save" them. Aside from denouncing the atrocities Spaniards committed against the Indians, Las Casas denied that Spain had the authority to undertake the conquest of its New World possessions. He contended that the Indians were docile and decent human beings, rational thinkers and could become pious Christians. Such traits confirmed the royal view that the Indians were free men— Christians were not permitted to enslave their brethren, nor could they justly reduce to slavery non-Christians who had not attacked Christendom. Spanish policies, and especially Spanish actions in America, he insisted, were barbarous, illegal and unjust.

Still, the *encomenderos* did have defenders. The most notable was the Aristotelian scholar Juan Ginés de Sepúlveda. Citing both the Bible and the classical philosophers, Sepúlveda denounced the heathenism of America's native's, arguing that such Indian practices as cannibalism, human sacrifice and idolatry deserved to be extinguished by any means. The Indians, he continued, were clearly inferior in every respect to the Spaniards and thus the laws of nature dictated that they be ruled as "the man rules over the woman, the adult over the child, the father over his children … the most powerful and most perfect … over the weakest and most imperfect."[2] That Spaniards had proved able to dominate them without difficulty was, for Sepúlveda, conclusive proof of their inferiority and fitness for subjugation. Besides, he stressed, the Indians had received and would continue to receive such benefits as civilization and Christianity from control by their Spanish masters.

*You should remember that authority and power are not only of one kind but of several varieties, since in one way and with one kind of law the father commands his children, in another the husband commands his wife, in another the master commands his servants, in another the judge commands the citizens, in another the king commands the peoples and human beings confined to his authority … Although each jurisdiction may appear different, they all go back to a single principle, as the wise men teach. That is, the perfect should command and rule over the imperfect, the excellent over its opposite …*

*And thus we see that among inanimate objects, the more perfect directs and dominates, and the less perfect obeys its command. This principle is even clearer and more obvious among animals, where the mind rules like a mistress and the body submits like a servant. In the same way the rational part of the soul rules and directs the irrational part, which submits and obeys. All of this derives from divine and natural law, both of which demand that the perfect and most powerful rule over the imperfect and the weaker …*

*The man rules over the woman, the adult over the child, the father over his children. That is to say, the most powerful and most perfect rule over the weakest and most imperfect. This same relationship exists among men, there being some who by nature are masters and others who by nature are slaves. Those who surpass the rest in prudence and intelligence, although not in physical strength, are by nature the masters. On the other hand, those who are dim-witted and mentally lazy, although they may be physically strong enough to fulfill all the necessary tasks, are by nature slaves. It is just and useful that it be this way. We even see it sanctioned in divine law itself, for it is written in the Book of Proverbs: "He who is stupid will serve the wise man." And so it is with the barbarous and inhumane peoples [the Indians] who have no civil life and peaceful customs. It will always be just and in conformity with natural law that such people submit to the rule of more cultured and humane princes and nations. Thanks to their virtues and the practical wisdom of their laws, the latter can destroy barbarism and educate these [inferior] people to a more humane and virtuous life. And if the latter reject such rule, it can be imposed upon them by force of arms. Such a war will be just according to natural law …*

*One may believe as certain and undeniable, since it is affirmed by the wisest authors, that it is just and natural that prudent, upright, and humane men should rule over those who are not. On this basis the Romans established their legitimate and just rule over many nations, according to St. Augustine in several passages of his work,* The City of God, *which St. Thomas [Aquinas] collected and cited in his work,* De rigimine principum. *Such being the case, you can well understand ... if you know the customs and nature of the two peoples, that with perfect right the Spaniards rule over these barbarians of the New World and the adjacent islands, who in wisdom, intelligence, virtue, and* humanitas *are as inferior to the Spaniards as infants to adults and women to men. There is as much difference between them as there is between cruel, wild peoples and the most merciful of peoples, between the most monstrously intemperate peoples and those who are temperate and moderate in their pleasures, that is to say, between apes and men.*

*You do not expect me to make a lengthy commemoration of the judgment and talent of the Spaniards ... And who can ignore the other virtues of our people, their fortitude, their humanity, their love of justice and religion? I speak only of our princes and those who by their energy and industriousness have shown that they are worthy of administering the commonwealth. I refer in general terms only to those Spaniards who have received a liberal education. If some of them are wicked and unjust, that is no reason to denigrate the glory of their race, which should be judged by the actions of its cultivated and noble men and by its customs and public institutions, rather than by the actions of depraved persons who are similar to slaves. More than any other country, this country [Spain] hates and detests depraved individuals, even those who have certain of the virtues that are common to nearly all classes of our people, like courage and the martial spirit for which the Spanish legions have always provided examples that exceed all human credibility ... And I would like to emphasize the absence of gluttony and lasciviousness among the Spaniards. Is there any nation in Europe that can compare with Spain in frugality and sobriety? Although recently I have seen the intrusion of luxury at the tables of the great as a result of commerce with foreigners, men of good will condemn this innovation, [and] it is to be hoped that in a short time the pristine and natural frugality of national customs may be restored ... How deeply rooted is the Christian religion in the souls of the Spaniards, even among those who live amidst the tumult of battle! I have observed many outstanding examples. The most notable [among] them, it appears to me, occurred after the sacking of Rome [in 1527]. There was scarcely a single Spaniard among those who died from the plague who did not order all the goods he had stolen from the Roman citizens returned in his last will and testament. Not a single other nation that I know of fulfilled this Christian duty, and there were many more Italians and Germans than Spaniards there. I followed the army and noted everything down scrupulously ... And what will I say of the gentleness and humanity of our soldiers, who even in battle, after the attainment of victory, expressed great concern and care in saving the greatest possible number of the conquered, protecting them against the cruelty of their allies [the Germans and Italians]?*

*Now compare these natural qualities of judgment, talent, magnanimity, temperance, humanity, and religion with those of these pitiful men [the Indians], in whom you will scarcely find any vestiges of humanness. These people possess neither science nor even an alphabet, nor do they preserve any monuments of their history except for some obscure and vague reminiscences depicted in certain paintings, nor do they have written laws, but barbarous institutions and customs. In regard to their virtues, how much restraint or gentleness are you to expect of men who are devoted to all kinds of intemperate acts and abominable lewdness, including the eating of human flesh? And you must realize that prior to the arrival of the Christians, they did not live in that peaceful kingdom of Saturn that the poets imagine, but on the contrary they made war against one another continually and fiercely, with such fury that victory was of no meaning if they did not satiate their monstrous hunger with the flesh of their enemies ... These Indians are so cowardly and timid that they could scarcely resist the mere presence of our soldiers. Many times thousands upon thousands of them scattered, fleeing like women before a very few Spaniards, who amounted to fewer than a hundred ...*

*In regard to those [of the Aztec and other Indian civilizations] who inhabit New Spain and the province of Mexico, I have already said that they consider themselves the most civilized people [in the New World]. They boast of their political and social institutions, because they have rationally planned cities and nonhereditary kings who are elected by popular suffrage, and they carry on commerce among themselves in the manner of civilized people. But ... I dissent from such an opinion. On the contrary, in those same institutions there is proof of the coarseness, barbarism, and innate servility of these men. Natural necessity encourages the building of houses, some rational manner of life, and some sort of commerce. Such an argument merely proves that they are neither bears nor monkeys and that they are not totally irrational. But on the other hand, they have established their commonwealth in such a manner that no one individually owns anything, neither a house nor a field that one may dispose of or leave to his heirs in his will, because everything is controlled by their lords, who are incorrectly called kings. They live more at the mercy of their king's will than of their own. They are the slaves of his will and caprice, and they are not the masters of their fate. The fact that this condition is not the result of coercion but is voluntary and spontaneous is a certain sign of the servile and base spirit of these barbarians. They had distributed their fields and farms in such a way that one third belonged to the king, another third belonged to the religious cult, and only a third part was reserved for the benefit of everyone; but all of this they did in such a way that they themselves cultivated the royal and religious lands. They lived as servants of the king and at his mercy, paying extremely large tributes. When a father died, all his inheritance, if the king did not decide otherwise, passed in its entirety to the oldest son, with the result that many of the younger sons would either die of starvation or subject themselves to an even more rigorous servitude. They would turn to the petty kings for help and would ask them for a field on the condition that they not only pay feudal tribute but also promise themselves as slave labor when it was necessary. And if this kind of servitude and barbaric commonwealth had not been suitable to their temperament and nature, it would have been easy for them to take advantage of the death of a king, since the monarchy was not hereditary, in order to establish a state that was freer and more favorable to their interests. Their failure to do so confirms that they were born for servitude and not the civil and liberal life ... Such are, in short, the character and customs of these barbarous, uncultivated, and inhumane little men. We know that they were thus before the coming of the Spaniards. Until now we have not mentioned their impious religion and their abominable sacrifices, in which they worship the Devil as God, to whom they thought of offering no better tribute than human hearts ... Interpreting their religion in an ignorant and barbarous manner, they sacrificed victims by removing the hearts from the chests. They placed these hearts on their abominable alters. With this ritual they believed that they had appeased their gods. They also ate the flesh of the sacrificed men ...*

*How are we to doubt that these people, so uncultivated, so barbarous, and so contaminated with such impiety and lewdness, have not been justly conquered by so excellent, pious, and supremely just a king as Ferdinand the Catholic was and the Emperor Charles now is, the kings of a most humane and excellent nation rich in all varieties of virtue?*

*War against these barbarians can be justified not only on the basis of their paganism but even more so because of their abominable licentiousness, their prodigious sacrifice of human victims, the extreme harm that they inflicted on innocent persons, their horrible banquets of human flesh, and the impious cult of their idols. Since the evangelical law of the New Testament is more perfect and more gentle than the Mosaic law of the Old Testament (for the latter was a law of fear and the former is a law of grace, gentleness, and clemency), so also [since the birth of Christ] wars are now waged with more mercy and clemency. Their purpose is not so much to punish as to correct evils. What is more appropriate and beneficial for these barbarians than to become subject to the rule of those whose wisdom, virtue, and religion have converted them from barbarians into civilized men (insofar as they are capable of becoming so), from being torpid and licentious to becoming upright and moral, from being impious servants of the Devil to becoming believers in the true God? They have already begun to receive the Christian religion, thanks to the prudent diligence of the Emperor Charles, an excellent and religious prince. They have already been provided with teachers learned in both the sciences and letters and, what is more important, with teachers of religion and good customs.*

*For numerous and grave reasons these barbarians are obligated to accept the rule of the Spaniards according to natural law. For them it ought to be even more advantageous than for the Spaniards, since virtue, humanity, and the true religion are more valuable than gold or silver. And if they refuse our rule, they may be compelled by force of arms to accept it. Such a war is just according to natural law ... Such a war would be far more just than even the war that the Romans waged against all the nations of the world in order to force them to submit to their rule [for the following reasons]. The Christian religion is better and truer than the religion of the Romans. In addition, the genius, wisdom, humanity, fortitude, courage, and virtue of the Spaniards are as superior to those same qualities among those pitiful little men [the Indians] as were those of the Romans vis-à-vis the peoples whom they conquered. And the justice of this war becomes even more evident when you consider that the Sovereign Pontiff, who represents Christ, has authorized it.*

Juan Ginés de Sepúlveda, *On the Reasons for the Just War among the Indians* (1547).
Reproduced courtesy of Digital History, http://www.digitalhistory.uh.edu/

## The Conquest of Mexico and Peru

If the West Indies had failed to provide Spain with significant material benefits, they did serve as an excellent base from which continued expansion to the mainland could begin. While Balboa was heading for the Pacific across Panama, Juan Ponce de León was searching for the fountain of youth in Florida. The fountain of youth and other mythical treasures were never found. But in 1519 a band of soldiers led by Hernán Cortés, a resident of Hispaniola since 1504 who had received a commission to explore on the mainland from the Cuban governor, Diego Velásquez, located a real source of wealth: the Aztec Empire. Like other Spanish *conquistadores* (conquerors) Cortés had been born in the arid western region of Extremadura, whose very name (which literally translates as "extremely hard") suggests the hardships geography and climate imposed on its residents. It was to Extremadura that many Spanish Jews had fled to escape the Inquisition, in the hope that the forbidding environment would deter their persecutors from pursuing them. Some historians have suggested that the toughness and determination displayed by Cortés and other conquistadors can be traced to their struggles to thrive as young men in Extremadura, where such traits were required if one were to survive.[3]

With 650 men and 16 horses, Cortés shipped to the coast of Mexico, landed near a Maya city, defeated the local native army, received gifts from the defeated Mayas (including a native woman, Malinali, or Doña Maria, who became his translator and mistress) and continued along the Yucatán coast until he found a good harbor. Since his commission from Velásquez strictly limited his activities to exploration along the Mexican coast, Cortés lacked the authority to do what he really wanted to do, which was to march to the interior where, according to reports by the coastal natives, a fabulously rich empire was located. His brilliant solution was at once both scrupulous in its strict adherence to legalities and shocking in its audacity: Cortés established a new municipality on the site, which he named Vera Cruz, appointed a town council composed of his subordinates, and received from that body a new mandate that sanctioned an expedition aimed at the Aztec kingdom in the heart of Mexico. When some objected to the enterprise he proposed, and urged that they return to Cuba, Cortés beached or burned his ships.

Cortés's sensitivity to the importance of acting legally by securing a document that authorized his activities typifies Spanish behavior throughout the era of exploration, conquest and colonization. In part, such behavior reflected the state of mind of the agents sent to execute a master plan created in Spain by superiors who expected their mandates to be carried out perfectly and without protest. Those who failed to obey faced the threat of the revocation of their privileges, in addition to severe punishment. Columbus, after all, had been returned to Spain from America in chains. But Spanish respect for the niceties of the law also derived from a perceived need to legitimize their activities in the New World—activities that gave them dominion over vast territories and all the inhabitants, and which promised to reward them with great wealth.

To deflect any criticism that their rivals might level, and to justify the exercise of power conferred by their sovereigns and by the pope, Spaniards in the New World were determined to demonstrate that they deserved what they had received and that they behaved in strict accordance with both human and divine (or natural) law.

In order to justify conquest itself, the Spanish maintained that they came to the New World to bring civilization and Christianity to the natives. If, in order to accomplish those worthy goals, it was necessary to subdue recalcitrant peoples by military action, Spaniards felt compelled to document that the resulting death and destruction should be blamed not on them, but rather on those who refused to accept domination. Thus in 1513 Juan López de Palacios Rubios, a lawyer, drafted the *Requerimiento* (Requirement) which all Spanish conquistadors were ordered to have read aloud to natives before engaging in combat with them.

*On the part of the King, Don Fernando, and of Doña Juana I, his daughter, Queen of Castille and León, subduers of the barbarous nations, we their servants notify and make known to you, as best we can, that the Lord our God, Living and Eternal, created the Heaven and the Earth, and one man and one woman, of whom you and we, all the men of the world at the time, were and are descendants, and all those who came after and before us. But, on account of the multitude which has sprung from this man and woman in the five thousand years since the world was created, it was necessary that some men should go one way and some another, and that they should be divided into many kingdoms and provinces, for in one alone they could not be sustained.*

*Of all these nations God our Lord gave charge to one man, called St. Peter, that he should be Lord and Superior of all the men in the world, that all should obey him, and that he should be the head of the whole Human Race, wherever men should live, and under whatever law, sect, or belief they should be; and he gave him the world for his kingdom and jurisdiction.*

*And he commanded him to place his seat in Rome, as the spot most fitting to rule the world from; but also he permitted him to have his seat in any other part of the world, and to judge and govern all Christians, Moors, Jews, Gentiles, and all other Sects. This man was called Pope, as if to say, Admirable Great Father and Governor of men. The men who lived in that time obeyed that St. Peter, and took him for Lord, King, and Superior of the universe; so also they have regarded the others who after him have been elected to the pontificate, and so has it been continued even till now, and will continue till the end of the world.*

*One of these Pontiffs, who succeeded that St. Peter as Lord of the world, in the dignity and seat which I have before mentioned, made donation of these isles and Tierra-firme to the aforesaid King and Queen and to their successors, our lords, with all that there are in these territories, as is contained in certain writings which passed upon the subject as aforesaid, which you can see if you wish.*

*So their Highnesses are kings and lords of these islands and land of Tierra-firme by virtue of this donation: and some islands, and indeed almost all those to whom this has been notified, have received and served their Highnesses, as lords and kings, in the way that subjects ought to do, with good will, without any resistance, immediately, without delay, when they were informed of the aforesaid facts. And also they received and obeyed the priests whom their Highnesses sent to preach to them and to teach them our Holy Faith; and all these, of their own free will, without any reward or condition, have become Christians, and are so, and their Highnesses have joyfully and benignantly received them, and also have commanded them to be treated as their subjects and vassals; and you too are held and obliged to do the same. Wherefore, as best we can, we ask and require you that you consider what we have said to you, and that you take the time that shall be necessary to understand and deliberate upon it, and that you acknowledge the Church as the Ruler and Superior of the whole world, and the high priest called Pope, and in his name the King and Queen Doña Juana our lords, in his place, as superiors and lords and kings of these islands and this Tierra-firme by virtue of the said donation, and that you consent and give place that these religious fathers should declare and preach to you the aforesaid.*

*If you do so, you will do well, and that which you are obliged to do to their Highnesses, and we in their name shall receive you in all love and charity, and shall leave you, your wives, and your children, and your lands, free without servitude, that you may do with them and with yourselves freely that which you like and think best, and they shall not compel you to turn Christians, unless you yourselves, when informed of the truth, should wish to be converted to our Holy Catholic Faith, as almost all the inhabitants of the rest of the islands have done. And, besides this, their Highnesses award you many privileges and exemptions and will grant you many benefits.*

*But, if you do not do this, and maliciously make delay in it, I certify to you that, with the help of God, we shall powerfully enter into your country, and shall make war against you in all ways and manners that we can, and shall subject you to the yoke and obedience of the Church and of their Highnesses; we shall take you and your wives and your children, and shall make slaves of them, and as such shall sell and dispose of them as their Highnesses may command; and we shall take away your goods, and shall do you all the mischief and damage that we can, as to vassals who do not obey, and refuse to receive their lord, and resist and contradict him; and we protest that the deaths and losses which shall accrue from this are your fault, and not that of their Highnesses, or ours, nor of these cavaliers who come with us. And that we have said this to you and made this Requisition, we request the notary here present to give us his testimony in writing, and we ask the rest who are present that they should be witnesses of this Requisition.*

Juan López de Palacios Rubios, *Requerimiento* (1513).[4]

Historian Patricia Seed has argued persuasively that the *Requerimiento* can be seen as the definitive Spanish document from the colonial era because it reflects so perfectly the attitudes, values and actions of Spain's agents both at home and in the Americas. Attention to the dictates of the law and to behaving in accord with instructions sent from Spain marked the behavior of Spanish officials throughout the colonial era. Even when faced with orders that made little sense given the realities they were encountering, or with instructions that were impossible to carry out, Spaniards steadfastly exhibited their determination to act as instructed. "I obey, but I do not enforce" was a phrase attributed to Spanish officials throughout the colonial era, perhaps first uttered by a viceroy when confronted by his obligation to follow a directive that, if implemented, might provoke resistance, even rebellion among the inhabitants.

From Vera Cruz Cortés's band moved overland in the direction of the Aztec capital Tenochtitlan (Mexico City). Along this route the Spaniards concluded alliances with native tribes, which were dominated by the Aztecs and chafed under their rule. One of the soldiers in his army, Bernal Díaz del Castillo, left a detailed narrative of the conquistador's exploits in a book he titled the *True History of the Conquest of Mexico* (written after 1554, first published in 1632). His account of one encounter with hostile natives as Cortés's army marched to the Aztec capital, is particularly interesting.

How Cortés assembles all the caziques of this province, and what further happened.

*I have above related that in this battle we took five prisoners, among whom were two chiefs. Aguilar, who understood their language, often discoursed with them, and from some remarks which they made, concluded that we might employ them as delegates to their countrymen. Having communicated his thoughts to Cortés, he proposed they should be set at liberty, and despatched with a message to the caziques and other inhabitants of the district. To this Cortés assented, ordering both the prisoners to be presented with blue glass beads, while Aguilar told them many things which he knew would please the inhabitants and prove advantageous to us. He assured them, that after this battle, which had been entirely of their own seeking, they had nothing further to fear from us, and commissioned them now to assemble all the caziques of the district, for we were very desirous of communicating with them. Everything Aguilar said was done with the view of inclining the Indians to make peace with us. The prisoners most willingly complied with our wishes, which they communicated to the caziques and principal personages among the inhabitants, telling them how we longed to become their friends. This message was in so far successful, that they resolved to send us fifteen of their Indian slaves with fowls, baked fish, and maise-bread. These slaves had their faces blackened, and were completely covered with ragged cloaks. When these personages appeared in the presence of Cortés he received them very friendly: Aguilar, on the contrary, asked them in an angry tone, why they had come with such painted faces—appearing rather to seek war than peace? If they were desirous of making peace, continued he, persons of rank should be deputed to us, not slaves. This they were to communicate to those who had sent them. We, however, treated these black faces very kindly, presenting them moreover with blue beads in token of peace, and in order to gain the good wishes of the inhabitants. And sure enough the very next day above thirty of the principal Indians, well dressed, appeared in our quarters, bringing with them, fowls, fruits, and maise-bread, and begged permission of Cortés to burn and bury the bodies of their fallen countrymen, in order that they might not create a pestilence in the air, or become a prey to the lions and tigers. This being granted, they brought along with them a great number of Indians to burn the bodies, and bury them according to their custom. Cortés himself went to watch their proceedings, when they assured him they had lost above 800 killed, without counting the wounded; adding, that at present they durst not enter into any treaty with us, as the day following all the chiefs and principal personages of the district would assemble to take our offers of peace into consideration.*

*Cortés, who profited by every circumstance, said smilingly to us: "It appears to me, gentlemen, that the Indians stand in great awe of our horses, and imagine that these and our guns alone fight the battle. A thought has just struck me which will further confirm them in this notion. You must bring here the mare of Juan Sedeño which foaled on board a short time ago, and fasten her here where I am now standing. Then bring also the stallion of the musician Ortiz, which is a very fiery animal, and will quickly scent the mare. As soon as you find this to be the case, lead both the horses to separate places, that the caziques may neither see the horses, nor hear them neigh, until I shall be in conversation with them." All this was accordingly done. He likewise ordered our largest cannon to be heavily loaded with gunpowder and ball.*

*A little after midday, forty caziques arrived in great state and richly clothed according to their fashion. They saluted Cortés and all of us, perfumed us with their incense, begged forgiveness for what had happened, and promised to be friendly for the future. Cortés answered by our interpreter Aguilar, reminding them, with a very serious look, how often he had wished them to make peace with us, and how, owing to their obstinacy, we were almost upon the point of destroying them with the whole of the inhabitants of this district. We were vassals of the mighty king and lord the emperor Charles, he further added, who had sent us to this country with orders to favour and assist those who should submit to his imperial sway, which we would assuredly do if they were amicably inclined towards us. If, however, they were not so, the* tepustles *(so the Indians called our cannon) would be fired off, which were already embittered against them in some measure on account of the attack they had made upon us. Cortés, at this moment, gave the signal for firing our largest cannon. The report was like a sudden clap of thunder, the ball whizzing along the hills, which could be distinctly heard as it was midday and not a breath of air stirring. The caziques who had never seen this before appeared in dismay, and believed all Cortés had said; who, however, desired Aguilar to comfort and assure them he had given orders that no harm should be done them. At this moment the stallion was brought and fastened at a short distance from the spot where Cortés and the caziques were holding the conference: as the mare was likewise near at hand, the stallion immediately began to neigh, stamp the ground and rear itself, while its eyes were continually fixed on the Indians who stood in front of Cortés's tent, as the mare was placed behind it. The caziques, however, thought the animal was making all these movements against them and appeared greatly agitated. When Cortés found what effect this scene had made upon the Indians, he rose from his seat, and walking to the horse, took hold of the bridle, and desired his servant to lead it away. Aguilar, however, was to make the Indians believe that he had ordered the horse not to do them any injury.*

*While all this was going on above thirty Indian porters (whom they term tamemes) arrived with fowls, baked fish, and various fruits: these porters, on account of their loads, had perhaps not been able to follow the caziques fast enough. A lively discourse was now kept up between Cortés and the caziques, who in the end left us perfectly contented, with the assurance that the following day they would return with a present.*

Bernal Díaz del Castillo, *The Memoirs of the Conquistador Bernal Díaz del Castillo Written by Himself Containing a True and Full Account of the Discovery and Conquest of Mexico and New Spain*, trans. by John Ingram Lockhart (London, 1844), 78–80.[5]

Díaz wrote his narrative three decades after the events he describes. He seems to have been motivated by the publication in 1552 of *The General History of the Indies* written by a priest in service to Cortés, Francisco Lopez de Gómara, who had never been in America. Bernal thought that Gómara's book gave too much credit to Cortés for the spectacular achievements of the men he led, while depriving the common soldiers in his army of glory they had rightly earned. In one memorable passage, Díaz contrasts the story of a battle between Cortés's forces and a native army as related by Gómara with what participants like him had actually witnessed:

*Francisco Lopez de Gómara, in his account of this battle, says, that previous to the arrival of Cortés with the cavalry, the holy apostle St. Jacob or St. Peter in person had galloped up on a gray-coloured horse to our assistance. I can only say, that for the exertion of our arms and this victory, we stand indebted to our Lord Jesus Christ; and that in this battle every individual man among us was set upon by such numbers of the enemy, that if each of them had merely thrown a handful of earth upon us we should have been buried beneath it. Certain it is, therefore, that God showed his mercy to us here, and it may, indeed, have been one of the two glorious apostles St. Jacob or St. Peter who thus came to our assistance. Perhaps on account of my sins I was not considered worthy of the good fortune to behold them; for I could only see Francisco de Morla on his brown horse galloping up with Cortés, and even at this very moment, while I am writing this, I can fancy I see all passing before my eyes just as I have related it; although I, an unworthy sinner, was not considered worthy of beholding one of the glorious apostles face to face: yet again I never heard any of the four hundred soldiers, nor ever Cortés himself, nor any of the many cavaliers, mention this wonder, or confirm its truth. We should certainly have built a church, and have called the town Santiago, or San Pedro de la Vitoria, and not Santa Maria de la Vitoria. If, therefore, what Gómara relates is true, then we must indeed have been bad Christians not to have paid greater respect to the assistance which God sent us in the person of his holy apostles, and for having omitted to thank him daily for it in his own church. Nevertheless, I should feel delighted if this historian has spoken the truth, although I must confess that I never heard this wonder mentioned before reading his book, nor have I ever heard any of the conquistadores speak of it who were present at the battle.[6]*

Note that Díaz's words both refute the account provided by Gómara and assert that it was the efforts of the soldiers themselves, as opposed to divine apostolic intervention, that led to the Spanish victory.

The nomadic Aztecs had arrived in the Valley of Mexico in the thirteenth century, established a settlement on an island in the valley's great lake, and within two centuries had transformed themselves from despised, uncultured and unwelcome outsiders into a dominant conquering power. They came to assert that they were, in fact, the descendants of the great Toltecs (whose language, Nahuatal, they spoke), who had abandoned the valley centuries before when their deity Quetzalcoatl departed. Legend had it that as he left, Quetzalcoatl had promised to return from across the sea to re-establish his sovereignty in the future. Under King Montezuma II, who had assumed power in 1502, the Aztecs had only recently succeeded in capturing some of the coastal towns. Therefore, many of the natives Cortés encountered on his march toward Tenochtitlan must have perceived him as a liberator—he was marching against the capital of their conquerors. In fact, the Aztecs may have intentionally chosen not to defeat some peoples, preferring instead to maintain a perpetual state of war, as that would allow them to secure captives to sacrifice to their Sun God who, they believed, required a steady diet of human blood. Thus, by the time he reached the Aztec capital in the fall of 1519, Cortés's small army had been reinforced by perhaps as many as several thousand native allies, both from groups the Aztecs had conquered and from whom they received tribute, and from others, like the Tlaxcalans, who were at war with the Aztecs. Diego Durán, a Spanish church official, compiled an account of the Aztecs which includes a vivid account of the way they used human sacrifice to accomplish not only religious but also political goals.

> Which treats of the cruel sacrifice of the Huaxtecs at the hands of the Aztecs. With a description of the Skinning Ceremony called Tlacaxipehualiztli. And how the lords of all the neighboring states and cities were invited to witness this spectacle and great festivities.

> *Many days passed after the return of the Aztecs from the war in the land of the Huaxtecs. Tlacaelel then reminded King Moteczoma of the work on the temple, which they had begun to build and said that it was necessary to carve a wide stone to serve as an altar or table upon which sacrifice would be made. This Tlacaelel, in addition to being bold and cunning in the trickery of war also invented devilish cruel and frightful sacrifices. He then told Moteczoma to order that the stone be carved and that in its carvings appear the war of liberation of their forebears from Azcapotzalco, so that this war might be given perpetual memory.*

> *Tlacaelel gathered the stone cutters and sculptors saying these words to them: "Master craftsmen our Lord wishes you to cut a large round stone which we will call* temalacatl, *which means "stone wheel." On it are to be inscribed our wars with the Tecpanecs, since this sculpture must be an eternal reminder of those admirable deeds. I beg you to give yourselves glory in this, since you will be remembered forever if it is well carved. Let it be done as soon as possible."*

> *The craftsmen were happy to carry out his orders and they sought a large stone about a yard*

*and a half wide. They made smooth its surface and represented in their carving the war with Azcapotzalco. This labor was very finely done and finished so swiftly that some days later they were able to notify the king that the table of sacrifice was ready. The king then ordered a base to be made for it to rest upon. And so a high platform was made slightly taller than a man, and the carved rock was placed upon it. Now that the stone had been set up, they called certain youths who lived in seclusion within the temple, and gave them the office of carrying out this sacrifice which the devil had invented and taught them. They were told, "Take care that every day you prepare yourselves to perform this sacrifice since the lords of all the cities and neighboring provinces will be invited to the feast and you must not put us to shame." The young men thanked them and promised to practice and rehearse according to the instructions that were given to them.*

*When the beginning of the month called Tlacaxipehualiztli, "Skinning of Men," approached they invited monarchs from the entire land: they called the kings of Texcoco and of Tacuba, the rulers of Chalco and Xochimilco, kings from the Marquesado, from Cohuixco, Matlatzinco and from the Mazahua tribes.*

*Once the guests had arrived the king gave them presents—fine mantles and loin cloths, rich clothes of feather work, wide sashes, sandals and lip-plugs of precious stones, golden ear-plugs and nose pendants. A great feast followed, with quantities of fowl, meat from the hunt, different breads, chocolate drinks and pulque. After the guests had eaten and drunk they were assigned booths adorned with flowers and reeds within which they could sit and watch. The strangers sat down in the decorated boxes and awaited the ceremony, which had been unknown till this time. The prisoners were brought out and placed in a line at a place called Tzompantitlan, which means something like "Mount Calvary" or "Place of Skulls." At this place there were long platforms upon which stood a great rack where the skulls of the sacrificial victims were strung and where they remained permanently as relics. The prisoners were arranged in a file and told to dance. All the victims were smeared with plaster, their heads were feathered and on the top of the head each wore some white feathers tied to his hair. Their eyelids were blackened and their lips painted red.*

*The priests who were to perform the sacrifice stood in a long row, according to their rank. Each one of them was disguised as a god. One of them wore the garb of Huitzilopochtli, Humming Bird on the Left; another was dressed as Quetzalcoatl, Plumed Serpent; another represented Toci, Our Grandmother; another was Yopi, the Yope; still another, Opochtzin, the Left-Handed One; another was Totec, Our Lord: and finally one of them wore the garments of Itzpapalotl, Obsidian Butterfly. One of them was disguised as a jaguar, another as an ocelot and yet another as an eagle. All carried their swords and shields, inlaid with gold and gems, and all these priests were covered with featherwork and rich jewels.*

*For all of these an arbor, beautifully adorned with flowers and paintings of the gods, had been prepared. This arbor was made of the branches and leaves of a tree called tzapotl; that is why it was called Tzapotl Calli, "House of Tzapotl." Within it were seats, also made of tzapotl wood, where all of them sat down according to age and rank. This arbor had been erected on the very summit of the pyramid, in a place called Yopico.*

*When the priests dressed as gods had been seated—and they were the ones who would perform the sacrifice—the elders called* Tecuacutin, *and the chanters of the temple, brought forth the drum, and to the rhythm of its beat they began to dance and sing.*

*The high priest, fully dressed for the rite, then came forth, with tall feathers in his diadem, his arms covered with golden bands, from which hung large, shining, green and blue feathers. Carrying in his hand the great knife of black stone called* ixcuahuac, *he went forward and took his place.*

*After he was seated, they brought out one of the prisoners from the land of the Huaxtecs and tied his neck with a rope which emerged from a hole in the middle of the great round stone. Once they had tied him they handed him a wooden sword and a shield; the sword was not equipped with blades but was feathered from top to bottom. At this point the high priest, who for this day was called "Drinker of the Night" and "Our Lord," rose from his seat and slowly began to descend the steps until he had reached the place where the prisoner was. He walked around the stone twice, sanctifying it, and having tied the victim again he returned to his seat.*

*An old man disguised as an ocelot appeared then and gave four wooden balls to the victim, telling him to try to defend himself with them. He wrapped a piece of cloth around the prisoner's body and gave him a little Divine Wine to drink. After this he withdrew, leaving the victim alone.*

*One of the men disguised as a god then approached the stone dancing, with his shield and sword in his hand; well protected with his helmet he went up to the place where the prisoner stood. The poor wretch upon the stone threw the wooden balls at him. These were evaded by the sacrificer if he was skillful, whereupon the prisoner picked up his feathered sword and defended himself the best he could.*

*Some of the victims possessed such ability that they wore out two or three attackers before they could be wounded. But as soon as the victim was wounded, four priests, painted black, with long braided hair, dressed in garments similar to chasubles, ascended the stone and laid the wounded man on his back, holding him down by the feet and hands. The high priest then rose from his seat, went to the stone and opened his chest with the knife. He took out his heart and offered the vapor that came out of it to the sun. As soon as the heart was cold he delivered it to certain ministers who placed it in a vessel called the* cuauhxicalli, *"eagle gourd," which was another large stone dedicated to the sun, containing in its center a concavity which was also used for another type of sacrifice.*

*These ceremonies were performed in the case of all the prisoners, each one in his turn. However, there were some who, on being given the shield and sword, felt the sword with their fingers. When they realized that the sword was not edged with stone but with feathers they cast it away and threw themselves willingly upon their backs on the stone. The priests then took hold of them and the high priest opened their chests and extracted their hearts. Some of the victims, such as those mentioned above, were unwilling to go through so much ceremonial, and they cast themselves upon the stone immediately, seeking a quick death. Whether one defended himself well or whether one fought badly, death was inevitable. That is why all those priests were required; when one was tired of sacrificing another would take his place. At the most it meant another half-hour of life.*

*After all the victims had died, the corpses were taken back to the place where, as live men, they had stood in a row, and the bodies cast down. Those who had taken part in the sacrifices entered certain rooms of the temple with the high priest, took off their ritual garb and, with great reverence, put it away in a clean place.*

*The lords from the provinces who had come to observe the sacrifice were shocked and bewildered by what they had seen and they returned to their homes filled with astonishment and fright.*

*Moteczoma now called those who had performed the sacrifice and ordered them to be dressed in fine mantles, loincloths and sandals, and thanked them for their skillful work. He commanded that they be given maize, chia seed, and cacao in great quantities. This was done to encourage others to imitate these exercises, which, according to the Aztecs, were filled with virtue and honor.*

*By ancient tradition, the feast was followed, the next day, by another celebration. At this time the king gave his noblemen fine mantles, rich loincloths and sandals, lip-plugs, ear-plugs. Shields, beautiful weapons, insignia and gold arm-bands. These were the rewards for men who were valiant.*

*Once the rewards had been distributed, those who had been sacrificed were flayed and the Tototectin, "Bird Lords," put on those skins and wore them. Carrying their shields in one hand and staffs covered with rattles in the other, they went from house to house. First they visited the houses of the nobility and then the homes of common people, asking for alms, wearing the skins all the time. The rich gave them mantles and loincloths and the common people gave them fistfuls of corn and other edibles.*

*For twenty days these men begged. At the end of this time they had gathered great quantities of clothing and food. The flayed skins had been worn in honor of the god of the feast.*

*When the twenty days had passed they took off the reeking skins and buried them in a special room in the temple. In this way ended the feast and the sacrifice of the Huaxtecs, which had been made to solemnize the first use of the carved stone. Here ends also the chapter on this subject which I found written in the Nahuatl tongue.*

Diego Durán, *The Aztecs*, trans. by Doris Heyden and Fernando Horasitas (New York, 1964), 109–13. Reproduced courtesy of University of Oklahoma Press.

When reports of the Spaniards' arrival on the coast reached Montezuma, the Aztec emperor was uncertain how to respond. Was Cortés an invader to be destroyed by the Aztecs' overwhelming numerical superiority? Or was Cortés, as some thought, the ancient Quetzalcoatl who had departed in the distant past but had promised to return? Montezuma sent emissaries who tried unsuccessfully to bribe Cortés into departing. An Aztec account of their mission has survived in the monumental *General History of the Things of New Spain*, written between 1540 and 1585 by Fray Bernardino de Sahagún, who compiled his history from the testimony of Native Indians in their own Nahuatl language.

**Figure 3.1.** Aztec ritual human sacrifice portrayed in the sixteenth-century Codex Magliabechiano (folio 70r). Biblioteca Nazionale Centrale, Florence.

*Sixth Chapter, in which it is told how Moctezuma's messengers returned here to Mexico. They came to relate to Moctezuma that which they had seen.*

*Thereupon [Cortés] left them; [the Spaniards] let them descend to their boats. And when they had climbed down to their boats, then they rowed vigorously. Each one rowed as hard as he could; some paddled with their hands.*

*With all their force they fled. They came saying to one another: "O warriors, [exert] all your strength! Row vigorously! Let us not be forced to do something [evil]; let nothing [evil] befall us!"*

*Speedily in the midst of the water they came hastening to the place called Xicalanco; there they no more than quickly restored their strength, so that once again they might hasten along with all their force. Then they came to reach Tecpantlayacac. Thereupon also they hastened along, they fled along. They came hastening to Cuetlaxtlan. Likewise they quickly left, [having] there restored their strength.*

*And the ruler of Cuetlaxtlan said to them: "Rest yet but a brief day! Restore your strength!"*

*But they said to him: "No, we shall only go hastening on. We shall warn the lord, the ruler Moctezuma. We shall tell him what we have seen, which is very terrifying, of which the like hath never been seen. Wilt thou perchance already be the first to hear it?"*

*Then speedily they set forth to go quickly to reach Mexico. It was deep night when they came to reach it; they entered it quite by night.*

*And while this was happening, [Moctezuma] enjoyed no sleep, no food. No one spoke more to him, Whatsoever he did, it was as if he were in torment. Oft times it was as if he sighed, became weak, felt weak. No longer did he enjoy what tasted good, what gave one contentment, what gladdened one.*

*Wherefore he said: "What will now befall us? Who indeed standeth [in command]? Alas, until now, I. In great torment is my heart; as if it were washed in chili water it indeed burneth, it smarteth. Where in truth [may we go], O our lord?"*

*Then [the messengers] demanded of those who guarded; they said to those who stood watch over his principal possessions: "Even if he sleepeth, tell him:*

*'They whom thou hast sent into the midst of the water have come.'"*

*But when they went to tell him, he then said: "I shall not hear it here; I shall hear it there in the Coacalli. There let them go." And he gave a command: he said: "Let two of the captives be covered with chalk."*

*And then the messengers went there to the Coacalli. Moctezuma also [went].*

*Thereupon before them the captives were slain; [they] cut open the captives' breasts; with their blood they sprinkled the messengers. For this reason did they do so, that they had gone to very perilous places; that they had gone to see, to look into the faces, the heads of the gods—had verily spoken to them.*

*Seventh Chapter, in which is related the account by which the messengers who had gone to see the boats reported to Moctezuma.*

*And when this was done, they thereupon reported to Moctczuma; so they told him how they had gone marveling, and they showed him what [the Spaniards'] food was like.*

*And when he had so heard what the messengers reported, he was terrified, he was astounded. And much did he marvel at their food.*

*Especially did it cause him to faint away when he heard how the gun, at [the Spaniards'] command, discharged [the shot]; how it resounded as if it thundered when it went off. It indeed bereft one of strength; it shut off one's ears. And when it discharged, something like a round pebble came forth from within. Fire went showering forth; sparks went blazing forth. And its smoke smelled very foul; it had a fetid odor which verily wounded the head. And when [the shot] struck a mountain, it was as if it were destroyed, dissolved. And a tree was pulverized; it was as if it vanished; it was as if someone blew it away.*

*All iron was their war array. In iron they clothed themselves. With iron they covered their heads. Iron were their swords. Iron were their crossbows. Iron were their shields. Iron were their lances.*

*And those which bore them upon their backs, their deer, were as tall as roof terraces.*

*And their bodies were everywhere covered; only their faces appeared. They were very white; they had chalky faces; they had yellow hair, though the hair of some was black. Long were their beards; they also were yellow. They were yellow-bearded. [The negroes' hair] was kinky, it was curly.*

*And their food was like fasting food—very large, white; not heavy like [tortillas]; like maize stalks, good-tasting as if of maize stalk flour; a little sweet, a little honeyed. It was honeyed to eat; it was sweet to eat.*

*And their dogs were very large. They had ears folded over; great dragging jowls. They had fiery eyes—blazing eyes; they had yellow eyes—fiery yellow eyes. They had thin flanks—flanks with ribs showing. They had gaunt stomachs. They were very tall. They were nervous; they went about panting, with tongues hanging. They were spotted like ocelots; they were varicolored.*

*And when Moctezuma so heard, he was much terrified. It was as if he fainted away. His heart saddened; his heart failed him.*

Fray Bernardo de Sahagún, *General History of the Things of New Spain*
*(Florentine Codex), Book 12—The Conquest of Mexico Part XIII,*
trans. by Arthur J. O. Anderson and Charles E. Dibble (Santa Fe, NM, 1975),
19–21. Reproduced courtesy of the University of Utah Press.

The Aztec ruler then sent forces to turn Cortés away, but in an attack at Cholula they failed to repel the invaders. Finally, the emperor invited Cortés and his men to enter Tenochtitlan. Bernal Díaz del Castillo has left us a vivid account of Cortés's meeting with the Aztec emperor.

The magnificent and pompous reception which the powerful Motecusuma gave to Cortés and all of us, on our entrance into the great city of Mexico.

*The following morning we left Iztapalapan accompanied by all the principal caziques above mentioned. The road along which we marched was eight paces in breadth, and if I still remember ran in a perfectly straight line to Mexico. Notwithstanding the breadth, it was much too narrow to hold the vast crowds of people who continually kept arriving from different parts to gaze upon us, and we could scarcely move along. Besides this, the tops of all the temples and towers were crowded, while the lake beneath was completely covered with canoes filled with Indians, for all were curious to catch a glimpse of us. And who can wonder at this, as neither men like unto ourselves, nor horses, had ever been seen here before!*

*When we gazed upon all this splendour at once, we scarcely knew what to think, and we doubted whether all that we beheld was real. A series of large towns stretched themselves along the banks of the lake, out of which still larger ones rose magnificently above the waters. Innumerable crowds of canoes were plying everywhere around us; at regular distances we continually passed over new bridges, and before us lay the great city of Mexico in all its splendour.*

*And we who were gazing upon all this, passing through innumerable crowds of human beings, were a mere handful of men, in all 450, our minds still full of the warnings which the inhabitants of Huexotzinco, Tlascalla, and Tlalmanalco, with the caution they had given us not to expose our lives to the treachery of the Mexicans. I may safely ask the kind reader to ponder a moment, and say whether he thinks any men in this world ever ventured so bold a stroke as this?*

*When we had arrived at a spot where another narrow causeway led towards Cojohuacan we were met by a number of caziques and distinguished personages, all attired in their most splendid garments. They had been despatched by Motecusuma to meet us and bid us welcome in his name; and in token of peace they touched the ground with their hands and kissed it. Here we halted for a few minutes, while the princes of Tetzcuco, Iztapalapan, Tlacupa, and Cojohuacan hastened in advance to meet Motecusuma, who was slowly approaching us, surrounded by other grandees of the kingdom, seated in a sedan of uncommon splendour. When we had arrived at a place not far from the town, where several small towers rose together, the monarch raised himself in his sedan, and the chief caziques supported him under the arms, and held over his head a canopy of exceedingly great value, decorated with green feathers, gold, silver, chalchihuis stones, and pearls, which hung down from a species of bordering, altogether curious to look at.*

*Motecusuma himself, according to his custom, was sumptuously attired, had on a species of half boot, richly set with jewels, and whose soles were made of solid gold. The four grandees who supported him were also richly attired, which they must have put on somewhere on the road, in order to wait upon Motecusuma; they were not so sumptuously dressed when they first came out to meet us. Besides these distinguished caziques, there were many other grandees around the monarch, some of whom held the canopy over his head, while others again occupied the road before him, and spread cotton cloths on the ground that his feet might not touch the bare earth. No one of his suite ever looked at him full in the face; every one in his presence stood with eyes downcast, and it was only his four nephews and cousins who supported him that durst look up.*

*When it was announced to Cortés that Motecusuma himself was approaching, he alighted from his horse and advanced to meet him. Many compliments were now passed on both sides. Motecusuma bid Cortés welcome, who, through Marina, said, in return, he hoped his majesty was in good health. If I still remember rightly, Cortés, who had Marina next to him, wished to concede the place of honour to the monarch, who, however, would not accept of it, but conceded it to Cortés, who now brought forth a necklace of precious stones, of the most beautiful colours and shapes, strung upon gold wire, and perfumed with musk, which he hung about the neck of Motecusuma. Our commander was then going to embrace him, but the grandees by whom he was surrounded held back his arms, as they considered it improper. Our general then desired Marina to tell the monarch how exceedingly he congratulated himself upon his good fortune of having seen such a powerful monarch face to face, and of the honour he had done us by coming out to meet us himself. To all this Motecusuma answered in very appropriate terms, and ordered his two nephews, the princes of Tetzcuco and Cojohuacan, to conduct us to our quarters. He himself returned to the city, accompanied by his two other relatives, the princes of Cuitlahuac and Tlacupa, with the other grandees of his numerous suite. As they passed by, we perceived how all those who composed his majesty's retinue held their heads bent forward, no one daring to lift up his eyes in his presence; and altogether what deep veneration was paid him.*

*The road before us now became less crowded, and yet who would have been able to count the vast numbers of men, women, and children who filled the streets, crowded the balconies, and the canoes in the canals, merely to gaze upon us? Indeed, at the moment I am writing this, everything comes as lively to my eyes as if it had happened yesterday; and I daily become more sensible of the great mercy of our Lord Jesus Christ, that he lent us sufficient strength and courage to enter this city: for my own person, I have particular reason to be thankful that he spared my life in so many perils, as the reader will sufficiently see in the course of this history: indeed I cannot sufficiently praise him that I have been allowed to live thus long to narrate these adventures, although they may not turn out so perfect as I myself could wish.*

*We were quartered in a large building where there was room enough for us all, and which had been occupied by Axayacatl, father of Motecusuma, during his life-time. Here the latter had likewise a secret room full of treasures, and where the gold he had inherited from his father was hid, which he had never touched up to this moment. Near this building there were temples and Mexican idols, and this place had been purposely selected for us because we were termed teules, or were thought to be such, and that we might dwell among the latter as among our equals. The apartments and halls were very spacious, and those set apart for our general were furnished with carpets. There were separate beds for each of us, which could not have been better fitted up for a gentleman of the first rank. Every place was swept clean, and the walls had been newly plastered and decorated.*

*When we had arrived in the great courtyard adjoining this palace, Motecusuma came up to Cortés, and, taking him by the hand, conducted him himself into the apartments where he was to lodge, which had been beautifully decorated after the fashion of the country. He then hung about his neck a chaste necklace of gold, most curiously worked with figures all representing crabs. The Mexican grandees were greatly astonished at all these uncommon favours which their monarch bestowed upon our general.*

*Cortés returned the monarch many thanks for so much kindness, and the latter took leave of him with these words: "Malinche, you and your brothers must now do as if you were at home, and take some rest after the fatigues of the journey," then returned to his own palace, which was close at hand.*

*We allotted the apartments according to the several companies, placed our cannon in an advantageous position, and made such arrangements that our cavalry, as well as the infantry, might be ready at a moment's notice. We then sat down to a plentiful repast, which had been previously spread out for us, and made a sumptuous meal.*

*This our bold and memorable entry into the large city of Temixtitlan-Mexico took place on the 8th of November, 1519. Praise be to the Lord Jesus Christ for all this. If, however, I have not exactly related every circumstance that transpired at the moment, the reader must pardon me for the present.*

Bernal Díaz del Castillo, *The Memoirs of the Conquistador Bernal Díaz del Castillo Written by Himself Containing a True and Full Account of the Discovery and Conquest of Mexico and New Spain*, trans. by John Ingram Lockhart (London, 1844), 221–3.

**Figure 3.3.** Hernán Cortés. Engraving by W. Holl, published in Charles Knight, *From a Picture in the Florence Gallery. Under the Superintendence of the Society for the Diffusion of Useful Knowledge* (n.d.). Library of Congress.

**Figure 3.2.** Portrait of Bernal Díaz del Castillo, by an unknown artist, published in Genaro García's first Guatemala edition of the *True History* in 1904.

Cortés has left a stunning description of the Aztec capital and of the Emperor Montezuma in a letter he wrote to King Charles V.

*IN order, most potent Sire, to convey to your Majesty a just conception of the great extent of this noble city of Temixtitan, and of the many rare and wonderful objects it contains; of the government and dominions of Muteczuma, the sovereign; of the religious rites and customs that prevail, and the order that exists in this as well as other cities appertaining to his realm: it would require the labor of many accomplished writers, and much time for the completion of the task. I shall not be able to relate an hundredth part of what could be told respecting these matters; but I will endeavor to describe, in the best manner in my power, what I have myself seen; and imperfectly as I may succeed in the attempt, I am fully aware that the account will appear so wonderful as to be deemed scarcely worthy of credit; since even we who have seen these things with our own eyes, are yet so amazed as to be unable to comprehend their reality. But your Majesty may be assured that if there is any fault in my relation, either in regard to the present subject, or to any other matters of which I shall give your Majesty an account, it will arise from too great brevity rather than extravagance or prolixity in the details; and it seems to me but just to my Prince and Sovereign to declare the truth in the clearest manner, without saying any thing that would detract from it, or add to it.*

*Before I begin to describe this great city and the others already mentioned, it may be well for the better understanding of the subject to say something of the configuration of Mexico, in which they are situated, it being the principal seat of Muteczuma's power. This Province is in the form of a circle, surrounded on all sides by lofty and rugged mountains; its level surface comprises an area of about seventy leagues in circumference, including two lakes, that overspread nearly the whole valley, being navigated by boats more than fifty leagues round. One of these lakes contains fresh, and the other, which is the larger of the two, salt water. On one side of the lakes, in the middle of the valley, a range of highlands divides them from one another, with the exception of a narrow strait which lies between the highlands and the lofty sierras. This strait is a bow-shot wide, and connects the two lakes; and by this means a trade is carried on between the cities and other settlements on the lakes in canoes without the necessity of travelling by land. As the salt lake rises and falls with its tides like the sea, during the time of high water it pours into the other lake with the rapidity of a powerful stream; and on the other hand, when the tide has ebbed, the water runs from the fresh into the salt lake.*

*This great city of Temixtitan [Mexico] is situated in this salt lake, and from the main land to the denser parts of it, by whichever route one chooses to enter, the distance is two leagues. There are four avenues or entrances to the city, all of which are formed by artificial causeways, two spears' length in width. The city is as large as Seville or Cordova; its streets, I speak of the principal ones, are very wide and straight; some of these, and all the inferior ones, are half land and half water, and are navigated by canoes. All the streets at intervals have openings, through which the water flows, crossing from one street to another; and at these openings, some of which are very wide, there are also very wide bridges, composed of large pieces of timber, of great strength and well put together; on many of these bridges ten horses can go abreast. Foreseeing that if the inhabitants of this city should prove treacherous, they would possess great advantages from the manner in which the city is constructed, since by removing the bridges at the entrances, and abandoning the place, they could leave us to perish by famine without our being able to reach the main land–as soon as I had entered it, I made great haste to build four brigantines, which were soon finished, and were large enough to take ashore three hundred men and the horses, whenever it should become necessary.*

*This city has many public squares, in which are situated the markets and other places for buying and selling. There is one square twice as large as that of the city of Salamanca, surrounded by porticoes, where are daily assembled more than sixty thousand souls, engaged in buying and selling; and where are found all kinds of merchandise that the world affords, embracing the necessaries of life, as for instance articles of food, as well as jewels of gold and silver, lead, brass, copper, tin, precious stones, bones, shells, snails, and feathers. There are also exposed for sale wrought and unwrought stone, bricks burnt and unburnt, timber hewn and unhewn, of different sorts. There is a street for game, where every variety of birds found in the country are sold, as fowls, partridges, quails, wild ducks, fly-catchers, widgeons, turtle-doves, pigeons, reedbirds, parrots, sparrows, eagles, hawks, owls, and kestrels; they sell likewise the skins of some birds of prey, with their feathers, head, beak, and claws. There are also sold rabbits, hares, deer, and little dogs, which are raised for eating and castrated. There is also an herb street, where may be obtained all sorts of roots and medicinal herbs that the country affords. There are apothecaries' shops, where prepared medicines, liquids, ointments, and plasters are sold; barbers' shops, where they wash and shave the head; and restaurateurs, that furnish food and drink at a certain price. There is also a class of men like those called in Castile porters, for carrying burthens. Wood and coals are seen in abundance, and brasiers of earthenware for burning coals; mats of various kinds for beds, others of a lighter sort for seats, and for halls and bedrooms. There are all kinds of green vegetables, especially onions, leeks, garlic, watercresses, nasturtium, borage, sorel, artichokes, and golden thistle; fruits also of numerous descriptions, amongst which are cherries and plums, similar to those in Spain; honey and wax from bees, and from the stalks of maize, which are as sweet as the sugar-cane; honey is also extracted from the plant called maguey, which is superior to sweet or new wine; from the same plant they extract sugar and wine, which they also sell. Different kinds of cotton thread of all colors in skeins are exposed for sale in one quarter of the market, which has the appearance of the silk-market at Granada, although the former is supplied more abundantly. Painters' colors, as numerous as can be found in Spain, and as fine shades; deerskins dressed and undressed, dyed different colors; earthenware of a large size and excellent quality; large and small jars, jugs, pots, bricks, and an endless variety of vessels, all made of fine clay, and all or most of them glazed and painted; maize, or Indian corn, in the grain and in the form of bread, preferred in the grain for its flavor to that of the other islands and terra-firma; patés of birds and fish; great quantities of fish, fresh, salt, cooked and uncooked; the eggs of hens, geese, and of all the other birds I have mentioned, in great abundance, and cakes made of eggs;, finally, every thing that can be found throughout the whole country is sold in the markets, comprising articles so numerous that to avoid prolixity, and because their names are not retained in my memory, or are unknown to me, I shall not attempt to enumerate them. Every kind of merchandise is sold in a particular street or quarter assigned to it exclusively, and thus the best order is preserved. They sell every thing by number or measure, at least so far we have not observed them to sell any thing by weight. There is a building in the great square that is used as an audience house, where ten or, twelve persons, who are magistrates, sit and decide all controversies that arise in the market, and order delinquents to be punished. In the same square there are other persons who go constantly about among the people observing what is sold, and the measures used in selling; and they have been seen to break measures that were not true.*

*This great city contains a large number of temples, or houses for their idols, very handsome edifices, which are situated in the different districts and the suburbs; in the principal ones religious persons of each particular sect are constantly residing, for whose use beside the houses containing the idols there are other convenient habitations. All these persons dress in black, and never cut or comb their hair from the time they enter the priesthood until they leave it; and all the sons of the principal inhabitants, both nobles and respectable citizens, are placed in the temples and wear the same dress from the age of seven or eight years until they are taken out to be married; which occurs more frequently with the first-born who inherit estates than with the others. The priests are debarred from female society, nor is any woman permitted to enter the religious houses. They also abstain from eating certain kinds of food, more at some seasons of the year than others. Among these temples there is one which far surpasses all the rest, whose grandeur of architectural details no human tongue is able to describe; for within its precincts, surrounded by a lofty wall, there is room enough for a town of five hundred families. Around the interior of this enclosure there are handsome edifices, containing large halls and corridors, in which the religious persons attached to the temple reside. There are full forty towers, which are lofty and well built, the largest of which has fifty steps leading to its main body, and is higher than the tower of the principal church at Seville. The stone and wood of which they are constructed are so well wrought in every part, that nothing could be better done, for the interior of the chapels containing the idols consists of curious imagery, wrought in stone, with plaster ceilings, and wood-work carved its relief, and painted with figures of monsters and other objects. All these towers are the burial places of the nobles, and every chapel in them is dedicated to a particular idol, to which they pay their devotions.*

*There are three halls in this grand temple, which contain the principal idols; these are of wonderful extent and height, and admirable workmanship, adorned with figures sculptured in stone and wood; leading from the halls are chapels with very small doors, to which the light is not admitted, nor are any persons except the priests, and not all of them. In these chapels are the images or idols, although, as I have before said, many of them are also found on the outside; the principal ones, in which the people have greatest faith and confidence, I precipitated from their pedestals, and cast them down the steps of the temple, purifying the chapels in which they had stood, as they were all polluted with human blood, shed in the sacrifices. In the place of these I put images of Our Lady and the Saints, which excited not a little feeling in Muteczuma and the inhabitants, who at first remonstrated, declaring that if my proceedings were known throughout the country, the people would rise against me; for they believed that their idols bestowed on them all temporal good, and if they permitted them to be ill-treated, they would be angry and withhold their gifts, and by this means the people would be deprived of the fruits of the earth and perish with famine. I answered, through the interpreters, that they were deceived in expecting any favors from idols, the work of their own hands, formed of unclean things; and that they must learn there was but one God, the universal Lord of all, who had created the heavens and the earth, and all things else, and had made them and us; that He was without beginning and immortal, and they were bound to adore and believe him, and no other creature or thing. I said every thing to them I could to divert them from their idolatries, and draw them to a knowledge of God our Lord. Muteczuma replied, the others assenting to what he said, That they had already informed me they were not the aborigines of the country, but that their ancestors had emigrated to it many years ago; and they fully believed that after so long an absence from their native land, they might have fallen into some errors; that I having more recently arrived must know better than themselves what they ought to believe; and that if I would instruct them in these matters, and make them understand the true faith, they would follow my directions, as being for the best. Afterwards, Muteczuma and many of the principal citizens remained with me until I had removed the idols, purified the chapels, and placed the images in them, manifesting apparent pleasure; and I forbade them sacrificing human beings to their idols, as they had been accustomed to do; because, besides being abhorrent in the sight of God, your sacred Majesty had prohibited it by law, and commanded to put to death whoever should take the life of another. Thus, from that time, they refrained from the practice, and during the whole period of my abode in that city, they were never seen to kill or sacrifice a human being.*

*The figures of the idols in which these people believe surpass in stature a person of more than the ordinary size; some of them are composed of a mass of seeds and leguminous plants, such as are used for food, ground and mixed together, and kneaded with the blood of human hearts taken from the breasts of living persons, from which a paste is formed in a sufficient quantity to form large statues. When these are completed they make them offerings of the hearts of other victims, which they sacrifice to them, and besmear their faces with the blood. For every thing they have an idol, consecrated by the use of the nations that in ancient times honored the same gods. Thus they have an idol that they petition for victory in war; another for success in their labors; and so for every thing in which they seek or desire prosperity, they have their idols, which they honor and serve.*

*This noble city contains many fine and magnificent houses; which may be accounted for from the fact, that all the nobility of the country, who are the vassals of Muteczuma, have houses in the city, in which they reside a certain part of the year; and besides, there are numerous wealthy citizens who also possess fine houses. All these persons, in addition to the large and spacious apartments for ordinary purposes, have others, both upper and lower, that contain conservatories of flowers. Along one of the causeways that lead into the city are laid two pipes, constructed of masonry, each of which is two paces in width, and about five feet in height. An abundant supply of excellent water, forming a volume equal in bulk to the human body, is conveyed by one of these pipes, and distributed about the city, where it is used by the inhabitants for drinking and other purposes. The other pipe, in the mean time, is kept empty until the former requires to be cleansed, when the water is let into it and continues to be used till the cleansing is finished. As the water is necessarily carried over bridges on account of the salt water crossing its route, reservoirs resembling canals are constructed on the bridges, through which the fresh water is conveyed. These reservoirs are of the breadth of the body of an ox, and of the same length as the bridges. The whole city is thus served with water, which they carry in canoes through all the streets for sale, taking it from the aqueduct in the following manner: the canoes pass under the bridges on which the reservoirs are placed, when men stationed above fill them with water, for which service they are paid. At all the entrances of the city, and in those parts where the canoes are discharged, that is, where the greatest quantity of provisions is brought in, huts are erected, and persons stationed as guards, who receive a certum quid of every thing that enters. I know not whether the sovereign receives this duty or the city, as I have not yet been informed; but I believe that it appertains to the sovereign, as in the markets of other provinces a tax is collected for the benefit of their cacique. In all the markets and public places of this city are seen daily many laborers and persons of various employments waiting for some one to hire them. The inhabitants of this city pay a greater regard to style in their mode of living, and are more attentive to elegance of dress and politeness of manners, than those of the other provinces and cities; since, as the Cacique Muteczuma has his residence in the capital, and all the nobility, his vassals, are in the constant habit of meeting there, a general courtesy of demeanor necessarily prevails. But not to be prolix in describing what relates to the affairs of this great city, although it is with difficulty I refrain from proceeding, I will say no more than that the manners of the people, as shown in their intercourse with one another, are marked by as great an attention to the proprieties of life as in Spain, and good order is equally well observed; and considering that they are a barbarous people, without the knowledge of God, having no intercourse with civilized nations, these traits of character are worthy of admiration.*

*In regard to the domestic appointments of Muteczuma, and the wonderful grandeur and state that he maintains, there is so much to be told, that I assure your Highness, I know not where to begin my relation, so as to be able to finish any part of it. For, as I have already stated, what can be more wonderful, than that a barbarous monarch, as he is, should have every object found in his dominions imitated in gold, silver, precious stones, and feathers; the gold and silver being wrought so naturally as not to be surpassed by any smith in the world; the stone work executed with such perfection that it is difficult to conceive what instruments could have been used; and the feather work superior to the finest productions in wax or embroidery. The extent of Muteczuma's dominions has not been ascertained, since to whatever point he dispatched his messengers, even two hundred leagues from his capital, his commands were obeyed, although some of his provinces were in the midst of countries with which he was at war. But as nearly as I have been able to learn, his territories are equal in extent to Spain itself, for he sent messengers to the inhabitants of a city called Cumatan, (requiring them to become subjects of your Majesty,) which is sixty leagues beyond that part of Putunchwn watered by the river Grijalva, and two hundred and thirty leagues distant from the great city; and I sent some of our people a distance of one hundred and fifty leagues in the same direction. All the principal chiefs of these provinces, especially those in the vicinity of the capital, reside, as I have already stated, the greater part of the year in that great city, and all or most of them have their oldest sons in the service of Muteczuma. There are fortified places in all the provinces, garrisoned with his own men, where are also stationed his governors and collectors of the rents and tribute, rendered him by every province; and an account is kept of what each is obliged to pay, as they have characters and figures made on paper that are used for this purpose. Each province renders a tribute of its own peculiar productions, so that the sovereign receives a great variety of articles from different quarters. No prince was ever more feared by his subjects, both in his presence and absence. He possessed out of the city as well as within, numerous villas, each of which had its peculiar sources of amusement, and all were constructed in the best possible manner for the use of a great prince and lord. Within the city his palaces were so wonderful that it is hardly possible to describe their beauty and extent; I can only say that in Spain there is nothing equal to them.*

*There was one palace somewhat inferior to the rest, attached to which was a beautiful garden with balconies extending over it, supported by marble columns, and having a floor formed of jasper elegantly inlaid. There were apartments in this palace sufficient to lodge two princes of the highest rank with their retinues. There were likewise belonging to it ten pools of water, in which were kept the different species of water birds found in this country, of which there is a great variety, all of which are domesticated; for the sea birds there were pools of salt water, and for the river birds, of fresh water. The water is let off at certain times to keep it pure, and is replenished by means of pipes. Each species of bird is supplied with the food natural to it, which it feeds upon when wild. Thus fish is given to birds that usually eat it; worms, maize, and the finer seeds, to such as prefer them. And I assure your Highness, that to the birds accustomed to eat fish there is given the enormous quantity of ten arrobas every day, taken in the salt lake. The emperor has three hundred men whose sole employment is to take care of these birds; and there are others whose only business is to attend to the birds that are in bad health.*

*Over the pools for the birds there are corridors and galleries, to which Muteczuma resorts, and from which he can look out and amuse himself with the sight of them. There is an apartment in the same palace in which are men, women and children, whose faces, bodies, hair, eyebrows, and eyelashes are white from their birth. The emperor has another very beautiful palace, with a large court-yard, paved with handsome flags, in the style of a chess-board. There were also cages, about nine feet in height and six paces square, each of which was half covered with a roof of tiles, and the other half had over it a wooden grate, skillfully made. Every cage contained a bird of prey, of all the species found in Spain, from the kestrel to the eagle, and many unknown there. There was a great number of each kind; and in the covered part of the cages there was a perch, and another on the outside of the grating, the former of which the birds used in the night time, and when it rained; and the other enabled them to enjoy the sun and air. To all these birds fowls were daily given for food, and nothing else. There were in the same palace several large halls on the ground floor, filled with immense cages built of heavy pieces of timber, well put together, in all or most of which were kept lions, tigers, wolves, foxes, and a variety of animals of the cat kind, in great numbers, which were also fed on fowls. The care of these animals and birds was assigned to three hundred men. There was another palace that contained a number of men and women of monstrous size, and also dwarfs, and crooked and ill-formed persons, each of which had their separate apartments. These also had their respective keepers. As to the other remarkable things that the emperor had in his city for his amusement, I can only say that they were numerous and of various kinds.*

*He was served in the following manner. Every day as soon as it was light, six hundred nobles and men of rank were in attendance at the palace, who either sat, or walked about the halls and galleries, and passed their time in conversation, but without entering the apartment where his person was. The servants and attendants of these nobles remained in the court-yards, of which there were two or three of great extent, and in the adjoining street, which was also very spacious. They all remained in attendance from morning till night; and when his meals were served, the nobles were likewise served with equal profusion, and their servants and secretaries also had their allowance. Daily his larder and winecellar were open to all who wished to eat and drink. The meals were served by three or four hundred youths, who brought on an infinite variety of dishes; indeed, whenever he dined or supped, the table was loaded with every kind of flesh, fish, fruits, and vegetables, that the country produced. As the climate is cold, they put a chafing-dish with live coals under every plate and dish, to keep them warm. The meals were served in a large hall, in which Muteczuma was accustomed to eat, and the dishes quite filled the room, which was covered with Gnats and kept very clean. He sat on a small cushion curiously wrought of leather. During the meals there were present, at a little distance from him, five or six elderly caciques, to whom he presented some of the food. And there was constantly in attendance one of the servants, who arranged and handed the dishes, and who received from others whatever was wanted for the supply of the table. Both at the beginning and end of every meal, they furnished water for the hands; and the napkins used on these occasions were never used a second time; this was the case also with the plates and dishes, which were not brought again, but new ones in place of them; it was the same also with the chafing-dishes. He is also dressed every day in four different suits, entirely new, which he never wears a second time. None of the caciques who enter his palace have their feet covered, and when those for whom he sends enter his presence, they incline their heads and look down, bending their bodies; and when they address him, they do not look him in the face, this arises from excessive modesty and reverence. I am satisfied that it proceeds from respect, since certain caciques reproved the Spaniards for their boldness in addressing me, saying that it showed a want of becoming deference. Whenever Muteczuma appeared in public, which was seldom the case, all those who accompanied him, or whom he accidentally met in the streets, turned away without looking towards him, and others prostrated themselves until he had passed. One of the nobles always preceded him on these occasions, carrying three slender rods erect, which I suppose was to give notice of the approach of his person. And when they descended from the litters, he took one of them in his hand, and held it until he reached the place inhere he was going. So many and various were the ceremonies and customs observed by those in the service of Muteczuma, that more space than I can spare would be required for the details, as well as a better memory than I have to recollect them; since no sultan or other infidel lord, of whom any knowledge now exists, ever had so much ceremonial in their courts.*

Hernán Cortés, "Second Letter of Hernando Cortés to Charles V,"
in Hernán Cortés, *The Dispatches of Hernando Cortés, The Conqueror of Mexico,
Addressed to the Emperor Charles V, Written During the Conquest,
and Containing a Narrative of Its Events* (New York, 1843).[7]

Once in the Aztec city the Spanish decided to protect themselves by holding Montezuma prisoner. They then proceeded to locate and seize the visible wealth of the Aztec capitol, mostly gold. The following spring, while Cortés was away dealing with a force sent by Cuba's governor to punish him for his disobedience, the Aztecs rebelled, drove the Spanish out of the city, and regained control. During the struggle Montezuma was killed, but no one knows who was responsible, the Spanish or his own people, resentful of the way he had given in to the invaders. Cortés recaptured the city in August after a major battle and remained in command until 1528 when he returned to Spain, defended his actions and received the title Marquis of the Valley. His writings are among the most important chronicles of the conquest.

## Peru

In 1531, after two previous attempts had failed, Francisco Pizarro, an experienced soldier acting with the support of King Charles V, led a successful assault on the other major Indian empire in Spanish America—that of the Incas in the Andes mountains of Peru. The Incas had created perhaps the best-ordered society in America, ruled by a chief who was also considered a god and who was married to his own sister. The people worked in tribute to their leaders who administered a kind of welfare state in which roads, buildings, terraced fields and waterworks were designed by architects and built by laborers who were employees of the government.

The Inca polity dated from the thirteenth century. Beginning in the middle of the fifteenth century the Incas created an empire, establishing by force their domination over virtually all the peoples in an area ranging from what is now Ecuador in the north to present day Argentina in the south. The conquered subjects paid tribute to and provided labor for the Incas and were required to adopt the Inca's language, Quecha. Among all the tribes they ruled, only the Aymara, in what is now Bolivia, were able to thwart the Inca's demand that they forsake their native tongue. The fierce Mapuche in the south (known to the Spanish as Araucanians) retained their independence from Inca rule entirely. Indeed, the Araucanians, using escaped Spanish horses that they captured and Spanish guns that they seized, also successfully resisted Spanish attempts to conquer them.

In command of an army even smaller than that led by Cortés against the Aztecs, Pizarro sailed from Panama and landed on the Pacific coast near the equator. Fortunate to enter the Inca Empire just when a civil war was in progress, Pizarro led each side to think he was its ally and then captured Atahualpa, the chief then occupying the throne. After much intrigue, and after securing a good deal of booty, the Spanish tried Atahualpa for a number of crimes (including polygamy). He was executed. The following years were filled with intrigue and conflict among the conquerors themselves. One of the casualties of the struggle for control was Pizarro himself, who was murdered in 1541 by the Spanish. A measure of stability finally was achieved by mid-century, but it was 1572 before the last serious claimant to the Inca throne, Tupac Amaru, was captured and executed by the Spanish.

The exploits of the conquistadors, and especially Cortés, roused many to seek to emulate his achievements. None did, but many tried heroically: Pánfilo de Narváez spent 1528 searching Florida for golden cities; Hernando de Soto left Florida by land in 1539 and headed to the Ozarks, then down the Mississippi River to the Gulf of Mexico in search of a similar prize; Francisco de Coronado looked for the seven cities of gold across the southwestern region of what is now the United States. But it was the conquest of the Inca Empire, and of the remnants of the Mayan civilization in Yucatan after a lengthy campaign of nearly two decades, which the Spanish won by 1545, that firmly established the bounds of the Spanish empire in America.

## Governing an Empire

The Spanish had discovered and conquered areas rich in two highly valuable resources: minerals and native populations accustomed to paying tribute to and to working for masters, or at least capable of being made to do so. To make their colonies profitable, Spanish leaders quickly perceived that they needed only to subdue, dominate and regulate the Indians to mine valuable minerals and till the soil. The existence of a useable labor force in the areas of the New World that Spain came to control meant that massive immigration from Spain was not essential to the success of its colonies. Since it was unnecessary to persuade large numbers of Iberians to come to America to perform harsh labor, the crown was able to create in its colonies as rigid and autocratic a regime as it desired—an ideal absolutist government. That is, the Spanish rulers did not have to promise liberty, self-government or freedom of religion to prospective colonists in order to attract a labor force. The purely material rewards to be gained from the domination of the natives in any given area through *encomienda* were sufficient to induce conquerors and their soldiers to remain in America after the conquest as the masters of mines and farms. The Spanish crown was not forced to reduce its power in the New World in order to persuade enough people to leave Spain for America to make the colonies pay. Spain sent neither peasants nor manual laborers to the New World. The Spaniards who came to America were soldiers, ranchers, mine owners, clergymen and officials. Most came not to enjoy liberty or freedom or to be part of an ideal society (that was the crown's and certain churchmen's business) but to make their fortunes.

Virtually from the outset of colonization in America Spanish rulers recognized that if their New World settlements were to prove beneficial to the mother country, then trade must be carefully regulated. Columbus's efforts had given the rulers of Castile title to the areas being settled, and Castilians were not anxious to share the wealth of America with other Spaniards. By law, only Castilians were permitted to engage in trade with Spanish America; and in 1503 the crown established the Casa de Contratación (House of Trade) in Seville to license commerce with the colonies and to inspect ships engaged in the colonial trade. To ensure even greater security, and maintain the exclusive rights of Castilians, policymakers decided to limit trade with America to two yearly convoys, which sailed from and returned to Seville. Furthermore, goods produced in America could be shipped legally only from specified ports in New Spain. Because such trade laws were so restrictive and because the colonists sought manufactured goods Spain could not supply, or higher rates for their own products than Sevillano merchants were willing to pay, the Spanish settlers carried out an extensive illicit trade with French, English and Dutch interlopers.

In 1524, King Charles I reorganized the Castilian Council, and formed the Council of the Indies whose appointed (by the king) members travelled with the royal court and legislated for America. The council exercised major judicial responsibilities in colonial matters, helped select men to fill vacant positions in the colonial administration and supervised their performance afterwards. Working with the council, the crown created a rigid, autocratic government for its colonies. Two major administrative areas were defined as viceroyalties, New Spain (Mexico, 1535) and New Castile (Peru, 1542), to be ruled in the king's name by viceroys, appointed by the king. Their annual salary of 60,000 pesos surely helped them to heed the king's orders that they keep from acquiring any personal interests in the areas they controlled. Advisory and judicial bodies called *audiencias* were created to assist the viceroys, to rule in their absence and to provide governance for the larger areas into which the viceroyalties were divided. Thus *audiencias* appeared at Santo Domingo, Mexico City, Panama, Lima, Guatemala and Bogota. Local affairs were administered by officials identified with a variety of titles, but with similar powers: *alcaldes*, *corregidores*, *gobernadores* and *mayores*. What is significant about them is that they were all appointed by higher officials, and in the later colonial period, by the crown itself. The *cabildos*, or town councils, were the only governmental institutions in which the people were represented.

Virtually all those appointed to important positions were *peninsulars*, or Spanish-born Spaniards. While men born in America of Spanish parents (Creoles) could aspire to lower offices in the colonial bureaucracy, higher positions were closed to them. For the crown not only relied on appointments in America to repay debts it incurred in Spain, but also regarded the Spanish upper class as uniquely fit to rule. Moreover, the crown doubtlessly feared that if high positions were given to native-born Americans its own authority might be threatened, since powerful men with permanent ties to America might evolve into a group able to oppose absolute rule and perhaps even encourage separation from Spain. The result of this policy was, of course, that Creoles increasingly resented both *peninsulars* and the system. Royal control extended even over the church in Spanish America. Papal bulls of 1501 and 1508 had determined that the crown (King Ferdinand) might exercise a broad range of ecclesiastical controls in the colonies. These included the authority to appoint ecclesiastics, to control church revenues, and to decide where churchmen were to be sent and what they might do. It is hardly surprising, therefore, that the church supported absolute rule by the crown, and, especially the missionary friars, supported the crown's assaults on *encomienda*. In spite of royal control over many aspects of its existence, the church grew rapidly in size, wealth and power. Some scholars have estimated that by the end of the colonial era the church owned half the land of Spanish America.[8] Such wealth proved attractive to many and the number of churchmen rose steadily, becoming so large that in 1611 the pope issued a bull suppressing certain religious houses. Immense size and wealth implies tremendous power, and this was certainly the case, particularly in instances where missionaries were entrusted with the supervision and care of groups of Indians. In these situations the churchmen exercised total authority, even regulating the sex lives of "their" natives.

Spaniards had, one might argue by pure chance, claimed areas in America whose indigenous native populations were large, had been conquered by and worked for masters prior to the appearance of the Spanish, and thus rather easily were induced to accept control by Europeans (who in many cases merely replaced Indian exploiters). While many Spaniards would have been content to settle in America and use this labor force to raise herds and grow crops, the attractiveness of the New World was magnified tremendously by the discovery of huge deposits of silver in the middle of the sixteenth century at Zacatecas and Guanajuato in Mexico and Potosí in Bolivia. The lure of silver proved so great that in 1550 the crown decreed that all conquests be stopped and that in the future any would-be conquistadors must apply to the king for a license.

### Reform and the Emergence of Spanish American Culture

The crown had consistently tried to limit the power of *encomenderos* in response to humanitarian pleas by men such as Las Casas and to political imperatives, which suggested that Spanish Americans with too much wealth and power might prove able to defy royal control. But with the conquest of the Valley of Mexico, Cortés opened a vast new area for exploitation whose large Indian population required control, and the crown had permitted *encomienda* to spread to the mainland. In 1542, King Charles I promulgated the New Laws of the Indies, a comprehensive legal code which guaranteed the rights of the Indians and severely restricted the powers of the *encomenderos*. New grants of *encomienda* were forbidden. Many existing grants were abolished immediately. Still others would expire with the death of the current *encomendero*. The reaction in America was overwhelming—rebellion was threatened by some and a number of officials outright refused to proclaim the laws. While the Spanish were willing to forsake certain liberties in order to reap the material rewards of life in America as masters of native laborers, putting an end to the system that permitted such exploitation would have made life in the New World, in their eyes, intolerable. The crown was forced to retreat, and by 1546 had agreed not to abolish *encomienda*. The king did manage, however, to take from the *encomenderos* their rights to Indian labor, leaving them only the collection of tribute. But a new system, *repartimiento*, under which settlers applied to local officials for a limited number of Indian laborers to perform specified tasks, did evolve. The "master" had to treat "his" Indians decently and pay them a designated wage, but *repartimiento* was still a kind of forced labor, which allowed the Spanish to secure workers for their farms and mines. Nonetheless, by the seventeenth century all such systems of labor control came to have less meaning. Due in some measure to harsh work, but primarily to diseases such as smallpox, the Indian population of New Spain had dropped from 25 million when Cortés landed to just over one million in 1605. This demographic catastrophe was noted by all Spain's critics in Europe and used to support the contention that Spaniards were the most cruel of all the Europeans who came to settle in the New World. But since disease is not confined to certain nationalities, it seems fair to suggest that had the more "liberal" English or the more "Indian-oriented" French colonized Mexico and South America, a similar annihilation of the native peoples would have occurred.

Nevertheless, the "Black Legend" that depicted the Spanish as uniquely brutal in their interaction with American natives has had an enduring impact. Images produced and published by the engraver Theodor de Bry, a Protestant, and his two sons in a series of books that circulated widely in Europe after 1590, popularized that view. The image below shows the Spanish explorer Vasco Núñez de Balboa in Central America with his troops, presiding over the execution of Indians, whom he ordered eaten alive by his war dogs.

**Figure 3.4.** Theodor de Bry, *Vasco Núñez de Balboa Executing Panamanian Native Americans by War Dogs for Same-Sex Practices* (1594). New York Public Library, Rare Book Room, De Bry Collection, New York. Balboa came to a bad end—he was beheaded after being accused of attempting to usurp power, a charge he vehemently denied as he was being led to the execution block.

Another engraving by de Bry depicts Spanish brutality and suggests the conquerors sanctioned cannibalism. Note the Spaniard in a shed selling or trading human body parts for a necklace.

**Figure 3.5.** Theodor de Bry, *Regionum indicarum per Hispanos Quosdam devastatarum verissima* (Spanish committing atrocities against Indians) (sixteenth century).

The decimation of the Indian population on the mainland paralleled that which had occurred in the West Indies a century earlier. The population of Native Americans in the valley of Mexico fell from over seven million in 1550 to just over a million in 1610. Just as they had done in the Indies, the Spanish responded by increasing the importation and use of blacks from Africa to resupply the depleted labor force. While both the crown and the church insisted that Indians—even those working under *encomienda*—were free people, no one argued that Africans ought to be similarly free. Unlike Indians, under Spanish law blacks could be, and in America were, slaves. This legal status meant that their bodies as well as their labor could be bought, sold or traded. They were property. All that was fine with the crown because if settlers relied on Africans to perform harsh labor with no rewards, then the Indians would not be forced to do so. Thus the crown's humanitarian policy toward Indians was served by African slavery; and so were its financial interests—those who received royal *asientos*, or licenses to engage in the slave trade, were required to share their profits with the crown. And, of course, the availability of black slaves meant that the socio-economic system whereby whites lived largely off the labor of non-whites was able to persist.

Spanish Americans had become accustomed to exploiting both the raw materials they found and the native population. Without some subordinate group to perform labor for whites, the rich resources of America could not have been used unless the Spanish had been willing to totally reorder the society they had created. That is, whites would have had to perform labor in mines and fields. Black slaves, therefore, freed the Spanish from having to face the social, economic and political consequences of such a reorganization. Spaniards were able merely to substitute black for Indian laborers in many cases, preserve their own domination and sense of superiority, and maintain the kind of society they had tried to build from the outset in the New World.

Had the Spanish not needed laborers, and had they lacked the capital to invest in purchasing a workforce, slavery could not have thrived in America. But workers were needed in the lucrative mining industry, and on the sugar plantations that appeared in the West Indies and parts of the mainland along with colonists from the Canary Islands where sugar was produced. Black slaves were in less demand on the large estates, or haciendas, where the owners, or *hacendados*, either cultivated European grains or raised herds of cattle, since these activities required less labor than mining or sugar production.

No matter what the industry, or whether in a city or on the countryside, the white population of Spanish America was in control. Creoles consistently sensed that Spanish-born Spaniards considered them inferior, and that was the case, but all whites were certain that they were superior to Indians, blacks and those of mixed parentage— *mestizos, mulatos, castos, coyotes*. To a great degree in colonial Spanish America, a person's heritage determined his or her social, economic and political position in society. Ancestry came to be so important, in fact, that persons troubled by fears that their "mixed" lineage would keep them from enjoying business or social privileges could hire professional genealogists to provide whatever documentation was required to establish their "purity." Spanish-American society had a fixed quality—patterns of white domination in all areas of life, and the consequent subordination of non-whites proved very durable, surviving well beyond the time when the colonial period itself ended in the nineteenth century.

## For Further Reading

de las Casas, Bartolomé, *History of the Indies* (New York, 1971).
Díaz del Castillo, Bernal, *The Discovery and Conquest of Mexico, 1517–1521*, ed. by Genaro García, trans. by A. P. Maudslay (Cambridge, MA, 2003).
de Sahagún, Fray Bernardo, *General History of the Things of New Spain* (Florentine Codex), trans. by Anderson and Dibble (Santa Fe, NM, 1975).
Elliott, J. H., *Empires of the Atlantic World: Britain and Spain in America 1492–1830* (New Haven, 2006).
Gibson, Charles, *Spain in America* (New York, 1966).
Hanke, Lewis, *The Spanish Struggle for Justice in the Conquest of the Americas* (Boston, 1965).
Leon-Portilla, Miguel, *The Broken Spears: The Aztec Account of the Conquest of Mexico* (Boston, 1990).
Parry, J. H., *The Spanish Seaborne Empire* (Berkeley, 1990).
_____, *The Spanish Theory of Empire in the Sixteenth Century* (Cambridge, 1940).
Thornton, John, *Africa and Africans in the Making of the Atlantic World, 1400–1800* (Cambridge, 1992).

## Notes

1 Bartolomé de Las Casas, quoted in Hugh Thomas, *Rivers of Gold* (London, 2003), 157–8.
2 Juan Ginés de Sepúlveda, *On the Reasons for the Just War among the Indians* (1547), ed. by S. Mintz and S. McNeil. Available online at http://www.digitalhistory.uh.edu/active_learning/explorations/spain/spain_sepulveda.cfm (accessed June 1, 2013).
3 Ida Altman, *Emigrants and Society. Extremadura and Spanish America in the Sixteenth Century* (Berkeley, Los Angeles, London, 1989); J. H. Elliott, *Empires of the Atlantic World: Britain and Spain in America 1492–1830* (New Haven and London, 2006), 24.
4 Available online at http://en.wikipedia.org/wiki/Requerimiento (accessed March 12, 2013).
5 Available online at http://www.gutenberg.org/files/32474/32474-h/32474-h.htm (accessed March 12, 2013).
6 Ibid.
7 Available online at http://mith.umd.edu/eada/html/display.php?docs=cortez_letter2.xml (accessed March 12, 2013).
8 Charles Gibson, *Spain in America* (New York, 1966), 84.

# Chapter Four

# INTERLOPERS: PIRATES, TRADERS, TRAPPERS, MISSIONARIES

*While the good Father was thus encouraging these good people, a wretched Iron renegade ... whom Father de Brebœuf had formerly instructed and baptized—hearing him speak Paradise and Holy Baptism, was irritated, and said to him, ... "[T]hou sayest that Baptism and the sufferings of this life lead straight to Paradise; thou wilt go soon, for I am going to baptize thee, and to make thee suffer well, in order to go the sooner to thy Paradise." The barbarian, having said that, took a kettle full of boiling water, which he poured over his body three different times, in derision of Holy baptism. And, each time that he baptized him in this manner, the barbarian said to him, with bitter sarcasm, "Go to Heaven, for thou art well baptized."*

—"A veritable Account of the Martyrdom and Blessed death of Father Jean de Brebœuf and of Father Gabriel L'Alemant, in New France, in the country of the Hurons, by the Iroquois, enemies of the Faith" (1649)

*They took the prisoners to the border of the water, and fastened them perfectly upright to a stake. Then each came with a torch of birch bark, and burned them, now in this place, now in that. The poor wretches, feeling the fire, raised so loud a cry that it was something frightful to hear; and frightful indeed are the cruelties which these barbarians practise towards each other. After making them suffer greatly in this manner and burning them with the abovementioned bark, taking some water, they threw it on their bodies to increase their suffering. Then they applied the fire anew, so that the skin fell from their bodies, they continuing to utter loud cries and exclamations, and dancing until the poor wretches fell dead on the spot.*

*As soon as a body fell to the ground dead, they struck it violent blows with sticks, when they cut off the arms, legs, and other parts; and he was not regarded by them as manly, who did not cut off a piece of the flesh, and give it to the dogs. Such are the courtesies prisoners receive.*

—Samuel de Champlain, "Second Voyage of Sieur. de Champlain to New France, in the Year 1610" (1613)[1]

## Spain's Challengers in America

The Portuguese had a solid claim to parts of America due to the voyages of Cabral and of Vespucci, and, of course, by the Treaty of Tordesillas. But they did little with their American territories during the time the Spanish were building their New World empire, largely because they were heavily committed to their profitable exploits in the Far East. The few permanent settlements established by the Portuguese in Brazil in this era were small and poor, serving mainly to secure Portugal's hold on the area and to provide ports for Portuguese ships engaged in the eastern trade. Brazil proved to be rich in dyewood, also known as brazilwood, a source of red dye. The Portuguese crown maintained a monopoly on the production and trade of this profitable resource. Disinclined to organize colonization efforts itself, the Portuguese crown chose to permit a few nobles to control affairs in Brazil—it granted them huge domains, called *captaincies*, and allowed the *captians* to rule without much interference from officials in the mother country. Beginning in the middle of the sixteenth century colonists turned to sugar planting as their primary source of income, using sugarcane imported from the Portuguese sugar islands of Madeira and Sao Tome. The crown had constructed the first sugar mills, called *engenhios*, in the 1550s. Soon individual *captians* introduced sugar production on their domains and production increased dramatically. Between 1550 and 1583, the number of *engenhios* in Brazil had grown from 5 to 115. By 1629, there were at least three hundred and fifty sugar mills producing a product for which the demand in Europe seemed insatiable.

Initially the sugar planters, many of whom had immigrated from Madeira and Sao Tome, relied on native slave labor to work on plantations modeled on those in the islands from which they had come. But as the Indian population declined under the impact of devastating diseases, the Portuguese turned to African slaves to meet their labor needs. As production soared and sugar came to dominate the Brazilian economy, the demand for African slaves rose accordingly. The Portuguese had long controlled areas in West Africa where slaves could be obtained. Historian Herbert Klein has calculated that between 1451 and 1700, 1,592,000 Africans were transported to the Americas as slaves. Of these, fully 610,000, or 38 percent, came to Brazil.[2] By the middle of the seventeenth century Brazil led the world in sugar production. Beneficial customs laws stimulated the rapidly growing trade in sugar.

In 1580, the Portuguese throne was left vacant when the king died without an heir, and Philip II of Spain, justifying his actions by citing his own rights to the throne, seized it for himself after leading an army into the nation. Philip did not intend to allow his new subjects in Brazil to exercise liberties his old subjects in New Spain might observe and come to demand for themselves. A viceroy was soon named, and in 1604 a Portuguese version of the Council of the Indies was created.

In unifying the crowns of Portugal and Spain, Philip had added to his wealth and power. But he had simultaneously come to rule an empire so visibly rich that many were determined to secure for themselves a share of the wealth. Spain's restrictive trade policies for such a huge empire meant that there would always be residents of Spanish America eager to deal with interlopers; tight supervision of every location where men could exchange goods would be impossible. By the start of the eighteenth century perhaps as much as 90 percent of the empire's trade was in violation of imperial regulations.

## Fish and the Fur Trade

From the beginning of the sixteenth century Europeans had been sailing to the North Atlantic off the coast of Newfoundland to exploit the vast supply of fish found there, especially the cod. John Cabot had reported after his 1497 voyage that the waters teemed with fish and the Corte-Real brothers, sailing for Portugal, had confirmed Cabot's assertion, adding that the land there would provide timber suitable for shipbuilding. Soon after the turn of the century an international community of French, English and Portuguese fisherman gathered in the area every summer, living in makeshift quarters on the shore where they dried, smoked and salted their catch. They returned to Europe in time to get their cargoes to market before winter, when dried fish served as a major source of sustenance for Europe's population. This body of fishermen was a crucial source of seamen for the continued exploration of America. Their experience in the North Atlantic proved of great value as leaders in England, France and the Netherlands became determined to seek their own route to the wealth of Asia via a northern passage that would not be interfered with by Portuguese or Spanish warships.

Fishermen returning to Europe from the Grand Banks surely disseminated some knowledge of the geography of the North American continent. Cartographers of the era typically depicted the Arctic area as dotted with islands that, in theory, could be navigated more easily than the southern tip of South America and the dangerous waters of Magellan's Strait, providing a much more straightforward route to the Far East. This assumption led the French ruler Francis I to hire an Italian seaman, Giovanni da Verrazano, in 1524 and instruct him to search the North American coast for a sea route through the continent to the orient. Verrazano sailed from the Carolinas to Nova Scotia, but found no northwest passage. Francis next engaged Jacques Cartier to conduct the search. He spent the year 1536 exploring the St. Lawrence River. Though unable to go beyond the rapids, he became convinced that the area had immense value even if it did not include a passage to the Pacific. In 1541, Cartier returned to North America, to attempt to establish a permanent settlement. However, the French found no ready wealth to plunder and learned how terrible a Canadian winter can be. They quickly gave up and returned home to France.

Later, Martin Frobisher, an Englishman hired by a private company organized to trade with China, sailed in 1576 to find a route his employers might use. Frobisher got sidetracked in America when he found what he thought was gold, and returned to England to have it assayed. Experts told him it was indeed gold, so he sailed back to North America, loaded more than a thousand tons of the "ore," and headed home to collect his fortune. His cargo proved to be worthless. Frobisher had found neither wealth nor a passage to China. Prospects for finding wealth seemed, at the time, much brighter far to the South.

As the sixteenth century progressed, Spain continued to be unable to provide her American colonies with the goods they sought, at prices the colonists thought they deserved. Thus a huge market existed which might be exploited if one were willing to risk the wrath of the Spanish navy. Sir John Hawkins, an Englishman, was ready to take on these risks in order to secure his share of that market, especially as Spain and England were then enjoying good relations. Hawkins intended to conform to Spanish trade regulations; he came to America prepared to pay duties on the cloth and slaves he wanted to sell, and even attempted to secure a license from Spanish authorities in America to engage in the commerce. He made his first voyage in 1562 with three vessels, which he led first to the Canaries where he found a Spaniard familiar with the Indies ports, then to Sierra Leone where he bought three hundred Africans from Portuguese slave traders, then to Hispaniola where he received a permit from local officials to sell his cargo. He paid all the required duties, persuaded the officials to provide him with letters certifying that he had complied with all the regulations, and sold his slaves for hides and sugar which he took to Europe where he made a very smart profit. He made a second voyage soon after this, selling his slaves in Venezuela and Panama for a good deal of silver. This delighted Elizabeth I and the members of her Privy Council who had helped finance the voyage (secretly, of course, since their participation in trade that Spanish leaders considered illegal might have serious consequences for relations between Spain and England). The Queen did forbid him from making further voyages, however, since the Spanish government had punished the West Indian officials who had cooperated with Hawkins, and the Spanish ambassador in London had made strong protests about his activities. Nonetheless, by 1567, Hawkins had convinced the Queen to permit him to lead one final expedition to the Indies. It proved a dismal failure. Hawkins's five ships were trapped by a Spanish fleet, which carried a new viceroy and had made false signals that a truce was in force. Three of Hawkins's ships were destroyed, and the surviving two (Hawkins's vessel and that of Francis Drake, his cousin) were severely damaged. In future, Englishmen who sailed to the Spanish West Indies came not as traders but as pirates. Among the most notorious was Francis Drake, whose experiences during his voyage with Hawkins left him with nothing but hatred for the Spanish.

Pirate communities had existed for some time in the islands of the Indies. They were loosely organized societies, different from many other American enterprises in that their members were all male. The pirates also shared an intense hatred of Spain and the Spanish. They did not share either race or nationality—*cimarrones*, escaped slaves from Spanish settlements, joined with the English, Dutch and especially French to plunder the wealth of Spanish America. Indeed, the French crown commonly granted licenses

**Figure 4.1.** Portrait of Sir John Hawkins (1581). National Maritime Museum, London.

to any captain willing to attack Spanish ships or Spanish towns in the New World. No coastal community felt entirely secure, and the Spanish crown received numerous pleas from local officials in the Indies for protection from the buccaneers. It was in response to pirate depredations that, toward the middle of the sixteenth century, the Spanish determined to employ the convoy system to safeguard trading ships and, under the direction of the gifted admiral Pedro Menendez, organized squadrons of warships to

**Figure 4.2.** Marcus Gheerhaerts the Younger, *Sir Francis Drake Wearing the Drake Jewel or Drake Pendant at his Waist* (1591). National Maritime Museum, London.

patrol the major shipping routes through the Antilles. Drake returned to America in 1571, scouted the coast of Panama and negotiated with groups of buccaneers. Together they formulated plans for a major raid on the Spanish treasure convoy while it proceeded by land across Panama to a Caribbean port. Drake's 70 men, reinforced by pirates and *cimarrones*, succeeded in capturing the convoy on land and loaded the silver on his ships, which sailed for England, arriving safely in 1573. Four years later Drake undertook his most famous exploit—to sail through the Straits of Magellan, contact the rulers of spice producing islands in the East, conclude formal trade agreements with them and continue sailing west until he had circumnavigated the globe. All this he accomplished, and more. For Drake also raided Spanish settlements, explored the North American Pacific coast (possibly in search of a northwest passage) and captured a Spanish galleon carrying a cargo of silver from Peru. His adventures earned him a level of fame achieved by few of his contemporaries. The depredations of Drake, Hawkins and their emulators were part of the series of events, which ultimately led to war between England and Spain in 1585. The culmination of that war, the disastrous (for Spain) attack on England by the Spanish Armada, left Spain visibly weakened.

## The Dutch

The Netherlands consisted of 17 provinces that through conquest, inheritance or purchase had come under the rule of the dukes of Burgundy during the fifteenth century. Philip II of Spain had inherited them from his father Charles. These seventeen separate states shared only a common king, and their sense of unity was almost wholly based on common attitudes—positive or negative—toward him. Philip was an aggressive monarch, and after 1560 he sent Spanish soldiers, Spanish officials and a Spanish governor to the Netherlands to enforce his laws. What was more distressing to people who were accustomed to less attention from kings who lived closer to their kingdoms than Philip did to the Low Countries, was that Philip's aggressiveness extended to religious matters. He was a Catholic determined to exterminate heresy (Protestantism), and Calvinism had begun to take root in the area.

Philip's decision to export the Inquisition from Spain to the Netherlands disregarded the pleas of the local nobility to keep it away, and as a result rebellion broke out. Philip responded by sending in not only the Inquisition but more troops and a harsh new governor. The result was a still greater sense of common purpose among the 17 provinces, and in 1576, after a decade of troubles, representatives of all the provinces met and decided to unite in order to expel the foreigners. When word reached Queen Elizabeth in England that the Spanish were planning to suppress the rebellion and then use the Netherlands as a base from which to launch an invasion of England (Protestant since Henry VIII's break with Rome), she formed an alliance with the rebels, which led to cooperation against Spain not only in Europe but in the waters of America as well, where English and Dutch captains ruthlessly attacked Spanish shipping and settlements.

Philip retaliated against England with his Armada in 1588. His 130 ships were confronted by Sir Francis Drake in command of two hundred heavily armed English vessels, lighter and more maneuverable than their Spanish counterparts. That portion of the Armada not blown apart by English gunners was blown against rocky coasts by the storm known thereafter as the "Protestant wind." By the time England and Spain achieved peace in 1604 both Philip and Elizabeth were dead. During the conflict, the Netherlands had divided into a pro-Spanish southern section and a rebellious northern section. In 1609, the northern provinces, now identified as the Dutch Republic (or United Provinces), likewise signed a treaty with Spain. Not only did Spain recognize them as an independent nation, but the Spanish also agreed that in America only those territories solidly controlled by Spain would be considered Spanish. Territories not both governed and settled by the Spanish were open for exploitation by any other power, a principle asserted by the new English King James I during his negotiations with the Spanish in 1604.

One result of Philip's forcible union of the Portuguese and Spanish crowns in 1580 was that at once all of Spain's enemies became Portugal's enemies. As long as Philip had ruled the Netherlands, spices from Portugal's far eastern trading centers had flowed into Antwerp and from there to points all over northern Europe. But with the Low Countries in revolt, Portuguese and Spanish warships closed sea lanes to merchantmen and Spanish officials closed the trade routes on land. If the Dutch wanted spices they would have to sail after them in their own ships. Fortuitously for potential traders, a Dutchman who had been a servant in India, Jan Huyghen van Linschoten, had returned home in 1592 and published a detailed account of the East, including vital navigational information. In 1595, a Dutch fleet set sail, following Linschoten's directions. The result was a trade agreement with a local Bantenese sultan. In 1598, five more fleets sailed—still more trading treaties were achieved, which is hardly surprising since the Dutch were first-rate sailors and perhaps even better businessmen. Only military power could prevent them from securing a major portion of the Far Eastern trade; and Portugal, committed to battle alongside Philip in Europe, was incapable of exerting much power in Asia. In 1602, to improve their negotiating position with local rulers in the East Indies, the Dutch government chartered the Dutch East India Company. In return for a trade monopoly and a grant of authority to wage war, create colonies and coin money, the Company would pay customs duties to and allow a degree of control over its operations by the government. While any Dutch citizen could buy shares in the Company, the major investors were Amsterdam's merchants. As long as the war with Spain lasted, the Dutch gladly shared the Far Eastern Trade with the English. An English East India Company had received a charter from Elizabeth in 1600 and it sent ships repeatedly to the Indies for more than a decade, or until the Dutch had made peace with Spain. For the Dutch thought James I of England far too friendly toward the Catholic power; and in any case, once freed of the need to fight for survival at home they decided to invest their resources in taking complete control of affairs in the East. This they accomplished by driving the Portuguese out of Malacca in 1641 and from Ceylon in 1658. By then the Dutch had become the major maritime power in the world.

The East India Company proved so successful that, in 1621, the Dutch government chartered a West India Company. Its trade monopoly extended to the west coast of

Africa, for the Dutch recognized that slaves would be a major commodity for the American market. Also, since the truce with Spain had just expired, it seemed reasonable to attack the enemy economically in as wide an area as possible. In 1624, the Company sent a heavily armed fleet against Bahia, in northeastern Brazil, a major sugar-producing area. Within a decade its forces managed to wrest control of about half the colony from the Portuguese. In 1628, 31 of the company's ships, commanded by Admiral Piet Heyn, captured the entire Spanish yearly convoy, which among other American products included the whole year's supply of treasure. The Dutch secured a base for supplying their Caribbean ships in 1634, when a force captured the island of Curaçao, just off the Venezuela coast.

The Dutch also moved to take control of a share of the North American Indian trade, which consisted almost entirely of furs. Henry Hudson had explored the river which bears his name for the East India Company in 1609, and thereby established the Dutch claim to what proved to be an area ideally located for such an enterprise—the Hudson cut into the center of an area whose native population was eager to exchange the furs of abundant animals (beaver, especially) for European manufactured goods. Starting with a fortified trading post near modern Albany, which they named Fort Orange (the Dutch rebellion against Spain had been led by William of Orange, known as William the Silent), by the middle of the century the Company's agents had erected a string of small communities along the Hudson, on Long Island and in New Jersey. In 1624, 30 families were sent to settle New Netherland, and under their governor Peter Minuit, who ruled with the advice of a council and without interference from an elected assembly, they established New Amsterdam on Manhattan Island in 1626. Minuit, of course, had purchased the site from local Indians for 24 dollars. After 1629, the Company granted patroonships to those wealthy enough to transport settlers to the tiny colony. The patroon not only controlled his land but exercised governmental prerogatives as well. These efforts produced so few visible achievements that the Company largely ignored the colony for many years. But the Dutch did manage to establish ties with the Indians under Peter Stuyvesant, who governed from 1646–64; the Dutch also permitted the settlers to elect an advisory assembly in 1647, and thus the colony finally began to grow. Such successes came only after their rivals in America, the French and the English, had gained an even greater foothold on the continent. But in a sense, the expansion of French and English colonization into North America, which soon would drive the Dutch out, was responsible for that growth. New Amsterdam became the center for a huge carrying trade between Europe and the American colonies of England, France and Spain—a trade largely carried on in Dutch bottoms.

During the seventeenth century the Dutch were the world's carriers. Their rivals admired the speed, economy and excellence with which the Dutch shipped all kinds of goods, especially by sea. In shipbuilding the Dutch were superior to the rest of Europe. They constructed boats specifically designed to handle different types of products—the "buss" for catching herring in the North Sea, the whaler for the waters off Greenland, the timber carrier for the Baltic, and most important the fluyt (flyboat) with a flat bottom and maximum cargo space for general goods. The Dutch offered the producers of raw materials cheaper rates, greater care for their cargoes and better credit terms than shippers of any other country. However, everyone recognized that if they were allowed to compete freely for the carrying trade the Dutch would dominate the world's commerce. This was especially true in the West Indies, where the French and English established settled colonies early in the seventeenth century, in areas not previously occupied by the Spanish. The French colonized Martinique and Guadeloupe under the direction of a company chartered by the government to trade and to populate the Outer Antilles. Using first white indentured servants (free laborers who voluntarily exchanged several years of labor for passage to America and support during their term of service) and later black slaves, the French cultivated tobacco. Dutch merchants taught the colonists the "mysteries" of sugar production, which they had learned in Brazil. Sugar soon came to dominate the economic life of the island colonies (and greatly stimulated the demand for slaves—which, of course, the Dutch could supply). The English settled in Barbados, where an economy quite similar to that in the French islands quickly developed. Together, the English and French colonized St. Kitts, where the warlike Carib Indians produced unity among the whites, grounded in their common fear of the natives. Both English and French settlers in the West Indies relied not on their home governments, but rather on the Dutch for most of their goods and for nearly all of their slaves. It was in response to the powerful economic threat posed by the Dutch that European governments erected stiff trade barriers in the form of commercial regulations for their empires. The Dutch, by their success, forced European leaders to pay greater attention to their colonies, and to devise more effective ways for administering them. If the colonies could be profitable to the Dutch who did not rule them, and whose people did not settle them, then they ought to prove even more profitable to nations that enjoyed governmental control over and shared common loyalties with the colonists.

### The French in North America

Under King Francis I the French had tried to build settlements in North America in Canada on the St. Lawrence River. A bitter winter and hostile Indians had ruined the experiment. But the French did not give up their hope of carving out an empire in America—they simply refocused their vision as to where such a foothold could be established, and saw Brazil. Although the Portuguese claimed the entire Brazilian coast, they could effectively control only parts of it. French corsairs had been active in the area for some years, trading, looting and building close ties with the Indians who hated the oppressive rule of their Portuguese masters. By mid-century, the French, without any systematic plan had come to control much of the territory along the coast. They launched a serious attempt to seize control of the colony in 1555 when Gaspard de Coligny, King Henry II's first minister and a Protestant, sent Nicolas de Villegaignon to

Rio de Janeiro at the head of a small force. But even when reinforced by 300 additional soldiers the next year, Villegaignon was unable to accomplish much more than merely holding onto his base. The Portuguese drove the French out of Rio in 1560, and had completely recaptured Brazil by 1603. Coligny's attempt to build another French base in Florida in 1561 was an even greater disaster than his efforts in Brazil. After attempts to settle near what is now Charleston, South Carolina in 1562 had failed under Jean Ribaut, Rene de Laudonniere succeeded in establishing a Huguenot (French Protestant) colony on the St. John's River. The Spanish were not the Portuguese, and it took them only one year to erect a rival base at St. Augustine, capture Fort Caroline (as the French had named their settlement) and slaughter the 132 soldiers they found there, as well as those they captured trying to escape.

The French, therefore, were left with Canada—an area no other power in Europe seemed to want. In spite of their previous failures in Canada, the French did know that the territory had valuable supplies of fish in its coastal waters, and even more valuable furs in its interior. Canada also had many Indians whose presence offered the French two potential benefits: they seemed quite eager to go into the woods and fetch beaver skins in return for European manufactured goods, and they were heathens whose souls might be saved thereby ensuring their eternal salvation and France's eternal glory. There was every reason to believe, moreover, that a northwest passage to the Far East did exist, and that it might be readily dominated by that European power which controlled the northern parts of North America. Thus even Canada might prove abundant and pay rewards to those who possessed it. But Canada was in one respect strikingly different from the abundant areas Spain had conquered. Canada's natives were not only good warriors; they were scattered in numerous small communities. Unlike the Aztecs and Incas, Canada's indigenous population could not be conquered by destroying a major metropolitan center or by deposing a single great ruler or dynasty. The French were not to find in Canada a ready-made labor force of docile natives accustomed to paying tribute or willing to be taught forced labor. If large-scale permanent settlements of Europeans were to be erected in Canada, a good many Frenchmen would have to be persuaded or coerced into leaving France for a life of labor in America (something virtually no potential Spanish colonist had to contemplate).

France was wracked by internal difficulties, most crucially the deadly mutual hatred between Protestants and Catholics. Both groups had evolved over a long period in France; both were well established and could exercise power (Coligny, after all, was a Protestant). Internal strife would plague France until Protestant and Catholic learned to love one another, but in the early seventeenth century neither group seemed amenable to such suggestions. Indeed, on August 24, 1572 the queen mother had initiated her own solution to the problem by arranging to have all the Huguenot leaders of France murdered while in Paris to celebrate a royal wedding. Among the victims in the St. Bartholomew's Day massacre was Coligny. Even the Edict of Nantes, by which King Henry IV declared that Huguenots would both be tolerated in France and enjoy all the liberties of Catholic Frenchmen, failed to eliminate the hatred that disunited Frenchmen. To many Protestants and Catholics, the mere presence of the other religion ensured that French society was impure. The more certain they were of the truth of their own religion the more galling it was to be unable to eradicate heretics. In such a social environment some Frenchmen came to look upon the open wilderness of Canada as a place to do more than get rich—they saw it as an opportunity to create a French society free of the imperfections and strife endemic to France. America, they realized, had vast open space where men might build real communities that conformed to an ideal vision and thereby eradicate all their previous mistakes. At minimum, there ought to be space enough in Canada for men to live as they saw fit and not be forced to associate with those whose proximity might lead to conflict.

Such considerations, however, were not uppermost in the minds of the duc de Montmorency (admiral of France) and Henry IV when, in 1603, they commissioned the Sieur de Monts lieutenant general and vice-admiral in Canada. The king and the admiral wanted gold or silver and a northwest passage, and expected de Monts to take 60 settlers there to secure the valuable things he might find. De Monts also would enjoy a 10-year monopoly on the fur trade and the authority to grant land. He and his chief associate, Samuel de Champlain, proceeded to establish a base of operations in Acadia, on the Atlantic coast where fish and furs were readily available. No northwest passage was found during the three years they spent there, but no one continued to doubt that white men could live the entire year in Canada. In 1607, de Monts lost his fur trade monopoly when other Frenchmen, perhaps witnessing the limited success his little all-male community was enjoying, succeeded in persuading the French government that if the trade were open to all, everyone (including the government) would benefit. By then, both de Monts and Champlain had decided that their major effort in future would have to be made inland, at a place where they could supervise the fur trade more carefully than was possible on the coast. Thus, in 1608, Champlain established Quebec on a site historian W. J. Eccles has called among "the best natural military strongpoints in North America. Whoever controlled it controlled access to the interior of the continent."[3] And that is precisely what Champlain sought. His primary goal was the creation of a center from which Frenchmen could secure and then protect for themselves the continental fur trade. After their first winter at Quebec, only 8 of the original 28 Frenchmen who established the post were still alive.

Good relations with the natives were crucial to Champlain's success. Quebec had to compete with other French trading posts downriver for the furs which the Indians supplied. In July 1609, Champlain accompanied a war party of Algonkian, Huron and Montagnai Indians formed to attack the Mohawks, part of the large and powerful Iroquois confederacy. He explored the route from the St. Lawrence to Lake Champlain. More important, near Ticonderoga, Champlain and his 60 companions confronted about two hundred Mohawks. Everyone wanted to fight, but since it was late they agreed to wait until morning to do battle. After a night during which each side

**Figure 4.3.** Inauthentic depiction of Samuel de Champlain by Théophile Hamel (1870), created after the one by Ducornet (d. 1856), which was based on a portrait of Michel Particelli d'Emery (d. 1650) by Balthasar Moncornet (d. 1668). Collection of the Governor General of Canada, La Citadelle, Quebec.

taunted the other with insults and declarations of courage, the war parties formed for battle in the morning. Little killing took place. For when Champlain fired his arquebus and two Mohawks fell, the remaining Mohawks fled. The Iroquois would soon overcome their initial shock and fear of European guns (and learn to use them themselves), but their hatred of the French did not pass so quickly. Champlain had initiated a pattern of Indian-European relations that would persist for nearly two centuries. The French could generally rely on alliances with the Hurons, while the Iroquois became the traditional allies of the English. In his *Voyages*, published in 1632, Champlain described the fight.

> *I set out accordingly from the fall of the Iroquois River on the 2d of July. All the savages set to carrying their canoes, arms, and baggage overland, some half a league, in order to pass by the violence and strength of the fall, which was speedily accomplished. Then they put them all in the water again, two men in each with the baggage; and they caused one of the men of each canoe to go by land some three leagues, the extent of the fall, which is not, however, so violent here as at the mouth, except in some places, where rocks obstruct the river, which is not broader than three hundred or four hundred paces. After we had passed the fall, which was attended with*

*difficulty, all the savages, who had gone by land over a good path and level country, although there are a great many trees, re-embarked in their canoes. My men went also by land; but I went in a canoe. The savages made a review of all their followers, finding that there were twenty-four canoes, with sixty men. After the review was completed, we continued our course to an island, three leagues long, filled with the finest pines I had ever seen. Here they went hunting, and captured some wild animals. Proceeding about three leagues farther on, we made a halt, in order to rest the coming night ...*

*We set out on the next day, continuing our course in the river as far as the entrance of the lake. There are many pretty islands here, low, and containing very fine woods and meadows, with abundance of fowl and such animals of the chase as stags, fallow-deer, fawns, roe-bucks, bears, and others, which go from the main land to these islands. We captured a large number of these animals. There are also many beavers, not only in this river, but also in numerous other little ones that flow into it. These regions, altho they are pleasant, are not inhabited by any savages, on account of their wars; but they withdraw as far as possible from the rivers into the interior, in order not to be suddenly surprised.*

*The next day we entered the lake, which is of great extent, say eighty or a hundred leagues long, where I saw four fine islands, ten, twelve, and fifteen leagues long, which were formerly inhabited by the savages, like the River of the Iroquois; but they have been abandoned since the wars of the savages with one another prevail. There are also many rivers falling into the lake, bordered by many fine trees of the same kinds as those we have in France, with many vines finer than any I have seen in any other place; also many chestnut-trees on the border of this lake, which I had not seen before. There is also a great abundance of fish, of many varieties: among others, one called by the savages of the country* Chaousarou *which varies in length, the largest being, as the people told me, eight or ten feet long. I saw some five feet long, which were as large as my thigh; the head being as big as my two fists, with a snout two feet and a half long, and a double row of very sharp and dangerous teeth ...*

*Continuing our course over this lake on the western side, I noticed, while observing the country, some very high mountains on the eastern side, on the top of which there was snow. I made inquiry of the savages, whether these localities were inhabited, when they told me that the Iroquois dwelt there, and that there were beautiful valleys in these places, with plains productive in grain, such as I had eaten in this country, together with many kinds of fruit without limit. They said also that the lake extended near mountains, some twenty-five leagues distant from us, as I judge. I saw, on the south, other mountains, no less high than the first, but without any snow. The savages told me that these mountains were thickly settled, and that it was there we were to find their enemies; but that it was necessary to pass a fall in order to go there (which I afterwards saw), when we should enter another lake, nine or ten leagues long ...*

*Now, as we began to approach within two or three days' journey of the abode of their enemies, we advanced only at night, resting during the day ...*

*When it was evening, we embarked in our canoes to continue our course; and, as we advanced very quietly and without making any noise, we met on the 29th of the month the Iroquois, about ten o'clock at evening, at the extremity of a cape which extends into the lake on the western bank. They had come to fight. We both began to utter loud cries, all getting their arms in readiness. We withdrew out on the water, and the Iroquois went on shore, where they drew up all their canoes close to each other and began to fell trees with poor axes, which they acquire in war sometimes, using also others of stone. Thus they barricaded themselves very well.*

*Our forces also passed the entire night, their canoes being drawn up close to each other, and fastened to poles, so that they might not get separated, and that they might be all in readiness to fight, if occasion required. We were out upon the water, within arrow range of their barricades. When they were armed and in array, they despatched two canoes by themselves to the enemy to inquire if they wished to fight, to which the latter replied that they wanted nothing else; but they said that, at present, there was not much light, and that it would be necessary to wait for daylight, so as to be able to recognize each other; and that, as soon as the sun rose, they would offer us battle. This was agreed to by our side. Meanwhile, the entire night was spent in dancing and singing, on both sides, with endless insults and other talk; as, how little courage we had, how feeble a resistance we would make against their arms, and that, when day came, we should realize it to our ruin. Ours also were not slow in retorting, telling them they would see such execution of arms as never before, together with an abundance of such talk as is not unusual in the siege of a town. After this singing, dancing, and bandying words on both sides to the fill, when day came, my companions and myself continued under cover, for fear that the enemy would see us. We arranged our arms in the best manner possible, being, however, separated, each in one of the canoes of the savage Montagnais. After arming ourselves with light armor, we each took an arquebuse, and went on shore. I saw the enemy go out of their barricade, nearly two hundred in number, stout and rugged in appearance. They came at a slow pace toward us, with a dignity and assurance which greatly amused me, having three chiefs at their head. Our men also advanced in the same order, telling me that those who had three large plumes were the chiefs, and that they had only these three, and that they could be distinguished by these plumes, which were much larger than those of their companions, and that I should do what I could to kill them. I promised to do all in my power, and said that I was very sorry they could not understand me, so that I might give order and shape to their mode of attacking their enemies, and then we should, without doubt, defeat them all; but that this could not now be obviated, and that I should be very glad to show them my courage and good-will when we should engage in the fight.*

*As soon as we had landed, they began to run for some two hundred paces toward their enemies, who stood firmly, not having as yet noticed my companions, who went into the woods with some savages. Our men began to call me with loud cries; and in order to give me a passage-way, they opened in two parts, and put me at their head, where I marched some twenty paces in advance of the rest, until I was within about thirty paces of the enemy, who at once noticed me, and, halting, gazed at me, as I did also at them. When I saw them making a move to fire at us, I rested my musket against my cheek, and aimed directly at one of the three chiefs. With the same shot, two fell to the ground; and one of their men was so wounded that he died some time after. I had loaded my musket with four balls. When our side saw this shot so favorable for them, they began to raise such loud cries that one could not have heard it thunder.*

*Meanwhile, the arrows flew on both sides. The Iroquois were greatly astonished that two men had been so quickly killed, altho they were equipped with armor woven from cotton thread, and with wood which was a proof against their arrows. This caused great alarm among them. As I was loading again, one of my companions fired a shot from the woods, which astonished them anew to such a degree that, seeing their chiefs dead, they lost courage, and took to flight, abandoning their camp and fort, and fleeing into the woods, whither I pursued them, killing still more of them. Our savages also killed several of them, and took ten or twelve prisoners. The remainder escaped with the wounded. Fifteen or sixteen were wounded on our side with arrow-shots; but they were soon healed.*

*After gaining the victory, our men amused themselves by taking a great quantity of Indian corn and some meal from their enemies, also their armor, which they had left behind that they might run better. After feasting sumptuously, dancing and singing, we returned three hours after, with the prisoners. The spot where this attack took place is in latitude 43 degrees and some minutes, and the lake was called Lake Champlain.*

> Samuel de Champlain, "The Voyages to the Great River St. Lawrence, Made by Sieur de Champlain, Captain in Ordinary to the King in the Marine, from the Year 1608 to that of 1612," in *Voyages of Samuel de Champlain, Vol. II. 1604–1610*, trans. by Charles Pomeroy Otis, ed. by Rev. Edmund F. Slafter (Boston, *c*. 1878).[4]

Champlain included this drawing of the encounter in his book.

**Figure 4.4.** An engraving based on a drawing by Samuel de Champlain of his 1609 voyage, published in Francis Parkman's *Historic Handbook of the Northern Tour: Lakes George and Champlain; Niagara; Montreal; Quebec* (1885).

Champlain was determined to establish a permanent French presence in America—to make Quebec a settled self-sustaining colony rather than a mere trading post. In 1617, he drafted a plea to the French government for financial help and asked that both settlers (400 families) and soldiers (300 troops) be sent to the colony. The benefits to France, Champlain maintained, would be numerous: the area was rich in fish, fur, minerals and wood; Canada was the likely location of the northwest passage, which, if controlled by the French, would give them a tremendous advantage in the Far Eastern trade and allow them to charge duties to the ships of other nations that wished to use the route; and finally, that if France did not move to establish its control then other nations surely would, and thereby exclude the French from all the benefits he had enumerated. The government in France did nothing. The church, however, took its first steps towards establishing its presence in Canada. In 1615, four Recollet (Franciscan) friars arrived at Quebec. They accomplished little. Ten years later the first five Jesuits arrived, followed the next year by three more. If the home government was unwilling or unable (King Louis XIII was preoccupied at the time with asserting his prerogative against a disobedient nobility, as well as the continuing disorders caused by Protestant-Catholic conflict) to help sustain the colony, at least the church had begun to show some interest in American affairs.

Already Champlain had taken steps on his own to ensure French control in Canada. The Indians were the key to success since they controlled the fur trade at its source in the

**Figure 4.5.** Portrait of Armand-Jean du Plessis, cardinal de Richelieu, painted by Philippe de Champaigne (*c.* 1640), in André Vachon, *Victorin Chabot et André Desrosiers, Rêves d'empire. Le Canada avant 1700.* Ministère des Approvisionnements et Services Canada.

**Figure 4.6.** Portrait of St. Jean de Brebœuf, published in R. G. Thwaites (ed.), *The Jesuit Relations* (1897).

woods and, by virtue of their sheer numbers, might at any moment they desired oust the Europeans by force. Champlain, therefore, dispatched some young men to live with the natives, to learn their languages and their customs, to explore their territories and to cement their growing ties to the French, specifically to the Frenchmen at Quebec rather than to Champlain's competitors based elsewhere in Canada. Most notable among these was Étienne Brûlé who set out in the winter of 1611–12 to live with the Algonkians. He adapted so rapidly and so well to their ways that soon he had become more Indian than Frenchman. He was the prototype *courier de bois* (roamer of the woods), the fur trapper who resembled the Indian in mores, clothing and way of life; and whose life in the woods served as a counter example to those Frenchmen who attempted to settle well-ordered, "civilized" communities in America. Brûlé came to a bad end—after he had robbed an Indian grave, the Hurons captured, killed and then ate him in 1632.

In 1623, Cardinal Richelieu became Louis XIII's first minister and, seeking to expand French influence overseas, he focused most of his energies on Canada. As did most Catholics in France, Richelieu both resented and wished to eliminate Huguenot influence (if not the Huguenots themselves), from society. But short of full-scale civil war such a goal could not be realized (even the queen mother had been content to slaughter only the Protestant leaders on St. Bartholomew's Day). In New France, however, where the Protestant population was small enough to be handled without excessive trouble, such ideals could be considered feasible. Indeed, one of the advantages of ruling Canada was that no group, Catholic or Protestant, was so deeply entrenched in a position of power that it could successfully withstand assaults from the French government. Canada was simply too "new" to display such vested interest groups. Richelieu therefore, in 1627, chartered the Company of the One Hundred Associates to administer and exploit the wilderness. This group, known also as the Company of New France, embraced government officials, merchants, noblemen and churchmen, each of whom invested 3,000 *livres* to create capital for the enterprise. The goals of at least some of the Company's shareholders were, if anything, more idealistic than mercenary. While none of the investors would be dismayed if the venture turned a profit, probably few invested solely in the hope that their shares would make them much wealthier than they already were. Rather, most wanted to foster the development in the New World of an ideal society, the major feature of which would be religious purity under the Church of Rome.

The Company received from the French government a monopoly on all trade in the colony but fishing. It also had title to, and enjoyed the right to grant, all land in Canada. The Company promised that within fifteen years it would transport at least four thousand settlers to the colony, and that all would be loyal Frenchmen and good Catholics. Virtually none of this was accomplished until 1633 when Champlain arrived from France as governor (appointed by both the Company and the king). In three ships he brought soldiers, workers and supplies. Most significant, some of the workers came with their wives and children, a sure sign that, unlike previous Frenchmen who had spent time in Canada, these men intended to stay.

Also significant was the system of granting land employed by the Company in Canada. The Company had promised the government that in return for the chartered privileges it received, it would populate Canada with four thousand settlers. Such a feat, while clearly worthwhile, would be prohibitively expensive. So the Company decided to grant feudal estates (*seigneuries*) to private individuals willing to undertake the effort and costs of peopling their lands. Such men would become, in effect, feudal lords (*seigneurs*) on their properties, with many of the privileges and responsibilities of feudal lords in medieval Europe. Beginning in 1634, this system of securing settlers had produced 70 grants of *seigneuries* by 1663 when the crown took possession of the colony. Thus the Company attempted to create in America what many desired France to be but everyone knew it could never be—an ideal, hierarchical, religiously pure, entirely French society composed of individuals perfectly content to fulfill their carefully defined role in that society and completely loyal to the crown.

According to the Company's charter, its major purpose was the spread of Christianity to the Indians. Indeed, the Company had even stated that any native who, after becoming a good Catholic, desired to go to France and live there would be permitted to do so. For in becoming a member of the church an Indian also became, they said, the equal of a Frenchman born in France. While converted Indians might consider themselves full subjects of the king of France and, therefore, entitled (in theory) to assimilate completely with the whites, the Jesuits in the colony insisted that the only way the natives could become good Catholics was to separate them completely from the whites. The example set by the *couriers de bois* distressed the Jesuits (and most officials) greatly. French leaders, as had their counterparts in other European colonizing nations, declared that among their main concerns in undertaking settlement in America was to bring civilization and Christianity to the heathens. What hope was there for the Indians, and thus for the leaders' inspirational motivating ideals if the end result of their efforts was not civilization of the savages but rather barbarization of Europeans?

Thus, when the Jesuits decided to effect a massive conversion to Christianity among the Hurons in their own territory, they began by closing the area to the *couriers de bois*. The Hurons were a settled people who farmed, fished and traded. They numbered about 20,000, scattered across 25 villages. Perhaps the main reason they aroused such attention by the French was their crucial economic function in Canada—they served as middlemen in the fur trade between the French and the Northern Algonkians.

Father Paul Le Jeune (1591–1664) came to Canada in 1632 as the superior of the Jesuit missions. Two years later he described the program he envisioned for converting the Indians. His narrative contains remarkably candid descriptions of both the challenges and the opportunities the missionaries would face.

On the means of converting the savages.

*The great show of power made at first by the Portuguese in the East and West Indies inspired profound admiration in the minds of the Indians, so that these people embraced, without an contradiction, the belief of those whom they admired Now the following is, it seems to me, the way in which to acquire an ascendancy over our Savages.*

*First, to check the progress of those who overthrow Religion, and to make ourselves feared by the Iroquois, who have killed some of our men, as every one knows, and who recently massacred two hundred Hurons, and took more than a hundred prisoners. This is, in my opinion, the only door through which we can escape the contempt into which the negligence of those who have heretofore held the trade of this country has thrown us, through their avarice.*

*The second means of commending ourselves to the Savages, to induce them to receive our holy faith, would be to send a number of capable men to clear and cultivate the land, who, joining themselves with others who know the language, would work for the Savages, on condition that they would settle down, and themselves put their hands to the work, living in houses that would be built for their use; by this means becoming located, and seeing this miracle of charity in their behalf, they could be more easily instructed and won. While conversing this Winter with my Savages, I communicated to them this plan, assuring them that when I knew their language perfectly, I would help them cultivate the land if I could have some men, and if they wished to stop roving,—representing to them the wretchedness of their present way of living, and influencing them very perceptibly, for the time being The Sorcerer, having heard me, turned toward his people and said, "See how boldly this black robe lies in our presence." I asked him why he thought I was lying. "Because," said he, "we never see in this world men so good as thou sayest, who would take the trouble to help us without hope of reward, and to employ so many men to aid us without taking anything from us; if thou shouldst do that," he added, "thou wouldst secure the greater part of the Savages, and they would all believe in thy words."*

*I may be mistaken; but, if I can draw any conclusion from the things I see, it seems to me that not much ought to be hoped for from the Savages as long as they are wanderers; you will instruct them today, tomorrow hunger snatches your hearers away, forcing them to go and seek their food in the rivers and woods. Last year I stammered out the Catechism to a goodly number of children; as soon as the ships departed, my birds flew away, some in one direction and some in another. This year, I hoped to see them again, as I speak a little better; but, as they have settled on the other side of the great river St. Lawrence, my hopes have been frustrated. To try to follow them, as many Religious would be needed as there are cabins, and still we would not attain our object; for they are so occupied in seeking livelihood in these woods, that they have not time, so to speak, to save themselves. Besides, I do not believe that, out of a hundred Religious, there would be ten who could endure the hardships to be in following them. I tried to live among them last Autumn; I was not there a week before I was attacked by a violent fever, which caused me to return to our little house to recover my health. Being cured, I tried to follow them during the Winter, and I was very ill the greater part of the time. These reasons, and many others that I might give, were I not afraid of being tedious, make me think that we shall work a great deal and advance very little, if we do not make these Barbarians stationary. As for persuading them to till the soil of their own accord, without being helped, I very much doubt whether we shall be able to attain this for a long time, for they know nothing whatever about it. Besides, where will they store their harvests? As their cabins are made of bark, the first frost will spoil all the roots and pumpkins that they will have gathered. If they plant peas and Indian corn, they have no place in their huts to store them. But who will feed them while they are beginning to clear the land? For they live only from one day to another, having ordinarily no provisions to sustain them during the time that they must be clearing. Finally, when they had killed themselves with hard work, they could not get from the land half their living, until it was cleared and they understood how to make the best use of it.*

*Now, with the assistance of a few good, industrious men, it would be easy to locate a few families, especially as some of them have already spoken to me about it, thus of themselves becoming accustomed, little by little, to extract something from the earth.*

*I know well there are persons of good judgment who believe that, although the Savages are nomadic, the good seed of the Gospel will not fail to take root and bring forth fruit in their souls, although more slowly, as they can only be instructed at intervals. They imagine also that, if a few families come over here, as they are already beginning to do, the Savages will follow the example of our French and will settle down to cultivate the land. I myself was impressed with these ideas, when we first came over .here; but the intercourse which I have had with these people, and the difficulty that men accustomed to a life of idleness have in embracing one of hard work, such as cultivating the soil, cause me to believe now that if they are not helped they will lose heart, especially the Savages at Tadoussac. As to those of the three rivers, where our French People are going to plant a new colony this year, they have promised that they will settle down there and plant Indian corn; this seems to me not altogether assured, but probable, inasmuch as their predecessors once had a good village in that place, which they abandoned on account of the invasions of their enemies, the Hiroquois.*

*The Captain of that region told me that the land there was quite good, and they liked it very much. If they become sedentary, as they are now minded to do, we foresee there a harvest more abundant in the blessings of Heaven than in the fruits of the earth.*

*The third means of making ourselves welcome to these people, would be to erect here a seminary for little boys, and in time one for girls, under the direction of some brave mistress, whom zeal for the glory of God, and a desire for the salvation of these people, will bring over here, with a few Companions animated by the same courage. May it please his divine Majesty to inspire some to so noble an enterprise, and to divest them of any fear that the weakness of their sex might induce in them at the thought of crossing so many seas and of living among Barbarians.*

*In the last voyage there came some women who were pregnant, and they easily surmounted these difficulties, as others had done before them. There is also some pleasure in taming the souls of the Savages, and preparing them to receive the seed of Christianity. And then experience makes us feel certain that God, who shows his goodness and power to all, has, nevertheless, for those who expose themselves freely and suffer willingly in his service, favors seasoned with so much sweetness, and succors them in the midst of their dangers with so prompt and paternal assistance, that often they do not feel their trials, but their pain is turned to pleasure and their perils to a peculiar consolation. But I would like to keep here, where we are, the children of the Hurons. Father Brebœuf leads us to hope that we shall have some, if he goes with our Fathers into those well-peopled countries, and if there is anything with which to found a seminary. The reason why I would not like to take the children of one locality [and teach them] in that locality itself, but rather in some other place, is because these Barbarians cannot bear to have their children punished, nor even scolded, not being able to refuse anything to a crying child. They carry this to such an extent that upon the slightest pretext they would take them away before they were educated. But if the little Hurons, or the children of more distant tribes, are kept here, a great many advantages will result, for we would not be annoyed and distracted by the fathers while instructing the children; it will also compel these people to show good treatment to the French who are in their country, or at least not to do them any injury. And, lastly, we shall obtain, by the grace of God our Lord, the object for which we came into this distant country; namely, the conversion of these nations.*

R. G. Thwaites (ed. and trans.), *The Jesuit Relations and Allied Documents:*
*Travels and Explorations of the Jesuit Missionaries in New France*
*1610–1791: Quebec, 1633–1634*, 73 vols (Cleveland, OH, 1898), VI: 145–54.

The Hurons probably wanted Christianity less than they wanted French trade goods. But the French made trade relations contingent on Huron acceptance of the Jesuit presence, and the fathers proceeded with great dedication and zeal. The Jesuits began their work by erecting missions in four Huron villages. They studied the natives' language and their customs, and performed many baptisms. But in 1640 disease (possibly smallpox) ravaged the Hurons, some of whom blamed the missionaries for the catastrophe. Even worse, at the end of the decade the Iroquois, traditional enemies of the Hurons and in the process of becoming traditional enemies of the French, launched savage attacks, destroying Huron villages and wrecking the missionaries' plans. Of the eighteen priests active in Huronia in 1647 the Iroquois assaults in 1648–9 allowed three to achieve martyrdom. Among them was Jean de Brebœuf, whose service in Canada was legendary. *The Jesuit Relations*, a 73-volume record of the activities of the order in Canada, includes a vivid description of de Brebœuf's death.

*At Three Rivers,*
*September 21, 1649.*

*A veritable Account of the Martyrdom and Blessed death of Father Jean de Brebœuf and of Father Gabriel L'Alemant, in New France, in the country of the Hurons, by the Iroquois, enemies of the Faith.*

*FATHER Jean de Brebœuf and Father Gabriel L'Alemant had set out from our cabin, to go to a small Village, called St. Ignace, distant from our cabin about a short quarter of a League, to instruct the Savages and the new Christians of that Village. It was on the sixteenth Day of March, in the morning, that we perceived a great fire at the place to which these two good Fathers had gone. This fire made us very uneasy; we did not know whether it were enemies, or if the fire had caught in some of the huts of the village. The Reverend Father Paul Ragueneau, our Superior, immediately Resolved to send someone to learn what might be the cause. But no sooner had we formed the design of going there to see, than we perceived several savages on the road, coming straight toward us. We all thought it was the Iroquois who were coming to attack us; but, having considered them more closely, we perceived that they were Hurons who were fleeing from the fight, and who had escaped from the combat. [T]hese poor savages caused great pity in us. They were all covered with wounds. One had his head fractured; another his arm broken; another had an arrow in his eye; another had his hand cut off by a blow from a hatchet. In fine, the day was passed in receiving into our cabins all these poor wounded people, and in looking with compassion toward the fire, and the place where were those two good Fathers. We saw the fire and the barbarians, but we could not see anything of the two Fathers.*

*This is what these Savages told us of the taking of the Village of St. Ignace, and about Fathers Jean de Brebœuf and Gabriel L'Allemant:*

*"The Iroquois came, to the number of twelve hundred men; took our village, and seized Father Brebœuf and his companion; and set fire to all the huts. They proceeded to vent their rage on those two Fathers; for they took them both and stripped them entirely naked, and fastened each to a post. They tied both of their hands together. They tore the nails from their fingers. They beat them with a shower of blows from cudgels, on the shoulders, the loins, the belly, the legs, and the face,—there being no part of their body which did not endure this torment." The savages told us further, that, although Father de Brebœuf was overwhelmed under the weight of these blows, he did not cease continually to speak of God, and to encourage all the new Christians who were captives like himself to suffer well, that they might die well, in order to go in company with him to Paradise. While the good Father was thus encouraging these good people, a wretched Iron renegade,—who had remained a captive with the Iroquois, and whom Father de Brebœuf had formerly instructed and baptized,—hearing him speak Paradise and Holy Baptism, was irritated, and said to him, "Echon," that is Father de Brebœuf's name in Huron, "thou sayest that Baptism and the sufferings of this life lead straight to Paradise; thou wilt go soon, for I am going to baptize thee, and to make thee suffer well, in order to go the sooner to thy Paradise." The barbarian, having said that, took a kettle full of boiling water, which he poured over his body three different times, in derision of Holy baptism. And, each time that he baptized him in this manner, the barbarian said to him, with bitter sarcasm, "Go to Heaven, for thou art well baptized." After that, they made him suffer several other torments. The 1st was to make hatchets red-hot, and to apply them to the loins and under the armpits. They made a collar of these red-hot hatchets, and put it on the neck of this good Father. This is the fashion in which I have seen the collar made for other prisoners: They make six hatchets red-hot, take a large withe of green wood, pass the 6 hatchets over the large end of the withe, take the two ends together, and then put it over the neck of the sufferer. I have seen no torment which more moved me to compassion than that. For you see a man, bound naked to a post, who, having this collar on his neck, cannot tell what posture to take. For, if he lean forward, those above his shoulders weigh the more on him; if he lean back, those on his stomach make him suffer the same torment; if he keep erect, without leaning to one side or other, the burning ratchets, applied equally on both sides, give him a double torture.*

*After that they put on him a belt of bark, full of pitch and resin, and set fire to it, which roasted his whole body. During all these torments, Father de Brebœuf endured like a rock, insensible to fire and flames, which astonished all the bloodthirsty wretches who tormented him. His zeal was so great that he preached continually to these infidels, to try to convert them. His executioners were enraged against him for constantly speaking to them of God and of their conversion. To prevent him from speaking more, they cut off his tongue, and both his upper and lower lips. After that, they set themselves to strip the flesh from his legs, thighs, and arms, to the very bone; and then put it to roast before his eyes, in order to eat it.*

*While they tormented him in this manner, those wretches derided him, saying: "Thou seest plainly that we treat thee as a friend, since we shall be the cause of thy Eternal happiness; thank us, then, for these good offices which we render thee,—for, the more thou shalt suffer, the more will thy God reward thee."*

*Those butchers, seeing that the good Father began to grow weak, made him sit down on the ground; and, one of them, taking a knife, cut off the skin covering his skull. Another one of those barbarians, seeing that the good Father would soon die, made an opening in the upper part of his chest, and tore out his heart, which he roasted and ate. Others came to drink his blood, still warm, which they drank with both hands,—saying that Father de Brebœuf had been very courageous to endure so much pain as they had given him, and that, by drinking his blood, they would become courageous like him.*

*This is what we learned of the Martyrdom and blessed death of Father Jean de Brebœuf, by several Christian savages worthy of belief, who had been constantly present from the time the good Father was taken until his death. These good Christians were prisoners to the Iroquois, who were taking them into their country to be put to death. But our good God granted them the favor of enabling them to escape by the way; and they came to us to recount all that I have set down in writing.*

*Father de Brebœuf was captured on the sixteenth day of March, in the morning, with Father L'Alemant, in the year 1649. Father de Brebœuf died the same day as his capture, about 4 o'clock in the afternoon. Those barbarians threw the remains of his body into the fire; but the fat which still remained on his body extinguished the fire, and he was not consumed. I do not doubt that all which I have just related is true, and I would seal it with my blood; for I have seen the same treatment given to Iroquois prisoners whom the Huron savages had taken in war, with the exception of the boiling water, which I have not seen poured on any one.*

*I am about to describe to you truly what I saw of the Martyrdom and of the Blessed deaths of Father Jean de Brebœuf and of Father Gabriel L'Alemant On the next morning, when we had assurance of the departure of the enemy, we went to the spot to seek for the remains of their bodies, to the place where their lives had been taken. We found them both but a little apart from each other. They were brought to our cabin, and laid uncovered upon the bark of trees,—where I examined them at leisure for more than two hours, to see if what the savages had told us of their martyrdom and death were true examined first the Body of Father de Brebœuf which was pitiful to see, as well as that of Father L'Alemant. Father de Brebœuf had his legs, thighs, and arms stripped of flesh to the very bone; I saw and touched a large number of great blisters, which he had on several places on his body, from the boiling water which these barbarians had poured over him in mockery of Holy Baptism. I saw and touched the wound from a belt of bark, full of pitch and resin, which roasted his whole body. I saw and touched the marks of burns from the Collar of hatchets placed on his shoulders and stomach. I saw and touched his two lips, which they had cut off because he constantly spoke of God while they made him suffer.*

Christophe Regnaut, "A veritable Account of the Martyrdom
and Blessed death of Father Jean de Brebœuf and of Father Gabriel L'Alemant,
in New France, in the country of the Hurons, by the Iroquois,
enemies of the Faith," in *The Jesuit Relations*, XXXIV: 23–37.

Although the Jesuit fathers had performed massive baptisms in Huron villages under attack, and thus offered eternal salvation to many Indians just prior to their deaths, the ideal Christian Indian society they believed they were creating was not saved.

More successful than the Huronia experiment, at least in achieving permanence, was the community of Montreal. Founded in 1641 by agents of a secret Catholic society in France under a grant from the Company, Montreal was intended to be a place set apart from the rest of Canada where the benefits of civilization (a school, a hospital, a church) would lure the natives who, once there, could be converted to Christianity. Located on an island, far from the mercantile center of the colony at Quebec, Montreal was designed to serve religious and humanitarian functions. But its location, at the junction of the Ottawa and St. Lawrence rivers, dictated that the community would develop in ways its founders did not envision. Within 20 years its residents had come to be as concerned with commerce as the residents of other American towns.

**Figure 4.7.** Claude Lefèbvre, *Colbert en grande tenue de l'ordre du Saint-Esprit* (c. 1666). Palace of Versailles.

**Figure 4.8.** Hyacinth Rigaud, *King Louis XIV of France* (1701). The Louvre, Paris.

Under the Company, New France had become more than a mere string of trading posts. Conversion work among the natives had proceeded. Ways of granting land and of ordering society had been devised. But the major economic activity in New France had not changed. Canada supported its white inhabitants by providing them with furs. Few had decided to leave France for life in the colony. For, in fact, the colony offered very little that might attract settlers. In 1627, when the Company was founded, 107 Europeans lived in New France. In 1641, after Montreal was founded the population stood at about five hundred whites. In 1663, the figure had risen to 2,500. But by then French leaders could see that the colonies of other nations, especially the English to the south, which had started no earlier and were blessed with no greater natural resources, had progressed far more than had Canada. In 1663, Louis XIV decided to take control of the colony himself.

Assisted by his first minister, Jean Baptiste Colbert, Louis XIV remodeled the colony along lines he deemed ideal. Able to exercise power without serious opposition, the king and the minister attempted to make French Canada what France could never be—the ideal absolutist state. Whatever had stood in the way of absolute rule by the king in France was either expelled from Canada or not allowed to enter the colony. Thus no lawyers were permitted to settle in Canada. No printing presses existed there. Unlike in France, here there was no independent hereditary judiciary to hear legal cases. Louis XIV intended to rule in Canada without opposition. The governmental system he and Colbert instituted in Canada reflected that attitude. By 1665 they had established royal government at Quebec, had given the fur trade monopoly to a new group, the Company of the West Indies, and had sent troops, ships and new officials to America. Under Louis XIV, two major administrators exercised power in Canada. Both were his appointees and served at his pleasure (he might dismiss them at any moment). The governor, always a professional soldier, looked after military matters and handled diplomatic tasks. The *intendant* had primary responsibility over the civil administration, the colony's finances and the judicial and police systems. Louis XIV and Colbert wisely assumed that this arrangement might lead to conflict between the two as each sought to consolidate or expand his own power. That was fine with the king, for if governor and *intendant* jealously watched each other then neither would become powerful enough to threaten absolute control by the crown. Local governors, also appointed to office, kept order in and were responsible for, the defense of the three principal areas other than Quebec around which settlement had developed: Acadia, Montreal and Trois Rivieres. Canada also was given a legislative body, the Superior or Sovereign Council. The twelve members who served alongside the governor, *intendant*, attorney general and bishop were all appointed by the king. The council's power was abolished by the crown in 1726, and after that the governor and *intendant* ruled alone.

Thus no institution of government in Canada under Louis and Colbert even remotely resembled a representative assembly. The militia system, organized in 1669, followed a similar pattern. The captains were all appointed by the governor. They were, however, nearly always common men and not *seigneurs*. Organized in the parishes, composed of all males between 16 and 60, the militia not only provided defense against attack, but also enforced the laws, arrested criminals and provided the *intendant* with information on local conditions. Authoritarian company rule had been replaced by even more restrictive royal government, if only because under the king's rule New France was totally subject to the will of one man. The crown did not increase the attractiveness of settling in Canada by its refusal to appoint Canadian-born Canadians to important colonial offices. Like the Spanish crown, the French probably feared that separatist movements might be encouraged, or its absolute control threatened if local men with close ties to the land and the people (and no ties to France or the king) were able to achieve positions of power. Thus, as in Spanish America, a rift developed in Canada between those born in the colonies and those born in the mother country. In 1664, one resident wrote, "good people may live here very comfortably; but not bad people, because they are too closely looked after here; therefore, I do not advise any such to come, because they might be expelled … or compelled to leave, as many have done already."[5] That few came to New France, and that many who did come either fled to the English colonies or took to the freedom of the woods in search of furs (as many as three hundred Canadians did so each year in the seventeenth century), suggests not that there were too few men suited to enjoying life in the colony but rather that there were too few who found the settled life the colony offered very attractive.

It was precisely that problem—the need to increase the number of settlers for Canada—that most distressed French leaders. The *seigneurial* system, designed to populate the countryside, proved ineffective since few Frenchmen seemed anxious to give up living in France to become the bottom layer of the social hierarchy in a feudal society. Many *seigneuries* had only one, or no inhabitants. The leaders did try to make life as tenants on feudal estates as attractive as possible to potential settlers. Some offices in New France were open to commoners—a significant change from the system functioning in France. Taxes were lower than in France. Land was readily available to any who wanted to use it and the feudal dues were virtually insignificant. Prospective "*habitants*" were offered mills to grind their grain, local churches to care for their souls and laws which declared that they could hunt and fish, and graze their livestock on the *seigneurial* common (for a small fee). The abundance of land, game and wood meant that the Canadian *habitant* had more to eat and lived a better life than his counterpart in Europe (he was surely warmer in winter, despite the harsher climate). The crucial need for settlers led the government to employ a wide variety of devices to increase the colony's population. Soldiers who had served in the colony were offered extra pay if they agreed to stay, and the government also promised to send decent women from France to become their wives. Early marriage was encouraged, bachelors were fined and parents who had more than 10 children received bonuses. But in spite of such efforts the population stood at only 10,000 in 1680.

Had the French taken more drastic steps and radically reorganized the political and social system, perhaps more Frenchmen would have migrated to Canada and fewer who did migrate would have continued on to the woods after only a quick glance at settled life on the estates. But the king viewed Canada as his opportunity to create the perfect society. Unfortunately, his vision of social perfection did not conform to less important people's perception of an ideal way of life. Even the colonial nobility—the *seigneurs*—found themselves unable to maintain the way of life the ideal plan prescribed for them. With few tenants to work and pay dues, they had to devise other ways to secure funds than charging fees for the use of mills (in 1688 only half the mills in Canada showed a profit) or for holding court and dispensing justice as feudal lords were supposed to do. Many came to participate in the fur trade, an endeavor considered far below the "station" of a *seigneur* by those who adhered to the master plan for a model society; yet it was one of the only ways that *seigneurs* could make enough money to survive at all, much less become rich. In spite of efforts to diversify the economy, the fur trade continued to be the economic life blood of the colony. Colbert ardently desired to keep the population centered in communities such as Quebec and Montreal, but every year Canada's best men scampered off to the woods in pursuit of the beaver. In spite of fixed prices for furs (set by the government), the trade still offered men the chance to turn a good profit. Indeed, engaging in the fur trade was the only way a man could secure wealth.[6]

Under Count Frontenac, the most forceful governor of the late seventeenth century, French explorers pushed the bounds of their empire in North America ever further from the center of power in Quebec. Robert Cavelier de La Salle reached the mouth of the Mississippi in April 1682, which had been explored by the Jesuit Father Jacques Marquette and the trader Louis Joliet nine years earlier. While such exploits opened a huge region to French traders, and allowed France to lay claim to the heart of the continent, they simultaneously greatly overextended the French leaders' ability to govern their empire and to defend it. Traders far distant from the governor and his power proved difficult to manage effectively; the areas they explored proved impossible to protect against interlopers without sending more settlers and troops than anyone believed possible.

## For Further Reading

Boucher, Philip P., *Les Nouvelles Frances: France in America, 1500–1815, An Imperial Perspective* (Providence, 1989).
Boxer, Charles R., *The Dutch Seaborne Empire: 1600–1800* (New York, 1970).
Dickason, Olive P., *The Myth of the Savage and the Beginnings of French Colonialism in the Americas* (Edmonton, 1997).
Eccles, W. J., *France in America* (New York, 1972).
Exquemelin, A. O., *The Buccaneers of America* (Baltimore, 1969).
Lane, Kris E., *Pillaging the Empire: Piracy in the Americas, 1500–1750* (Armonk, 1998).
Nash, Gary B., *Red, White, and Black: The Peoples of Early America* (Englewood Cliffs, NJ, 1974).
Pagden, Anthony, *Lords of all the World: Ideologies of Empire in Spain, Britain and France, c. 1500–c. 1800* (New Haven, 1995).
Schmidt, Benjamin, *Innocence Abroad: The Dutch Imagination and the New World, 1570–1670* (Cambridge, 2001).

# Notes

1 Samuel de Champlain, "Second Voyage of Sieur. de Champlain to New France, in the Year 1610," in *Voyages of Samuel de Champlain, Vol. II. 1604–1610*, trans. Charles Pomeroy Otis, ed. by Rev. Edmund F. Slafter (Boston, *c.* 1878).

2 Herbert S. Klein, *The Atlantic Slave Trade* (Cambridge, 1999), 210.

3 W. J. Eccles, *France in America* (New York, 1972), 19.

4 Available online at http://www.gutenberg.org/ebooks/6749 (accessed March 12, 2013).

5 Pierre Boucher, *True and Genuine Description of New France Commonly Called Canada* (Paris, 1664) as quoted in Mason Wade, *The French Canadians: 1760–1945* (Toronto, 1955), 23.

6 One of the steps French leaders might have taken to increase the colony's population would have been to open Canada to immigration by Huguenots or non-French settlers. Strict adherence to their vision of New France as an ideal society composed of French Catholics and converted natives kept them from doing so. After 1627 Richelieu and his successors made a concerted effort to eradicate heresy (Protestantism) in New France, and Huguenots in the colony were forced to convert. Some remained in the colony as "secret Protestants." Others departed and took refuge with the English or the Dutch to the south. Whether many Huguenots would have found life in Canada attractive, had the policy been changed, is an open question. However, Huguenots had a long history of persecution in France and some might well have been eager to take advantage of the opportunity to leave France yet maintain their identity as French by settling in Canada.

# Chapter Five

# PROFIT AND PIETY: THE ENGLISH SETTLEMENTS

*And the diminishing of [the Spanish] forces by sea is to be done either by open hostility, or by some deceptive means, as by giving license under letters patent to discover and inhabit some strange place, ... by which means the doing of the contrary shall be imputed to the executor's fault, your Highness's letters patent being a manifest show that it was not your Majesty's pleasure so to have it. After the public notice of which fact, your Majesty is either to avow or to disavow both them and the fact, as league breakers, leaving them to pretend it as done without your knowledge ...*

—Sir Humphrey Gilbert to Queen Elizabeth I (November 6, 1577)

*Oh, that you did see my daily and hourly sighs, groans, and tears, and thumps that I afford mine own breast, and rue and curse the time of my birth, with holy Job. I thought no head had been able to hold so much water as hath and doth daily flow from mine eyes.*

—Richard Freethorne to his parents in England from Virginia (April 3, 1623)

*We shall be as a Citty upon a Hill, the eies of all people are upon us; soe that if wee shall deale falsely with our god in this worke we have undertaken and soe cause him to withdraw his present help from us, wee shall be made a story and a by word through the world, wee shall open the mouthes of enemies to speake evill of the ways of god ...*

—John Winthrop, "A Model of Christian Charity" sermon on board the *Arbella* en route to America (1630)

## The English in North America

Cabot, Frobisher and Hawkins had all sailed in American waters for England. Yet none had taken serious steps toward creating permanent settlements on the North American continent. Perhaps the first Englishman to advocate such activities was Sir Humphrey Gilbert, a gentleman from the West Country near the small ports of Bristol, Dartmouth,

**Figure 5.1.** Sir Humphrey Gilbert (*c.* 1584). Provincial Archives of Newfoundland and Labrador (PANL B16–18), St. John's, Newfoundland.

**Figure 5.2.** Queen Elizabeth I, the *Armada Portrait* by George Gower (1588). Painted to commemorate the victory over the Spanish fleet, the artist places Elizabeth's right hand over the Earth, symbolizing her dominion.

Exeter, Plymouth and Southampton—that part of England where many sailors and explorers made their homes.

Gilbert was an adventurer with many interests (including alchemy) who had participated in English colonization of Ireland (where he displayed his capacity for brutality in suppressing a rebellion of the "wild Irish"), and the author of lengthy tracts. His favorite topic was the expansion of England by sea and the colonization by Englishmen of distant lands that would serve his nation and his monarch by increasing their prestige, power and wealth. International rivalry occupied his thoughts, especially England's religious and political conflict with Spain. In one of his treatises, prepared for Elizabeth in 1577, Gilbert calmly outlined a master plan whereby the Spanish could be deceived into thinking the English were preparing an expedition of discovery and exploration which, in fact, would be used to raid Spanish shipping and settlements in the West Indies. The result, he gleefully predicted, would be the decimation of Spanish sea power, from which England's rivals might never fully recover. That was a consequence he welcomed, and he urged Elizabeth to act without mercy and without concern for the fate even of those of her subjects who might have to be sacrificed in the process. Gilbert titled his essay, "A Discourse How Hir Majestie May Annoy the King of Spayne," and was more than willing to lead the expedition he had proposed.

A discourse how her majesty may annoy the king of Spain.

*I am bold, most excellent Sovereign, to exercise my pen touching matters of state, because I am a simple member of this Commonwealth of England, and do not offer myself therein as an instructor, or a reformer, but as a wellwisher to your Majesty and my country, wherein the meanest or simplest ought not to yield themselves second to the best or wisest. In this respect I hope to be pardoned, if through want of judgment I be mistaken herein. And so to the matter.*

*The safety of principates, monarchies, and commonwealths rests chiefly in making their enemies weak and poor and themselves strong and rich, both of which God has specially wrought for your Majesty's safety, if your Highness does not overlook good opportunities for the same, when they are offered. For your neighbors' misfortunes through civil wars have weakened and impoverished them both by sea and land and have strengthened your Majesty's Realm ...*

*First, your Highness ought undoubtedly to seek the kingdom of heaven, and upon that foundation to believe that there can never be constant and firm league of amity between those princes whose division is planted by the worm of their consciences. Therefore, their leagues and fair words ought to be held but as mermaid's songs or sweet poisons that abuse with outward plausibility, and gay shows. For in truth as in such leagues there is no assurance, so Christian princes ought not for any reason combine themselves in amity with such as are at open and professed war with God himself. For non est consilium contra deum. So that no state or commonwealth can flourish where the first and principal care is not for God's glory and for the advancing of the policies of His spiritual kingdom. This done, your Majesty is to think that it is more than time to pare their nails by the stump, that are most ready pressed to pluck the crown (as it were in spite of God) from your Highness's head, not only by foreign force, but also by stirring up home factions. And therefore the best way is first to purge, or at least to protect your own kingdom from their suspected adherents, I mean not by banishment, or by fire and sword, but by diminishing their abilities by purse, credit and force. Then to foresee by all diligent means that your suspected neighbors may not have opportunity to recover breath whereby to repair their decayed losses; which for your safety is principally to be done by further weakening their navies and preserving and increasing your own.*

*And the diminishing of their forces by sea is to be done either by open hostility, or by some deceptive means, as by giving license under letters patent to discover and inhabit some strange place, with special proviso for the safety of those whom policy requires to have most annoyed, by which means the doing of the contrary shall be imputed to the executor's fault, your Highness's letters patent being a manifest show that it was not your Majesty's pleasure so to have it. After the public notice of which fact, your Majesty is either to avow or to disavow both them and the fact, as league breakers, leaving them to pretend it as done without your knowledge, either in the service of the Prince of Orange or otherwise.*

*This cloak being had for the Kingdom, the way to work the feat is to set forth under such a pretext of discovery certain ships of war to the New Land, which with your good license I will undertake without your Majesty's charge; in which place they shall certainly once in the year meet all the great shipping of France, Spain, and Portugal. There I would capture and bring away with their freights and ladings the best of those ships and burn the worst, and those that I take, carry into Holland or Zealand. Or as a pirate, I would conceal myself and my men for a small time upon your Majesty's coasts, under the friendship of some certain vice-admiral of this realm who may be afterwards committed to prison, as if in displeasure for the same. For the men, six months' provision of bread and four of drink should be laid in some apt place, together with [munitions] to serve for the number of five or six thousand men …*

*The setting forth of shipping for this service will amount to no great matter, and the return shall certainly be with great gain, for the New Land fish is a principal and rich and everywhere saleable merchandise; and by the gain thereof, the shipping, victual, munition, and the transporting of five or six thousand soldiers may be defrayed.*

*It may be said that a few ships cannot possibly distress so many, and that although by this service you take or destroy all the shipping you find of theirs in those places, yet are they but subjects' ships, their own particular navies being nothing lessened thereby, and therefore their forces shall not so much be diminished, as it is supposed. To this I answer:*

*There is no doubt to perform it without danger. For although they may be many in number, and great of weight, yet are they furnished with men and [munitions] like fishers, and when they come upon the coasts, they do always disperse themselves into sundry ports, and do disbark the most of their people into small boats for the taking and drying of their fish, leaving few or none aboard their ships, so that there is as little doubt of the easy taking and carrying them away as of the decaying thereby of those princes' forces by sea. For their own ships are very few, and of small strength in respect of the others, and their subjects' shipping being once destroyed, it is likely that they will never be repaired, partly through the decay of the owners, and partly, through the losses of the trades whereby they maintained the same. For every man that is able to build ships does not dispose his wealth that way, so that their shipping being once spoiled, it is likely that they will never be recovered to the like number and strength. And if they should, it will require a long time to season timber for that purpose, in which time we shall have good opportunity to proceed in our further enterprises. And all the meantime the foresaid princes [of France, Spain and Portugal] shall not only be disappointed of their forces as aforesaid, but also lose great revenues which by traffic they formerly gained, and shall in addition endure great famine for want of such necessary victuals, etc., as they formerly enjoyed by those voyages.*

*It may also be objected that although this may be done in act, yet it is not allowable, being against your Majesty's alliance, for although by the reach of reasons men's eyes may be obscured, yet unto God nothing is hidden, which I answer thus:*

*I hold it as lawful in Christian policy to prevent a mischief in good time as to revenge it too late, especially seeing that God Himself is a party in the common quarrels now afoot, and since His enemy is malicious disposition towards your Highness, and since His Church, although manifestly seen, is by His merciful providence not yet thoroughly felt.*

*Further it may be said that if this should be done by Englishmen under any disguise, yet will that cut us off from all traffic with those that shall be annoyed by such attacks, and thereby utterly undo the state of Trade, decay the maintenance of the shipping of this realm and also greatly diminish your Majesty's customs, to which I reply thus:*

*To prevent these dangers (although your Highness may at first attack the French, Spanish, and Portuguese) there needs none to be touched but the Spaniards and Portuguese or the Spaniards alone by the want of whose traffic there is no necessity of such decay and losses, as partly appeared by the late embargo between your Majesty and them. And the forces of the Spaniards and Portuguese being so much decayed as aforesaid, the French of necessity shall be brought under your Highness' eye. This assures your Majesty, the case being as it is, that it were better a thousand fold thus to gain the start of them, rather than yearly submit ourselves to having all the merchant ships of this realm fall into their hands, whereby they shall be armed at our costs to beat us with rods of our own making, and ourselves thereby deprived both of our own wealth and strength.*

*And touching the continuance of traffic wherewith to increase and maintain our shipping and your Majesty's revenues and also to provide that the prices of southern wares shall not be so enhanced to the detriment of the commonwealth, there may be good means found for the preventing thereof, as hereafter follows:*

*It is true that if we should endure the loss of those [southern] trades and not recover those commodities by some other means, your Majesty might be both hindered in shipping and customs, to the great decay of the commonwealth. But if your Highness will permit me with my associates either overtly or covertly to perform the aforesaid enterprise, then with the gain thereof there may be easily such a competent company transported to the West Indies as may be able not only to dispossess the Spaniards thereof, but also to provide forever your Majesty and realm with those islands, and thereby not only counterbalance but by far surmount with gain the aforesaid supposed losses. Besides the gold and silver mines, there is the profit of the soil and the inward and outward customs from there, by which means your Highness's doubtful friends, or rather apparent enemies, shall not only be made weak and poor, but with that yourself and realm made strong and rich both by sea and by land, as well there as here. And where both is wrought under one, it brings a most happy conclusion. So that if this may be well brought to pass (whereof there is no doubt), then will we have hit the mark we shot at and won the goal of our securities to the immortal fame of your Majesty. For when your enemies shall not have shipping nor means left them whereby to maintain shipping to annoy your Majesty, nor your subjects be any longer forced for want of other trades to submit themselves to the danger of arrest, then of necessity this realm, being an island, shall be discharged from all foreign perils if all the monarchies of the world should join against us, so long as Ireland shall be in safekeeping, the league of Scotland maintained, and further amity concluded with the Prince of Orange and the King of Denmark. By which means also your Majesty shall graft and glue to your crown in effect all the northern and southern sea routes of the world, so that none shall then be able to cross the seas except subject to your Highness's devotion, considering the great increase of shipping that will grow and be maintained by those long voyages extending themselves so many sundry ways. And if I may perceive that your Highness should like this enterprise, then will I most willingly express my simple opinion which way the West Indies may without difficulty be more surprised and defended, without which resolution it were but labor lost. But if your Majesty would like to do it at all, then would I wish your Highness to consider that delay does often prevent the performance of good things, for the wings of man's life are plumed with the feathers of death. And so submitting myself to your Majesty's favorable judgment, I cease to trouble your Highness any further. November 6, 1577.*

*Your Majesty's most faithful servant and subject.*

*H. GYLBERTE*

D. B. Quinn (ed.), *The Voyages and Colonizing Enterprises
of Sir Humphrey Gilbert* (London, 1940), 170–74.

Granted a charter in 1578 to undertake overseas colonization, Gilbert left England to discover new territories but probably (no one is certain) looked only for other ships, which, many think, he plundered as a pirate. In 1583, he set out again to found a colony in the New World. At the head of five ships that carried 260 colonists he sailed off in June and had reached Newfoundland by August. There he encountered the summer residents of the area, the international fishing community, to whom he pompously announced that he was taking possession of the area for Elizabeth, that they must accept the Church of England, and that they must honor the queen. Sailing on, he lost one vessel on a reef and another when the crew decided to quit the expedition. Now Gilbert himself decided to return to England. But his ships ran into a storm on the way. Gilbert disappeared with his ship and was never heard from again.

Among those in whom Gilbert had fostered an interest in American colonization was his younger half-brother, Sir Walter Raleigh. When Gilbert failed to survive his voyage of 1583, Raleigh determined to carry on with the endeavor and in 1584 secured a charter from Elizabeth, who displayed great fondness for him, to plant his own colony in America. Raleigh laid his plans with care. Before sending colonists out, he engaged Philip Amadas and Arthur Barlow to make a preliminary voyage to locate a suitable spot for England's first permanent settlement in America. Having sailed along the coast, they returned with a highly favorable report about the area south of Chesapeake Bay. Indeed, two days before reaching the area, Barlow wrote, the water "smelt so sweet ... as if we had bene in the midst of some delicate garden." The land, he continued, was "so full of grapes ... that I thinke in all the world the like abundance is not to be found." And when he described the natives he and Amadas had met as "most gentle, loving, and faithfull, voide of all guile and treason, and such as live after the manner of the golden age," how could Raleigh be anything but enthusiastic?[1] Raleigh named this paradise (which he had not seen) Virginia, after Elizabeth.

By 1585 a full-scale expedition was ready to sail for Virginia commanded by Ralph Lane and Richard Grenville.

**Figure 5.3.** Sir Walter Raleigh, by the French School (sixteenth century). Kunsthistorisches Museum, Vienna/ Bridgeman Art Library.

**Figure 5.4.** Sir Richard Grenville, by an unknown artist (1571). National Portrait Gallery, London.

One of the members of the party was John White, an artist who enjoyed remarkable success in his work. His drawings of the Indians, wildlife and plants are masterpieces in their own right, and the best visual record we have of how the Indians lived in the area around Roanoke Island where the colony was planted.

But the settlement itself failed. Lane claimed the Indians were generally hostile, and the settlers preferred looking for gold to working in an effort to produce food. The colonists came to believe that the Indians, on whom they depended for survival, were about to desert them, and when Drake happened by on his way home after attacking Spanish St Augustine, the entire community boarded his vessels and departed. Just two

**Figure 5.5.** Dancing Secotan Indians in North Carolina, John White (1585). British Museum, London.

**Figure 5.6.** Village of the Secotan in North Carolina, John White (1585). British Museum, London.

**Figure 5.7.** Warrior of the Secotan Indians in North Carolina, John White (1585). British Museum, London.

weeks later a supply ship Raleigh had sent out to provision the colony arrived and found no one left to supply. Since only four colonists had perished over the winter at Roanoke, the temporary settlement proved that Englishmen could survive in Virginia, even when they did not work very hard. So Raleigh prepared a second expedition in 1587. The 150 settlers included women and children—these colonists, unlike their predecessors at the site (all males), intended to stay. Among them were Ananias Dare and his wife, Elenora, the daughter of John White, the colony's governor. They gave their daughter, the first English child born in America, the name Virginia. Just after the colony was settled, while White was in England seeking support for the infant colony, Philip II sent his Armada against England. White was unable to return to Virginia to see how the colonists fared until 1590, upon which he discovered that the entire community had vanished. Perhaps the Indians rose up and killed them. But no adequate explanation of just what did happen at Roanoke has ever been provided.

These first tentative steps by Englishmen toward establishing a permanent presence in America failed to produce a community that survived. However, such endeavors, as well as the feats of Spanish, French and Portuguese explorers inspired Ralcigh's friend, the scholar Richard Hakluyt, to compile narratives of their voyages, which he published in 1589. He not only called upon the English nation to take part actively in the continuing quest to Europeanize the entire globe; he promoted, advocated and generally popularized such activities, stimulating general interest among Englishmen in imperial adventures.

After peace was made with Spain, other Englishmen would be eager to share in the glories Hakluyt described. Some had already participated in colonization schemes "overseas," in Ireland. Early English preconceptions about how to deal with American Indians may have been based on their prior experiences with the "wild Irish." And the struggle with Spain, especially the splendid victory at sea over the Armada, had left Englishmen with great pride and self-confidence. Ships and men who had defeated a mighty Spanish fleet, investors probably reasoned, should perform very well against any natives who might oppose English attempts to settle colonies in America. Moreover, even after the pacific King James I arranged a peace treaty with the Spanish in 1604, hatred for Spain did not end in England. Many resented the fact that what previously had been legal attacks on the shipping of the enemy were now to be called acts of piracy. One way to use their sea power, to strike an indirect blow at the Spanish and to secure wealth was for Englishmen to colonize the New World—which is precisely what advocates such as Hakluyt had been urging, and what promoters now determined to do.

## Virginia

Two groups of English investors finally acted on such ideas in 1606. Their goal was quite simple—they wanted to sponsor American colonization in order to make money. It was not that there were no Englishmen at the beginning of the seventeenth century who wanted to use America to support ideal communities; rather these Englishmen were mostly merchants, not social planners. They had devised a way in which risky ventures such as financing an American colony could attract sufficient investment capital to work. Rather than one man paying for the entire project (and thereby standing to make or lose a fortune), they suggested that many men invest smaller amounts in a joint stock company (and thereby stand to make or lose less). James I acceded to their requests for authority to undertake American colonization, and granted each group a charter. The Virginia Company of Plymouth was to colonize the northern portion of English America. They set to work at once. But the colony established under their direction in Maine from 1607–1608 collapsed when Englishmen learned how cold a winter in Maine could be. The Virginia Company of London proved more successful than the group based in Plymouth. In December 1606, they sent three ships, the *Susan Constant*, the *Godspeed* and the *Discovery* to America with just over one hundred male settlers. Not until May did they reach the mouth of a river that led inland, which they sailed up until they came to a peninsula where they founded their first settlement. They named the river and the town in honor of their monarch, James.

Both the settlers and the company were optimistic about the future in Virginia. The example of Spanish America played a powerful role in shaping both the expectations and the behavior of those who undertook voyages to the New World after the middle of the sixteenth century—the notion that all of America would prove to be abundant in easily accessible wealth (gold, precious stones, docile Indians who would become willing laborers for European masters) was one of the most durable myths of the entire era of exploration and settlement. That legend surely worked on the minds of the first settlers at Jamestown. Preoccupied by the search for quick riches and not predisposed to perform manual labor (the men had assumed from the outset that, at most, they would have to overawe some Indians and collect some gold—they did not come prepared to work in the fields or to build durable edifices), the settlers were having great difficulty in surviving. Their troubles were compounded when disease made many of those it did not kill too sick to perform much work. (Jamestown was built on an easily defended peninsula which, unfortunately, was full of malaria-carrying mosquitoes.)

Perhaps the major reason Virginia did not seem to offer much promise was that the company failed to give its colony strong leadership. The original method of governing Virginia was through a small council in America, which had no independent power. Instead, it merely acted on behalf of another council at home in England, which in turn received its instructions from King James. Such a situation produced only chaos as no one in Virginia had the authority to decide what to do. A young member of the Virginia council, Captain John Smith, who at age 27 had enough self-esteem to believe he could succeed, seized control of affairs. His self-confidence, derived from military exploits as a mercenary soldier earlier in life, and perhaps bolstered by his release from capture by Virginia's natives during an exploration expedition in 1607 (which he later attributed to rescue by the Indian chief's 11-year-old daughter Pocahontas) proved well placed.[2] He soon had the colonists at work (proclaiming that only those who labored would eat) planting corn, fortifying their settlement and procuring a cargo of cedar wood to send back to England. He explored and mapped the surrounding area, and insisted that the only way to make Virginia a success was to assume an aggressive posture toward the natives, thereby gaining both their assistance and their admiration. His ideas worked. The Indians provided sufficient corn to the settlers to keep them from starving. But Smith pursued his policies with such vigor that reports reached the company describing him as a tyrant and claiming he had been cruel to the natives. The company decided to make changes, but did not reward Smith for saving its enterprise by proving that with adequate leadership Virginians might perform sufficient labor to make the colony a profitable venture. Smith was not named governor. Injured in an accidental gunpowder explosion in 1609, he left for England and never returned to Virginia.

In 1609, the company secured a new charter, which gave a council in England the authority to name a single governor who would control the colony through the exercise of extensive powers. A campaign was started, which aimed at securing new investors who could buy stock in the company, and the capital thus raised allowed the company to provide 9 ships to sail for Virginia with 600 settlers. Those who paid for their passage were given shares in the company, while the rest received their transportation to America in return for their agreement to work for the company for seven years. In 1616, at the end of that period, all who owned company stock would receive land, any profits would be divided and the servants (those whose passage was paid for by the company) would be freed. The plan was ambitious and might have succeeded had not the new governor, Lord De La Warr, been detained in England and his deputy Sir Thomas Gates drowned when one of the ships was lost at sea. The 400 colonists who finally arrived in Virginia safely, therefore, came without a leader who could claim to exercise legitimate authority, and thus merely added to an already disorganized population. Only in 1611, when a new governor, Thomas Dale, arrived and enforced discipline similar to that in the army (a policy followed by his successor, Samuel Argall) did the settlers accomplish the work necessary to ensure their survival, much less to turn a profit for the company.

In fact, the colony had cost the company so much (£50,000), and had returned so little, that many shareholders may have wished that their goal had been the creation of an ideal society rather than mere profit making. For at least then they might have derived some satisfaction from the enterprise. But since their motive had been economic gain, their only hope lay in finding something that could be produced in Virginia and shipped to England at a profit. The soil had failed to yield gold, silver or precious stones. But it might be used for planting, and the company launched experiments in the colony to find what would grow best there and cost most in European markets. The colonists cut cedar and sassafras, they planted grapes, they tried to manufacture silk, they investigated the possibility of producing iron and tar, but all their efforts led to little tangible gain. Then, in 1612, John Rolfe (Pocahontas's future husband) planted tobacco from the West Indies in the soil of Virginia. It thrived in its new environment. Though it was not valued as highly by Europeans as that grown further south, Virginia tobacco would sell to those who believed Spanish claims that was a certain cure for most diseases, as well as to those who cared less about its medicinal values than the pure pleasure they derived from smoking. Virginians had at last discovered a cash crop and they turned to its cultivation eagerly. Economically, the future seemed to promise much.

Unfortunately for those who had invested in the colony, the development of tobacco as a profitable crop coincided with the expiration of the terms of service of those sent to Virginia in 1609. Now that there was something to grow, shareholders had no one to grow it for them. All they did have was the land itself. A profit still might be made, however, if many settlers could be persuaded to go to Virginia, take up land and plant tobacco. Land granted by the company could be taxed by the company. Thus, in 1618, members of the Virginia Company inaugurated a new program for their colony, a program designed specifically to make life there highly attractive to potential immigrants. They chose Sir Edwin Sandys, who never left England, to administer it. The company established a "headright system" for allocating land, under which anyone who paid for the passage to Virginia of any person would receive 50 acres. The more settlers any given person sent (and paid for) the larger his plantation would be. Land granted under the headright system would be taxed at the rate of 1 shilling for every 50 acres. Such taxes were called "quitrents" and were intended to provide the company a steady, if not phenomenally large, income. The company also formally ended the harsh discipline imposed by Dale and Argall, promising that in future Virginians would be subject to the laws of England and entitled to the rights of Englishmen. Moreover, the governor would not only rule along with an appointed council, but now would have to reckon with an assembly of representatives elected by the people to make the laws to which they were subject. Virginia's first 22 burgesses from 11 areas met to draft laws in 1619, and thereby began a trend that set the English colonies apart from those of other European colonial powers. Englishmen who came to America from that moment on expected that they would enjoy the same rights and privileges as Englishmen living in England, including a measure of representative government. The company concluded its new program for Virginia by sending out additional servants, who received their passage and a share of whatever profits their seven years' labor for the company produced, and numerous craftsmen with a variety of skills.

The vision of America Englishmen had prior to actual settlement included an image of Indians who, once subdued or befriended, would provide help to the settlers and might even perform the heavy labor required to make colonies prosper. That is what the Spanish had done with "their" Indians, and there was every reason to hope Virginia's natives were similar to those who lived in Spanish America. Although Lane's reports about Indian attitudes toward Englishmen and the fate of Raleigh's "lost colony" at Roanoke may have caused some to have second thoughts about their notion of

**Figure 5.8.** Indian massacre of 1622, depicted as a woodcut by Matthaeus Merian (1628), based on an engraving by de Bry.

North America's natives, Barlow's account plus the accumulated experience of Spaniards who had relied on Indian labor for nearly a century seemed to give reason to anticipate that similar developments could be expected in Virginia. The reality of life in the new colony, however, quickly dispelled English visions of a life of ease at Jamestown supported by Indian labor for Protestant masters. The native ruler, Chief Powhatan, was not impressed by such a blueprint for the social and economic organization of the colony. The natives he ruled with great efficiency were far too powerful to be coerced into doing what they and their chief did not want to do. The marriage of his youngest daughter, Pocahontas, to colonist John Rolfe did lead to a period of cooperation between the natives and the colonists. But after Powhatan's death, his younger brother Opechancanough assumed leadership. In 1622, the Indians chillingly disproved any notions that all American natives were as easily dominated as the Aztecs, Incas and Caribbean Indians had been. In that year they attacked the English settlers and left 347 corpses as testimony to their attitude and their power.

The reorganization program of 1618 succeeded in attracting settlers—approximately 4,000 came to the colony between 1618 and 1624. Unfortunately, a very large percentage of these immigrants arrived ill prepared and poorly provisioned. Many were hungry, and most simply died in Virginia. In 1625, fewer than 1,300 people composed the colony's official population. One white servant, Richard Freethorne, described the reality of life and death in the colony in a letter to his parents, written in the spring of 1623. "Wee are in great danger," he wrote, "for our Plantation is very weake, by reason of the dearth [of food], and sickness, of our companie, for wee came but twentie … and they are halfe dead just; and wee looke everie hower when two more should goe, … and our Lieutenant is dead, and his father, and his brother, and … of the last yeares 20 [new settlers] … there is but 3 left …" The letter is the most evocative description of life in the colony, and is especially remarkable for having been written by a servant.

Loving and kind father and mother:

*My most humble duty remembered to you, hoping in God of your good health, as I myself am at the making hereof. This is to let you understand that I your child am in a most heavy case by reason of the nature of the country, [which] is such that it causeth much sickness, [such] as the scurvy and the bloody flux and diverse other diseases, which maketh the body very poor and weak. And when we are sick there is nothing to comfort us; for since I came out of the ship I never ate anything but peas, and loblollie (that is, water gruel). As for deer or venison I never saw any since I came into this land. There is indeed some fowl, but we are not allowed to go and get it, but must work hard both early and late for a mess of water gruel and a mouthful of bread and beef. A mouthful of bread for a penny loaf must serve for four men which is most pitiful. [You would be grieved] if you did know as much as I [do], when people cry out day and night—Oh! that they were in England without their limbs—and would not care to lose any limb to be in England again, yea, though they beg from door to door. For we live in fear of the enemy every hour, yet we have had a combat with them on the Sunday before Shrovetide, and we took two alive and made slaves of them. But it was by policy, for we are in great danger; for our plantation is very weak by reason of the death and sickness of our company. For we came but twenty for the merchants, and they are half dead just; and we look every hour when two more should go. Yet there came some four other men yet to live with us, of which there is but one alive; and Our Lieutenant is dead, and [also] his father and his brother. And there was some five or six of the last year's twenty, of which there is but three left, so that we are fain to get other men to plant with us; and yet we are but 32 to fight against 3,000 if they should come. And the nighest help that we have is ten miles of us, and when the rogues overcame this place [the] last [time] they slew 80 persons. How then shall we do, for we lie even in their teeth? They may easily take us, but [for the fact] that God is merciful and can save with few as well as with many, as he showed to Gilead. And like Gilead's soldiers, if they lapped water, we drink water which is but weak. And I have nothing to comfort me, nor there is nothing to be gotten here but sickness and death, except [in the event] that one had money to layout in some things for profit. But I have nothing at all—no, not a shirt to my back but two rags nor no clothes but one poor suit, nor but one pair of shoes, but one pair of stockings, but one cap, [and] but two bands. My cloak is stolen by one of my own fellows, and to his dying hour [he] would not tell me what he did with it; but some of my fellows saw him have butter and beef out of a ship, which my cloak, I doubt [not], paid for. So that I have not a penny, nor a penny worth, to help me to either spice or sugar or strong waters, without the which one cannot live here.*

*For as strong beer in England doth fatten and strengthen them, so water here doth wash and weaken these here [and] only keeps [their] life and soul together. But I am not half [of] a quarter so strong as I was in England, and all is for want of victuals; for I do protest unto you that I have eaten more in [one] day at home than I have allowed me here for a week. You have given more than my day's allowance to a beggar at the door; and if Mr. Jackson had not relieved me, I should be in a poor case. But he like a father and she like a loving mother doth still help me.*

*For when we go up to Jamestown (that is 10 miles of us) there lie all the ships that come to land, and there they must deliver their goods. And when we went up to town [we would go], as it may be, on Monday at noon, and come there by night, [and] then load the next day by noon, and go home in the afternoon, and unload, and then away again in the night, and [we would] be up about midnight. Then if it rained or blowed never so hard, we must lie in the boat on the water and have nothing but a little bread. For when we go into the boat we [would] have a loaf allowed to two men, and it is all [we would get] if we stayed there two days, which is hard; and [we] must lie all that while in the boat. But that Goodman Jackson pitied me and made me a cabin to lie in always when I [would] come up, and he would give me some poor jacks [to take] home with me, which comforted me more than peas or water gruel. Oh, they be very godly folks, and love me very well, and will do anything for me. And he much marvelled that you would send me a servant to the company; he saith I had been better knocked on the head. And indeed so I find it now, to my great grief and misery; and [I] saith that if you love me you will redeem me suddenly, for which I do entreat and beg. And if you cannot get the merchants to redeem me for some little money, then for God's sake get a gathering or entreat some good folks to layout some little sum of money in meal and cheese and butter and beef. Any eating meat will yield great profit. Oil and vinegar is very good; but, father, there is great loss in leaking. But for God's sake send beef and cheese and butter, or the more of one sort and none of another. But if you send cheese, it must be very old cheese; and at the cheesemonger's you may buy very good cheese for twopence farthing or halfpenny, that will be liked very well. But if you send cheese, you must have a care how you pack it in barrels; and you must put cooper's chips between every cheese, or else the heat of the hold will rot them. And look whatsoever you send me—be it never so muchlook, what[ever] I make of it, I will deal truly with you. I will send it over and beg the profit to redeem me; and if I die before it come, I have entreated Goodman Jackson to send you the worth of it, who hath promised he will. If you send, you must direct your letters to Goodman Jackson, at Jamestown, a gunsmith. (You must set down his freight, because there be more of his name there.) Good father, do not forget me, but have mercy and pity my miserable case. I know if you did but see me, you would weep to see me; for I have but one suit. (But [though] it is a strange one, it is very well guarded.) Wherefore, for God's sake, pity me. I pray you to remember my love to all my friends and kindred. I hope all my brothers and sisters are in good health and as for my part I have set down my resolution that certainly will be; that is, that the answer of this letter will be life or death to me. Therefore, good father, send as soon as you can; and if you send me any thing let this be the mark.*

    *ROT    ~~IMT~~    Richard Frethorne*

                      *Martin's Hundred*

*The names of them that be dead of the company [that] came over with us to serve under our Lieutenants:*

| | | | |
|---|---|---|---|
| *John Flower* | *Rich. Smith* | *Jos. Johnson* | *a little Dutchman* |
| *John Thomas* | *John Olive* | *our lieutenant, his* | *one woman* |
| *Thos. Howes* | *Thos. Peirsman* | *father, and brother* | *one maid* |
| *John Butcher* | *William Cerrel* | *Thos. Giblin* | *one child* |
| *John Sanderford* | *George Goulding* | *George Banum* | |

*All these died out of my master's house, since I came; and we came in but at Christmas, and this is the 20th day of March. And the sailors say that there is two-thirds of the 150 dead already. And thus I end, praying to God to send me good success that I may be redeemed out of Egypt. So vale in Christo.*

*Loving father, I pray you to use this man very exceeding kindly, for he hath done much for me, both on my journey and since. I entreat you not to forget me, but by any means redeem me; for this day we hear that there is 26 of [the] Englishmen slain by the Indians. And they have taken a Pinnace of Mr. Pountis, and have gotten pieces, armor, [and] swords, all things fit for war; so that they may now steal upon us and we cannot know them from [the] English till it is too late—[till the time] that they be upon us—and then there is no mercy. Therefore if you love or respect me as your child, release me from this bondage and save my life. Now you may save me, or let me be slain with infidels. Ask this man—he knoweth that all is true and just that I say here. If you do redeem me, the company must send for me to my Mr. Harrod; for so is this Master's name.*

*April, the second day*

*Your loving son,*

*Richard Frethorne*

*Moreover, on the third day of April we heard that after these rogues had gotten the pinnace and had taken all furnitures [such] as pieces, swords, armour, coats of mail, powder, shot and all the things that they had to trade withal, they killed the Captain and cut off his head. And rowing with the tail of the boat foremost, they set up a pole and put the Captain's head upon it, and so rowed home. Then the Devil set them on again, so that they furnished about 200 canoes with above 1,000 Indians, and came, and thought to have taken the ship; but she was too quick for them which thing was very much talked of, for they always feared a ship. But now the rogues grow very bold and can use pieces, some of them, as well or better than an Englishman; for an Indian did shoot with Mr. Charles, my master's kinsman, at a mark of white paper, and he hit it at the first, but Mr. Charles could not hit it. But see the envy of these slaves, for when they could not take the ship, then our men saw them threaten Accomack, that is the next plantation. And now there is no way but starving; for the Governor told us and Sir George that except the Seaflower [should] come in or that we can fall foul of these rogues and get some corn from them, above half the land will surely be starved. For they had no crop last year by reason of these rogues, so that we have no corn but as ships do relieve us, nor we shall hardly have any crop this year; and we are as like to perish first as any plantation. For we have but two hogsheads of meal left to serve us this two months, if the* Seaflower *do stay so long before she come in; and that meal is but three weeks bread for us, at a loaf for four [men] about the bigness of a penny loaf in England—that is but a halfpenny loaf a day for a man. Is it not strange to me, think you? But what will it be when we shall go a month or two and never see a bit of bread, as my master doth say we must do? And he said he is not able to keep us all. Then we shall be turned up to the land and eat barks of trees or molds of the ground; therefore with weeping tears I beg of you to help me. Oh, that you did see my daily and hourly sighs, groans, and tears, and [the] thumps that I afford mine own breast, and [the way I] rue and curse the time of my birth, with holy Job. I thought no head had been able to hold so much water as hath and doth daily flow from mine eyes.*

*But this is certain: I never felt the want of father and mother till now; but now, dear friends, full well I know and rue it, although it were too late before I knew it.*

*I pray you talk with this honest man. He will tell you more than now in my haste I can set down.*

*Your loving son*
*Richard Frethorne*
*Virginia, 3rd April, 1623*

Richard Freethorne, letter to his father and mother, March 20, April 2 and 3, 1623.[3]

Settlers had flocked to Virginia to enjoy the benefits its promoters had advertised. But without food, clothing, shelter and immunity to disease they died off nearly as fast as they came.

Their chances of survival were not improved by the harsh labor inflicted on many of the newcomers. Since tobacco prices were high, servants were exploited mercilessly and a lucrative trade developed in human laborers. In 1624, responding to complaints that Englishmen were being terribly abused in Virginia, King James launched an investigation into the company's activities, took away its charter and decided to rule the colony himself. Here too a pattern was established that would be repeated time and again, although it would be quite some time before anyone would take note of it as such. The English crown, after relying on private initiative and private capital to get an American colony established, subsequently revoked the governmental rights specified in the original charter and seized that authority for itself. But in 1624, Englishmen in Virginia did not feel threatened by royal actions that their descendants would perceive as a king's attempts to engross power and deprive them of their liberties. Such impressions of the crown would make little sense to Americans for many years.

## Slavery in English America

Africans first came to Virginia in 1619 when a Dutch ship arrived in Jamestown in need of provisions and traded its cargo of "twenty and odd" blacks for food and water.

Whether these newcomers were purchased by the company or by private colonists is not known. Neither is their precise status. In English America they could not legally be slaves, since English law made no provision for chattel slavery. Thus, the first black Virginians were defined as servants, whose labor for a specified and limited period belonged to whomever "owned" it, and who, in turn, might sell it or trade it away to another temporary master. Gradually over a period of many years slavery came to be accepted by the English in America as a legal status. While that status did occasionally apply to Indians, it came to be associated almost exclusively with blacks. Our own modern images of slaves seem always to color them black. While few Americans can conjure up in their minds images of Indian slaves, many readily conceive of them as "noble savages," courageous and skillful defenders of their way of life, and pre-modern conservationists—all very positive images. Why did slavery come to be associated in America exclusively with blacks? And why, in American folklore, do Indians seem to fare better—to be more frequently portrayed in a favorable way—than blacks?

Englishmen knew that the Portuguese and Spanish had enslaved Africans. To the Iberians, blacks were Moors and Moors were the hated enemies of Christendom. During the re-conquest of the Iberian peninsula, Muslims commonly sold Christian captives as slaves and Christians did the same to their Muslim prisoners. In the mid-fifteenth century, the pope had sanctioned slavery of Moors and pagans; and a sixteenth-century Brazilian statute authorized the enslavement of Indians captured in a "just war." It was possible, therefore, for Englishmen to assuage moral concerns by assuming that blacks being sold "qualified" for slavery because of their religion or because they had been taken prisoner fairly. The Book of Genesis relates the story of Noah's curse on his son Ham, whose own son Canaan would be "a servant to servants" because Ham had offended him.[4] Africans were considered by many Europeans to be the direct descendants of Ham. When Englishmen attempted to describe Africans, they bolstered, consciously or subconsciously, an unflattering image. *White* connoted cleanliness, goodness and purity. *Black* implied corruptness, dirtiness, evilness or foulness. Reports from the first Europeans to encounter Africans, seamen engaged in exploration, were unanimous in describing the natives as *black*. What struck Europeans about Africans was their blackness, an image that tells us as much about the observers as it does about the observed.

If the European cultural heritage promoted racism against Africans, the fact that blacks arriving in America had, to white eyes, no culture at all worked to reinforce racist images. Commonly, captives from many different tribes were crowded together on the same slave ship. Whites of this era never saw blacks as members of their own African civilizations, some of which were quite advanced. Europeans encountered blacks either when they arrived in America, and thus already in chains, or when they had already been captured and were huddled together in African ports waiting to be shipped to the colonies. In either case, whites saw blacks only as captives lacking in culture, religion or any traits which would have promoted viewing them as something other than debased, fit only to serve. The voyage to America—the Middle Passage—not only stripped Africans of their own culture, heritage and nationality; it also stripped them of their pride. Bound in chains and possibly unable to communicate effectively with their fellow prisoners (the captives on any given slave ship might speak different African languages), they were unable to band together to organize any unified or effective resistance.

Native Americans, on the other hand, met Europeans in radically different circumstances. While many whites despised their "heathen ways" and were appalled by their "barbaric acts," Indians were viewed in their native land and in the context of their own civilizations. Those civilizations did lead many Europeans to comment on their primitive and savage aspects (cannibalism, heathenism, immorality). But Europeans simultaneously found much to admire in Native American cultures. European reports pointed out how honest Indians were, how friendly they acted toward one another, how skillfully they dealt with the challenges of life in a wilderness setting. Unlike Africans, Native Americans were seen as complete humans, as capable of living in freedom and solving life's problems. Europeans who observed all this, and left a record of what they saw (such as the artist John White), portrayed for Europeans aspects of Indian culture which struck them both as positive, as well as negative.

Indeed, some Europeans spoke and wrote about Indian America in almost idyllic terms, describing a race of candid, simple, generous, noble humans who lived in what seemed to be total contentment without private property, material goods or the laws considered essential to survival, much less happiness, in the Old World. Confronting Indian culture, many Europeans were struck by what they perceived as real shortcomings in their own "advanced" cultures—Indians displayed virtues which typified life in a golden past that Europeans had lost. In a sense then, Europeans not only admired, but also envied some aspects of Indian life in the wilderness.

Blacks, on the other hand, meeting Europeans only after they had been taken from their African civilizations, never had the chance to impress them with their own native cultures. The circumstances of these very different first encounters deprived Africans of a major advantage enjoyed by the Indians in countering the creation of racist images in European minds.

Native Americans also were surrounded by members of their own tribes, and by other tribal groups—their sheer numbers led the colonists, at least during the early years of settlement, to seek to establish peaceful relationships with them. Not only did the English know that Indians had the potential strength to annihilate them by force, but they also recognized that the Indians knew more about surviving in America than they did. Europeans depended on Indians to teach them what and where to plant, and what and where to hunt and fish. Africans, imported by force, could never provide such assistance because they knew nothing of America. The English (and the French) also depended on the Indians for animal furs. They thus controlled a major source of wealth for the colonists. Finally, Indians were adept at and seemingly quite willing to fight—qualities the Europeans admired. In purely practical terms, Indians were often too powerful to permit themselves to be enslaved, and even if they became captured and enslaved they knew the wilderness better than the settlers and thus were better equipped to run off successfully at the first opportunity. For all these reasons Indian slavery, though attempted in the English colonies, did not succeed. Some Indians who had been captured in battle were shipped to the West Indies as slaves. There, lacking the knowledge of the land and the support of their larger tribal group, which on the mainland allowed them to counter European efforts to dominate or subjugate, such Indian slaves faced the same diminished ability to resist their oppressors as did African slaves.

There is no doubt that Native Americans were victims of racial prejudice in the colonial era, or that the legacy of negative stereotypes of Indians persists to the present. However, unlike African Americans, Native Americans have historically been portrayed in popular culture as heroic and noble defenders of a culture that has elicited admiration. It is not only books and movies that convey such an image. More than a few entities, most notably college and professional sports teams, have chosen to identify with Native Americans, precisely because in the popular mind the figure or name of the Indian evokes a host of positive associations. Though caricatures and stereotypes are inevitably offensive (and often hurtful) there is no doubt that names such as Blackhawks, Seminoles, Braves, Indians, Utes and even Redskins were chosen because of the positive implications of identifying with Native Americans.[5]

Given the racial prejudice against blacks, and the need for labor once a cash crop had been found, it is not surprising that the European settlers gradually narrowed their labor pool to black slaves. Before 1640 a Maryland statute used the term "slave" for the first time; and in the 1640s in Virginia and Maryland laws made distinctions between English and African servants. Estate inventories consistently valued black more highly than European servants; likely, because they were worth more due to the much longer time period during which it was expected they would work. If blacks were in servitude for life it becomes easier to understand why, when white and black "servants" were charged with committing the same type of crime, the whites were punished by having time added to their terms of service while the blacks were sentenced to corporal punishment. In this era, some blacks were freed after serving a number of years. Once free they took up land and built homes. A few may even have come to own slaves of their own. But the number of such cases diminished over time.

Towards the end of the seventeenth century a number of factors led colonists in Virginia and Maryland to write laws that not only defined but supported black slavery. A huge number of black "servants" had been imported, and the English settlers feared they might prove dangerous if not carefully watched and controlled. By the middle of the seventeenth century the English had discovered what crops would thrive in American soil and return a profit, and knew that these could best be grown on farms worked by many laborers. Some leaders must have feared that if labor needs were met by bringing ever more white indentured servants to the colonies, these workers, once freed from service, might turn into a class of disorderly residents (a dispossessed lower class) whose activities might threaten the peace and stability of society. Slaves, of course, could never become such a threat to ordered society because, unlike indentured servants, they would serve and thereby be controlled as long as they lived. Moreover, in a society where land was plentiful and workers in short supply, white laborers were coming to demand wages so high that, if free men were hired to do basic agricultural tasks, profits to landowners would be cut drastically. Crucially important in the transition from servitude to slavery was the recognition that English settlements had matured.

By the last quarter of the century settlers had achieved a level of existence in America wherein workers no longer were dying off rapidly—landowners could feel fairly secure in investing a good bit of their capital in slaves and assume that those they imported to work would live long enough to make such an expenditure worthwhile. Settlers knew that Africans were able to endure hard work and to survive in harsh conditions. Only in the twentieth century did we come to understand that the gene which predisposes some Africans to sickle cell anemia simultaneously confers a degree of immunity to malaria, which would have made this possible.

These developments did not take place all at once. The process by which slavery came to be seen as a legitimate answer to the labor problem in the English colonies was slow. That is, slavery was not adopted immediately, nor was the institution a given at the outset. Indeed, we do not see slave codes legislated for many years. But by the last quarter of the century it seemed a sound answer to a sufficient number of whites that slavery was legitimized and institutionalized, with its meaning defined in the statute books.

## Puritanism and New England

The Virginia Company's reforms of 1618 had made its colony (taken over by the king after 1624) a very appealing place to Englishmen who were looking for a new home and new opportunities. But England claimed to possess other parts of the continent than Virginia, and there were some Englishmen who were determined to make use of it. The Virginia Company of Plymouth still held rights to the area north of the colony built on Chesapeake Bay, but did not know what to do with it. In 1620, 40 wealthy and powerful Englishmen secured these rights from the company along with a charter to rule the area from the king. Their leader was Sir Ferdinando Gorges, a prominent member of the company who now dreamed of carving out a number of feudal estates in the wilderness, which he and his colleagues might rule without interference. But just when Gorges' Council for New England (as the new group was named in its charter) was getting organized, a small band of radical Protestants aboard a ship called the *Mayflower* was making a landfall at a place near Cape Cod they named Plymouth. This group, the Pilgrims of American lore, were adherents to their own brand of Protestantism, which they called Puritanism.

Among the commonest images of early America is that of the Puritan. Generations of Americans have thought of Puritans as unemotional, unloving, intense, nasty, intolerant, religious fanatics. H. L. Mencken suggested that Puritanism was the lingering fear that "someone, somewhere might be happy." Others have sought to characterize Puritans with claims that they outlawed bear baiting not because it gave pain to the bear but because it gave pleasure to the observers. Such perceptions are so durable they may never be eradicated, but tell us little that is valid about these people.

Puritans were Calvinists and were convinced that when Adam committed the original sin in the Garden of Eden he had corrupted all future humans. Tainted with sin, man was inherently bad and, therefore, deserved eternal damnation. That was only just. But Puritans also believed that God could only be understood in superlatives—He was all powerful, all knowing, all pure, all good, all merciful and all just. If God's absolute justice demanded Him to damn all men, His absolute goodness, kindness and mercy led Him to offer salvation. Not to all humans, to be sure, only to some of Adam's descendants. Since God possessed absolute knowledge, He must have known before creation that Adam would commit sin. He also had known those men and women who would be saved from the fate all deserved. But humans were not capable of comprehending the divinity. They could never know which of them were predestined for either damnation or salvation. Since, as Calvin had shown, a man's deeds on Earth could have no bearing whatsoever on his eternal fate (as that had been decided by an all-knowing God before creation), the best any human could do was strive to live as if he were saved: honestly, decently, obediently, kindly, charitably, religiously. The reason humans ought to try to live such holy lives, Puritans reasoned, was that while no one could be certain who was saved, generally those who were able to lead godly lives did so because God had given them the divine grace necessary for salvation. If a man had received grace (which only God could bestow on those predestined to receive it), he would be able to lead such a pious life.

In some cases, humans actually could identify the moment at which they believed they received grace, which was commonly accompanied by an emotion-filled conversion experience. But because even the saved were still fallible, believers could never be certain that they—even those who appeared to live the most pure lives—were really saved. Indeed, claiming with absolute assurance that one had received grace was perceived to signal just the opposite. Since all Puritans had to maintain doubts about their eternal fate, they strove ever harder to live decent lives. Puritans recognized that simply striving to lead a good life might be a sign of salvation—those who were saved would want to follow God's laws, though as mere men they could never follow them perfectly.

Puritanism did not imply that its adherents forsake the world and its pleasures. God had created everything, including those aspects of life that were enjoyable. Men should enjoy life's pleasures, which God had generously provided but, Puritans cautioned, should not become so deeply involved in them that they lost sight of God and His laws.

They must perform their worldly tasks; indeed, God took satisfaction in seeing men do the jobs He had created for them. If one worked hard and became successful, that might be a sign of God's favor. Men only had to guard against losing sight of the reason for such hard work. Money, honor and power in and of themselves were not goals for which men ought to strive. However, if they resulted as "by-products" of a godly life devoted to fulfilling a certain function in life, they could surely be seen as proof of a life well spent. The Puritans reasoned that God visibly manifested His will in the lives of men, societies and states. He had given humans His master plan for life in the Bible. The more closely they adhered to its strictures the better they would fare in this world.

If obedience to God's laws determined the success, prosperity, health and peace of a community, then it followed that all who lived in that community must obey His rules. Deviation from them would bring down God's wrath and since He was all powerful no one would benefit from a display of divine vengeance. Therefore, in creating new communities Puritans, at the outset, drafted statements of principle and purpose, which specified how all members of the society were to live. Everyone who joined the community was expected formally to signify acceptance of the rules outlined in such a social covenant, and thereby be bound to fulfill its obligations and conform to its rules. If anyone deviated from the strictures for behavior set forth in such compacts or in the Bible, the civil authorities would act to enforce conformity and punish misdeeds. Failure by them to do so would endanger the entire community, for all would certainly suffer if they tolerated flagrant violation of God's laws.

It was precisely such fears that troubled Puritans in England. The name "Puritan" derived from their strident cries for reform both in the Anglican Church and in English society—they wanted, in a word, to purify England. They were certain that the English government permitted far too much sinful behavior by their countrymen, who, like the Puritans, enjoyed life's pleasures, but unlike them carried their enjoyment to excesses. Even more distressing were a number of practices in the established (state-supported) Church of England, which seemed to Puritans to be readily recognizable as legacies from the hated Church of Rome. Puritans specifically pointed out that bishops, kneeling in church, priestly vestments, altars and religious courts had not been sanctioned by the Bible, and made the Church of England different from that of Rome only in name. Ostentation, wealth and ornament had no legitimate religious role, according to Puritan thinking. Yet these seemed to receive much emphasis from the leaders of England's state church, and in their eyes corrupted it.

Some Puritans, Presbyterians, suggested that a general supervisory board should exercise power over individual congregations, which would admit as members anyone who wished to join. More radical Puritans, called Congregationalists, stressed that what was wrong with the Anglican Church was, in large measure, due to the inability of individual congregations to exercise independent power over their own affairs (choose their own officers such as ministers and teachers) or control their own members (expel from Christian fellowship the clearly ungodly).

Congregationalists were divided when they considered possible courses of action for the future. The Non-Separatists argued that even though it did retain corrupt practices, the Church of England was, nevertheless, a true church and, therefore, Puritans should work from within to reform it. The Separatists believed that the established church was so fouled that it could not be cleansed. The only recourse for those who wished to live holy lives and escape the punishment God was sure to inflict if the church continued as it was, Separatists argued, was to leave the Anglican church and perhaps to leave England and settle elsewhere. Non-Separatists responded that in departing England, they would be deserting their fellow reformers in a time when all true Christians (Protestants) should act in unity, in order to be as strong as possible for the struggle against corruption. Such pleas for solidarity failed in some cases because many Separatists had already been persecuted by the government. A growing number came to believe that if they and their ideas were to survive at all, a new home must be found.

America was already seen as an ideal location to transform ideas of an ideal society into reality. But the Spanish who had done so, and the French who were about to initiate social experiments in the freedom of a new world, acted as agents of their home governments. The "ideal" absolutist Catholic societies in New Spain and those which would be built in New France (with feudalism added to the plan) received support from the respective Spanish and French crowns, which ardently desired to achieve in America what they could not accomplish in Europe. Separatist Puritans wanted to use America in exactly that way, but they were a dissenting group—men and women whose plans had to be tried in America because the home government prevented their realization in England.

The group of Puritans, which would be called Pilgrims by later generations, formed the first English American community to follow this pattern. It had originated in Scrooby in 1607. Its members hated not merely the degree of evil tolerated by their government at home but the relics of Roman Catholicism they saw in the established Church of England. Also distressing was the fate of those who agreed with them—two Separatists had been executed for their activities, while others had been sent to rot in prisons. Fearing a similar fate, and uncomfortable living in a region whose residents were not reluctant to display their contempt for such radical troublemakers, they decided in 1608 to seek a new home.

Their first choice was the Netherlands whose government and citizens exhibited a remarkable degree of tolerance for people who held "different" views. Settling in Leyden, the Scrooby Separatists did find that they could practice religion as they saw fit. But the price seemed very high as these English refugees watched unhappily as their children slowly became Dutch and were exposed to a wide spectrum of religious views. English Separatists were not the only religious dissenters who had sought refuge with the Dutch, and many different groups used the freedom Holland offered to espouse their religious ideas. Seeking to hold onto both their religion and their nationality, the group turned to America, where the recent liberal reorganization in Virginia attracted their attention.

In 1620, 102 English emigrants boarded the *Mayflower* and set off for the New World. Among them were about 40 members of the Scrooby group of Separatists (28 of the 69 adult settlers on board were members of the Leyden congregation). They had contracted to work seven years for a group of investors, the Merchant Adventurers, who had agreed to pay their expenses and, when the term of service expired, divide with the group any profits its labor had produced. The majority of the passengers (including Miles Standish, who would become the Pilgrims' military leader) had been recruited by merchants to populate the colony and provide needed skills and labor in the new settlement.

Virginia was a big place, and there was a huge amount of unsettled land available. Perhaps the Pilgrims actually intended to settle well to the north of Jamestown, where they could do as they pleased with as little direct observation from colonial officials as possible. Whether intended or not, the *Mayflower* made its landfall so far to the north of Jamestown that the group found itself in an area beyond the jurisdiction of the Virginia Company. Under no one's immediate control, the Pilgrims explored the area and decided that they would stay. But they needed to organize and, like all Puritans, the Scrooby group knew that everyone had to agree to live as God had told them to live, especially since in this wilderness they would require a great deal of divine help. So on November 21, 41 adult males signed the Mayflower Compact, which bound everyone (adult males were expected to control the behavior of wives and children, so their formal agreement was not deemed necessary) to conform to laws "for the general good."

In the name of God, Amen. We whose names are under-written, the loyal subjects of our dread sovereign Lord, King James, by the grace of God, of Great Britain, France, and Ireland King, Defender of the Faith, etc.

*Having undertaken, for the glory of God, and advancement of the Christian faith, and honor of our King and Country, a voyage to plant the first colony in the northern parts of Virginia, do by these presents solemnly and mutually, in the presence of God, and one of another, covenant and combine our selves together into a civil body politic, for our better ordering and preservation and furtherance of the ends aforesaid; and by virtue hereof to enact, constitute, and frame such just and equal laws, ordinances, acts, constitutions and offices, from time to time, as shall be thought most meet and convenient for the general good of the Colony, unto which we promise all due submission and obedience. In witness whereof we have hereunder subscribed our names at Cape Cod, the eleventh of November [New Style, November 21], in the year of the reign of our sovereign lord, King James, of England, France, and Ireland, the eighteenth, and of Scotland the fifty-fourth. Anno Dom. 1620.*

| | | | |
|---|---|---|---|
| *John Carver* | *James Chilton* | *John Rigdale* | *Richard Clark* |
| *William Bradford* | *John Craxton* | *Edward Fuller* | *Richard Gardiner* |
| *Edward Winslow* | *John Billington* | *John Turner* | *John Allerton* |
| *William Brewster* | *Richard Warren* | *Francis Eaton* | *Thomas English* |
| *Isaac Allerton* | *John Howland* | *Moses Fletcher* | *Edward Doten* |
| *Miles Standish* | *Steven Hopkins* | *Digery Priest* | *Edward Liester* |
| *John Alden* | *Edward Tilly* | *Thomas Williams* | *John Goodman* |
| *Samuel Fuller* | *John Tilly* | *Gilbert Winslow* | *George Soule* |
| *Christopher Martin* | *Francis Cook* | *Edmond Margeson* | |
| *William Mullins* | *Thomas Rogers* | *Peter Brown* | |
| *William White* | *Thomas Tinker* | *Richard Bitteridge* | |

William Bradford, "The Mayflower Compact" (1620).[6]

When John Carver, their first elected governor died, the Pilgrims chose William Bradford to lead them. Except for five years, when others served in the post, Bradford was re-elected annually from 1621 until 1657. Bradford supervised their efforts to overcome the hardships they faced as a consequence of building a community far to the north of Virginia, coming to America with no prior experience in dealing with life in a wilderness (they knew neither how to hunt nor how to fish) and arriving with inadequate supplies (the English merchants failed promptly to send the provisions which had been promised).

More than half the settlers perished during the first winter at Plymouth, but Puritans were not easily discouraged. An assembly composed of the governor, a number of elected assistants and the freemen (adult males who could vote), which met each year as the General Court, governed the community. In 1626, the Pilgrims negotiated an agreement with the Merchant Adventurers that allowed them to purchase the shares of most of the investors. Eight of the leading settlers joined with three of the merchants, who agreed to invest even more money in the colony—the debt was to be paid by profits from the fur trade, over which the company held a monopoly. With the dissolution of the joint stock company the cattle were divided among the settlers and every free adult male received 20 acres of land. By 1629–30, most of the original Leyden group had reached Plymouth. After 1636, the General Court included two representatives, or deputies, elected by the residents of each town in Plymouth colony (Plymouth never secured a royal charter). If nothing else, the Pilgrims had proved that even in the harshest of American environments, determined settlers could survive. They did not find gold, silver or Indian civilizations to plunder, but they seemed content with what, by their standards, were even greater rewards. For they were serving God as He had indicated men and women should, and looking after themselves. By 1640, the colony's population had climbed to nearly a thousand. Bradford's account of the Pilgrims' achievements in his history of the colony is both a testimony to their dedication, courage and abilities, as well as a record of the challenges they faced as they attempted to realize their vision of an ideal society.

From the outset, Plymouth's population had lacked the homogeneity that might have ensured uniform adherence to the standards of behavior the Pilgrim founders desired. Only a minority of the original *Mayflower* passengers, after all, came from the Scrooby/Leyden Puritans who initiated the enterprise. Given that the majority of other settlers (who the Pilgrims referred to as "strangers") were not primarily motivated to immigrate by their desire to establish a society free of the defects that plagued England, it is hardly surprising that Bradford's history includes examples of wickedness. Perhaps the most unusual was a case of bestiality that compelled him to explain how such perfidy could infect a settlement created to follow God's plan for humanity.

*Besids y occation before mentioned in these writings concerning the abuse of those 2. children, they had aboute y same time a case of buggerie fell out amongst them, which occasioned these questions, to which these answers have been made.*

*And after y^e time of y^e writig of these things befell a very sadd accidente of the like foule nature in this govermente, this very year, which I shall now relate. Ther was a youth whose name was Thomas Granger; he was servant to an honest man of Duxbery, being aboute 16. or 17. years of age. (His father & mother lived at the same time at Sityate.) He was this year detected of buggery (and indicted for y^e same) with a mare, a cowe, tow goats, five sheep, 2. calves, and a turkey. Horrible it is to mention, but y^e truth of y^e historie requires it. He was first discovered by one y accidentally saw his lewd practise towards the mare. (I forbear perticulers.) Being upon it examined and comitted, in y^e end he not only confest y^e fact with that beast at that time, but sundrie times before, and at severall times with all y^e rest of y^e forenamed in his indictmente; and this his free-confession was not only in private to y^e magistrats, (though at first he strived to deney it,) but to sundrie, both ministers & others, and afterwards, upon his indictment, to y^e whole court & jury; and confirmed it at his execution. And wheras some of y^e sheep could not so well be knowne by his description of them, others with them were brought before him, and he declared which were they, and which were not. And accordingly he was cast by y^e jury, and condemned, and after executed about y^e 8. of Sept^r, 1642. A very sade spectakle it was; for first the mare, and then y^e cowe, and y^e rest of y^e lesser catle, were kild before his face, according to y^e law, Levit: 20. 15. and then he him selfe was executed. The catle were all cast into a great & large pitte that was digged of purpose for them, and no use made of any part of them.*

*Upon y^e examenation of this person, and also of a former that had made some sodomiticall attempts upon another, it being demanded of them how they came first to y^e knowledge and practice of such wickednes, the one confessed he had long used it in old England; and this youth last spoaken of said he was taught it by an other that had heard of such things from some in England when he was ther, and they kept catle togeather. By which it appears how one wicked person may infecte many; and what care all ought to have what servants they bring into their families.*

*But it may be demanded how came it to pass that so many wicked persons and profane people should so quickly come over into this land, & mixe them selves amongst them? seeing it was religious men y begane y work, and they came for religions sake. I confess this may be marveilled at, at least in time to come, when the reasons therof should not be knowne; and y more because here was so many hardships and wants mett withall. I shall therfore indeavor to give some answer hereunto. And first, according to y̌ in y̌ᵉ gospell, it is ever to be remembred that wher y̌ᵉ Lord begins to sow good seed, ther y̌ᵉ envious man will endeavore to sow tares. 2. Men being to come over into a wildernes, in which much labour & servise was to be done aboute building & planting, &c., such as wanted help in y̌ respecte, when they could not have such as y̌ᵒ would, were glad to take such as they could; and so, many untoward servants, sundry of them proved, that were thus brought over, both men & women kind: who, when their times were expired, became families of them selves, which gave increase hereunto. 3. An other and a maine reason hearof was, that men, finding so many godly disposed persons willing to come into these parts, some begane to make a trade of it, to transeport passengers & their goods, and hired ships for that end; and then, to make up their fraight and advance their profite, cared not who y̌ᵉ persons were, so they had money to pay them. And by this means the cuntrie became pestered with many unworthy persons, who, being come over, crept into one place or other. 4. Againe, the Lords blesing usually following his people, as well in outward as spirituall things, (though afflictions be mixed withall,) doe make many to adhear to y̌ᵉ people of God, as many followed Christ, for y̌ᵉ loaves sake, John 6. 26. and a mixed multitud came into y̌ᵉ willdernes with y̌ᵉ people of God out of Eagipte of old, Exod. 12. 38; so allso ther were sente by their freinds some under hope y̌ they would be made better; others that they might be eased of such burthens, and they kept from shame at home y̌ would necessarily follow their dissolute courses. And thus, by one means or other, in 20 years time, it is a question whether y̌ᵉ greater part be not growne y̌ᵉ worser.*

William Bradford, *Bradford's History of "Plimoth Plantation." From the Original Manuscript. With a Report of the Proceedings Incident to the Return of the Manuscript to Massachusetts* (Boston, 1898), 475–7.[7]

## Massachusetts Bay

The Pilgrims and other Separatists might have been the only Puritans to seek new homes in America had James I ruled forever. Although James I displayed no affection for them, he did nothing sufficiently ominous to drive Non-Separating Puritans away from their home. But James died in 1625 and his son Charles I did not promise to be a king Puritans would love. Married to a Catholic, he favored such ecclesiastics as William Laud, whom he named bishop of London and then archbishop of Canterbury and who wanted little more than he wanted to eradicate Puritanism in England. Laud seemed determined to bring the Church of England back closer to the Church of Rome, beginning with the removal of Puritan ministers from their ecclesiastical posts. Even Non-Separatists could not tolerate these developments, but they had no recourse, not even to Parliament (where Puritans had some strength) since Charles proclaimed in 1629 that, in future, he would rule England without it. If they remained in England, their leaders now knew, the Puritans would be swept away along with all the sinners and disbelievers, when God demonstrated how just He could be.

Now Non-Separatist eyes turned toward America. In the open space of a new world they would build an ideal community, a "city on a hill" where men might live according to God's ordinances.[8] God, in turn, would surely be pleased and the resulting prosperity, happiness, peace and security He would dispense to them would prove to all mankind that the Puritan way was God's way and must someday come to be everyone's way.

In 1628, the New England Company, whose members included Puritans, secured rights to settle in America that had originally been granted to the Dorchester Adventurers, whose attempts to settle a colony north of Boston, at Cape Ann, had failed. The New England Company confirmed these rights by securing from the Council for New England a charter to settle the area north of Plymouth. Finally, in March 1629, the renamed Massachusetts Bay Company, under the control of the Puritans, gained royal sanction for colonization when the king granted them a charter. The king was generous—his charter gave the company's shareholders complete governmental rights over its colony. Significantly, the charter did not specify where the company was to hold the meetings necessary to conduct the business of settling, supplying and governing its territory. The Puritans realized that if the company was moved to America, and if the shareholders moved with it, they would be governed entirely by themselves and shielded by the Atlantic from the watchful eyes of Charles I and his churchmen. Thus they determined to hold future meetings of the Massachusetts Bay Company in Massachusetts.

They needed a leader; in choosing a substantial squire, attorney and magistrate in the Court of Wards and Liveries, John Winthrop of Groton manor, Suffolk county (one of the four counties of East Anglia where Puritanism had taken especially deep root), they displayed excellent judgment. Like most Puritans, Winthrop was deeply concerned about the impending disasters God might at any moment inflict on England. And he considered his faith more important than the material comforts of life at Groton manor. In 1630, he led 1,000 settlers to Massachusetts, and they rapidly spread out into a number of settlements around the bay. Before the "Great Migration" ceased in 1640, perhaps as many as 20,000 others left England for Massachusetts Bay.

Under the charter, Winthrop and the comparatively few company members in the colony could exercise power themselves. But the Puritans knew that God held entire communities responsible for the behavior of every individual. Obedience to God's rules would ensure success; and the best way to guarantee that success was to commit them to communal goals by sharing with them the power to formulate those goals. Thus, in 1631, one hundred male colonists were given the title "freeman," which meant that they could vote on questions considered by the company and participate in decisions about their own government and society. The freemen of the company were, the charter stipulated, to meet four times a year as the General Court, to make laws and judge legal cases. Since such tasks could not be managed easily by such a large group, Winthrop gave the lawmaking tasks over to his council of 18 "assistants," who, like the governor, were selected annually by vote of all freemen.

**Figure 5.9.**  Portrait of Massachusetts Bay Colony governor John Winthrop, by an unknown artist (seventeenth century). American Antiquarian Society.

The freemen demanded in 1634 that they be given a still greater voice in framing the colony's laws, and after that date voters in Massachusetts elected every year a governor, a deputy governor, the 18 assistants and many representatives of local towns or "deputies" to meet together as the General Court and govern the colony. Thus Puritan Massachusetts Bay became the most democratic society in either North or South America. The fact that the freemen elected all the colony's government officials did not threaten Puritan control of the commonwealth. For most of the first freemen had been Puritans, and in future church membership would become a prerequisite required of all new freemen.

Both the king and the wilderness had been very generous to the Puritans. The king had provided a charter which, when read a certain way, had allowed Winthrop and his companions to formulate plans for a community without having to make concessions to anyone. And America had provided them with a place to put that community—a place where the Puritans did not need to make compromises with any pre-existing institutions. In Massachusetts Bay these community builders could start with what one scholar has called a "clean slate."[9] Enjoying both the authority and the opportunity to do as they wished, they proceeded to build an ideal Puritan society. Their government enforced both divine and human laws, required that everyone go to church and barred any potential disturbers of the harmony that had been achieved.

Individual congregations governed themselves and disciplined their own members. They hired (and could discharge) their own ministers, and votes of congregation members determined whether or not an applicant for membership would be accepted. Soon after their arrival in America, Puritans began to require of applicants for church membership not only that they lead decent lives (one of their major complaints about the Church of England had been that it admitted to membership even those whose lives were openly scandalous); they also wanted to be fairly certain they had received grace and thus were saved. Votes of the members also decided who would be censured and, when that step failed to bring about changed behavior, who would be excommunicated. But in Puritan Massachusetts, excommunication carried with it no civil penalties. For the Puritan church laid claim to no secular authority and possessed no power to coerce.

Neither, of course, did the ministers. Puritans were certain that when the church and its churchmen exercised power on behalf of the state, they filled positions in the community which, according to divine instructions, they were not meant to occupy. God had, in the Bible, provided humans with a blueprint for their societies. He had established all offices, all positions in which men might exercise power, and those who filled such positions in society derived their power from Him and must use it for the general good. God had provided a civil administration to enforce laws, restrain the sinful tendencies inherent in all men, and thereby maintain order, peace, harmony and stability in society. For ministers to involve themselves in such tasks was clearly a violation of their prescribed role, which God intended to involve instructing, preaching, praying and persuading. In Puritan Massachusetts Bay, religious services were held in the meetinghouse, where such secular events as town meetings also took place. Marriage involved a civil, not a religious, ceremony. And, of course, clergymen were barred from seeking or holding political office. For while taxes collected by the state paid ministerial salaries, and the civil authorities enforced God's laws on all men, Massachusetts Bay was no theocracy. Participation by the church in the civil administration of any society, in Puritan eyes, smacked of Roman Catholicism.

Massachusetts Bay thus offered immigrants a governmental and religious structure which many found very attractive. The colony also offered prospective settlers land, which was distributed by the General Court to towns, and by towns to individuals. Any group of colonists that desired to establish a town formally petitioned the General Court for a grant of land. It was not only groups recently arrived in the colony that made such petitions. Long-time settlers, feeling crowded or simply wanting to make a fresh start, might seek land. So might segments of the population of old towns which had been torn apart by disagreements. If the Court acceded to the request, the petitioners found themselves the proprietors of a new town and were responsible for distributing the land they had been granted. Puritans displayed a good deal of common sense—they seldom squandered their blessings. Such was the case when they parceled out land. Each adult male commonly received several tracts of land scattered over a wide area within the new town's boundaries—a lot for his house, another for timber and grazing, and one or more for planting. But the proprietors always held a good deal of their original grant of land in reserve. Looking to the future they set aside enough land at the outset to meet the needs of their children, as well as the requirements of any new settlers they might permit to join their community. From the start of settlement in Massachusetts Bay, all freemen (and after 1648 all free adult males) participated and could vote in the town meetings, which governed the colony's many communities.

In 1635, a group of Puritans petitioned the General Court for a grant of land on which they could build a new "plantation" south of Watertown. Their request was granted and the new town of Dedham came into existence. Writing about the town's founding, historian Kenneth A. Lockridge notes, "Since Adam awoke in Paradise there had been no moments in which mankind had been given a clean slate, but the founders of Dedham came as close as men had ever come."[10] Among their first acts was to draft a covenant that all the heads of households signed.

The Covenant

1    *We whose names ar here vnto subscribed, doe. in the feare and Reuerence of our Allmightie God, Mutually: and seuerally pmise amongst our selues and each to other to pffesse and practice one trueth according to that most pfect rule. the foundacion where of is Euerlasting Loue:*

2    *That we shall by all meanes Laboure to keepe off from vs all such. as ar contrarye minded. And receaue onely such vnto vs as be such as maybe pbably of one harte, with vs as that we either knowe or may well and truely be informed to walke in a peaceable conuersation with all meekenes of spirit for the edification of each other in the knowledg and faith of the Lord Jesus: And the mutuall encouragm' vnto all Temporall comforts in all things: seekeing the good of each other out of all which may be deriued true Peace.*

3    *That if at any time difference shall arise betwene pties of our said Towne. that then such ptie and pties shall p'sently Referre all such difference. vnto som one. 2 or 3 others of our said societie to be fully accorded and determined. without any further delaye. if it possibly may bee:*

4    *That euery man that now. or at any time heereafter shall haue Lotts in our said Towne shall paye his share in all such Rates of money. and charges as shall be imposed vpon him Rateably in pportion with other men As allso become freely subiect vnto all such orders and constitutions as shall be necessariely had or made now or at any time heere after from this daye fore warde. as well for Loueing and comfortable societie in our said Towne as allso for the psperous and thriueing Condicion of our said Fellowshipe especially respecting the feare of God in which we desire to begine and continue. what so euer we shall by his Loueing fauoure take in hand.*

5    *And for the better manefestation of our true resolution heere in. euery man so receaued: to subscribe heere vnto his name. there by obligeing both himself and his successors after him for euer. as we haue done.*

*Names subscribed to the Couenant as followeth:*

| | | | |
|---|---|---|---|
| Robert: Feke | Michaell Metcalfe | Michaell: Bacon | Thomas: Fuller |
| Edward: Alleyn | John Morse | Robert Onion | Thomas: Payne |
| Samuell: Morse | John Allin | Samuell Milles | John: Fayerbanke |
| Philemon Dalton | Anthony: Fisher | Edward Colver | Henry Glover |
| John: Dwight | Thomas: Wight | Thomas Bayes | Thomas Hering |
| Lambert: Generye | Eleazer: Lusher | George Bearstowe | John Plimption |
| Richard: Euered | Robert: Hiusdell | John: Bullard | George Fayerbanke |
| Ralph: Shepheard | John Luson | Thomas: Leader | Tymoth Dwight |
| John: Huggin | John: Fisher | Joseph Moyes | Andr: Duein |
| Ralph: Wheelock | Thomas: Fisher | Jeffery Mingeye | Joseph Ellice |
| Thomas Cakebread | Joseph Kingsberye | James: Allin | Ralph Freeman |
| Henry: Philips | John Batchelor | Richard Barber | Joh: Rice |
| Timothie Dalton | Nathaniell | Thomas: Jordan | Danll Ponde |
| Thomas Carter | Coaleburne | Joshua: Fisher | John Hovghton |
| Abraham Shawe | John: Roper | Christopher Smith | Jonathan |
| John Coolidge | Martin Philips | John Thurston | Fayerbank Jur: |
| Nicholas Philips | Henry Smyth | Joseph Clarke | James Vales |
| John: Gaye | John: Fraerye | Thomas: Eames | Thomas Metcalfe |
| John Kingsbery | Thomas Hastings | Peter Woodward | Robert Crossman |
| John Rogers | Francis Chickering | Thwaits | William Avery |
| Francis Austen | Thomas: Alcock | Strickland | John Aldus |
| Ezekiell Holleman | William: Bullard | John: Guild | John: Mason |
| Joseph Shawe | Jonas Humphery | Samuell Bulleyne | Isaac Bullard |
| William: Bearstowe | Edward Kempe | Robert Gowen | Cornelus Fisher |
| John: Haward | John Hunting | Hugh Stacey | John Partridge |
| Thomas: Bartlet | Tymothie Dwight | George: Barber | James Draper |
| Ferdinandoe Adams | Henry: Deengaine | James Jordan | James Thorpe |
| Daniell: Morse | Henry Brocke | Nathaniell | Samuell Fisher |
| Joseph: Morse | James: Hering | Whiteing | Benjamin Bullard |
| John Ellice | Nathan Aldus | Beniamine Smith | Ellice Woode |
| Jonathan | Edward Richards | Richard: Ellice | Thomas Fisher |
| Fayerbanke | Michaell Powell | Austen: Kalem | |
| John: Eaton: | John Elderkine | Robert: Ware | |

*The Early Records of the Town of Dedham, Massachusetts. 1636–1659.*
*A Complete Transcript of Book One of the General Rixords of the Town,*
*Together with the Selectmen's Day Book, Covering a Portion of the*
*Same Period, Being Volume Three of the Printed Records of the Town,*
ed. by Don Gleason Hill (Dedham, MA, 1892).[11]

The Puritans had departed England on what the Reverend Samuel Danforth (1626–1674) described as an "errand into the wilderness."[12] In their view their mission in America had universal significance since it involved the salvation of the entire world. Prepared with God's instructions for organizing and sustaining an ideal community, they were determined to follow those plans so carefully that God must surely prosper them. Winthrop had proclaimed the significance of their communal experiment in a shipboard sermon while en route to America in 1630. He declared:

> We shall be as a Citty upon a Hill, the eies of all people are uppon us; soe that if wee shall deale falsely with our *god* in this worke wee have undertaken and soe cause him to withdraw his present help from us, wee shall be made a story and a by word through the world, wee shall open the mouthes of enemies to speake evill of the wayes of god.[13]

Failure to live as God instructed would not only thus keep others from living as all men should, but would at the same time spell the ruin of their own community. For, Winthrop pointed out, "If our heartes shall turne away soe that wee will not obey, but shall be seduced and worshipp ... [only] our [own] pleasures and proffitts ... we shall surely perishe ..."[14]

Puritans believed God dealt with humans through formal contractual agreements, or covenants, which had been revealed in the Bible. He had entered into a pact with Adam, promising humans salvation in return for obedience to His laws. But Adam had broken this "Covenant of Works" when he sinned, which meant all his descendants deserved eternal damnation. But the all-merciful God had then given man a second chance. In the "Covenant of Grace," God assures Abraham that He will save all who believe in Him, who have faith.[15] The only problem for men was that they were so tainted by original sin that, left to themselves, they could not fulfill their part of the contract. To do so they required saving grace, which God dispensed in ways that defied human comprehension.

Now, in moving to Massachusetts Bay, Winthrop stressed, the group he led had entered its own covenant with the Lord. In delivering them safely to America, God would signify His acceptance of the pact and have met His obligations to them. Now they must comply with their obligations under the compact, and live as God said all humans should. Their reward would be so stunning, as God took pleasure in their work and dispensed His blessings on them, that the entire world would learn the truth of what Puritans had been saying since the middle of the sixteenth century.

Given such a frame of reference for viewing their endeavor, Puritans could not tolerate dissent. Nathaniel Ward, a lawyer who became a minister, and the author of the colony's first code of laws, wrote that anyone who did not wish to live as Puritans lived "shall have free liberty to keep away from us," noting that "God does nowhere in his word tolerate Christian states to give toleration to ... adversaries of His truth, if they have power in their hands to suppress them."[16] But because humans, as they well knew, were flawed creatures, few expected that the colony would never be forced to deal with dissenters. Fortunately for the Puritans, the free land of America, which had permitted them to erect their ideal community in the first place, also allowed them to preserve its peace and its purity. For those who became convinced that they knew of an even better way to live than did the majority, and threatened to disrupt the unanimity that was considered so crucial to success, there was open space available were they could go to live as they wished.

## The Founding of Rhode Island

In 1631, a Separatist named Roger Williams came to Massachusetts Bay. Preaching from the pulpit of the Salem church as minister, Williams proclaimed a number of views that to many listeners endangered the entire Puritan experiment. Williams hated the corrupt Church of England, said so, and openly advised everyone else to reject it. He suggested, again quite openly, that since English agents had not discovered the area, and since the king had never paid the Indians for what was their land until they sold it, the crown had no authority to give anyone a charter to settle there. Even if there were truth in his assertions, the colony's leaders realized, permitting Williams to announce such views publicly might prove suicidal. Were the king to learn that the government he had chartered tolerated such behavior and such ideas, then he might very well revoke the charter which had allowed the Puritans to do largely as they pleased. Equally dangerous were Williams's notions about the proper relationship between the church and the state. He wished to separate them completely, and leave the churches to care for their members themselves. Thus, the civil authorities should not, he stressed, even enforce such laws as those which required residents to attend church or observe the Sabbath. That struck many as a rather distressing prospect—men and women who by nature were imperfect and inclined to sin would be unrestrained from following their worst inclinations. God surely would respond to such a breach of His covenant with the Puritans by inflicting harsh punishments on them, the rest of the world would observe how poorly the Puritans fared and the notion of a city on a hill would retain only negative value. In 1636, the authorities banished Williams and he moved to Rhode Island, where his views continued to develop, but where they threatened no one's master plan for an ideal community. In 1644, he secured a charter from the largely Puritan parliament, which provided Rhode Island with a government similar to that of Massachusetts Bay. But in Rhode Island taxes were not used to pay ministers' salaries and voting was not a privilege exercised exclusively by church members.

Soon after the colony's leaders had managed to restore order by expelling Williams, the harmony they sought was again threatened, this time by a woman. Anne Hutchinson, married to a Lincolnshire merchant, had come to admire a vigorous Puritan minister, John Cotton, whose views would have led him to prison had he not fled to

Massachusetts Bay in 1633. The next year the Hutchinsons followed him to the colony. Anne quickly assumed an important role in Boston. Each week she held meetings in her home where the town's women discussed their ministers' sermons. These discussions became so popular that soon men began to attend—it seemed that everyone wanted to hear what this extremely intelligent woman had to say. Her message ignited one of the most serious controversies of the colony's early years when she began to criticize the local ministers. She asserted that in emphasizing the notion that external behavior could be a sign of salvation, they were leading people away from orthodox Puritan beliefs that stressed the impossibility of identifying with certainty those who had received grace, and toward an attitude that good works might influence God to grant grace. Even worse, she claimed that those who were saved—those who had already received grace—need not obey the laws or conform to the views of the larger community, since they were filled with the Holy Spirit and it should direct their behavior. Only Cotton and her brother-in-law, the reverend John Wheelwright, she claimed, were preaching sound doctrine, an assertion which obviously dismayed the colony's other ministers, especially when many in their own congregations seemed increasingly attentive to what Anne was saying. The colony divided into pro- and anti-Hutchinson groups, and the controversy soon spilled over into politics. Finally, Anne was compelled to appear before the authorities, where she insisted that her opinions were correct because she had experienced a direct revelation from God (to Puritans that was blasphemy). Like Williams, she was banished, and she joined him in Rhode Island before moving on to New York where, in 1643, Indians killed her and 12 others in her family.

## Connecticut

Virginia and Massachusetts failed to lure every Englishman who sought to settle in America. In 1636, Thomas Hooker, a minister at Cambridge, MA, led his congregation into the Connecticut Valley. The Dutch settlers already living there could do nothing to keep the intruders out. Once settled they adopted the Fundamental Orders, which provided for government by an elected governor and magistrates. As in Rhode Island, church membership was not a prerequisite for exercising the franchise. Connecticut received a royal Charter in 1662, which allowed it to annex the small colony of New Haven, which had been founded by other Puritans. No matter how their governments were organized, the various colonies of New England nevertheless shared one common characteristic—all were definitely Puritan colonies. And though separated by different governments, they could cooperate when the need arose. Thus, in 1637, a combined force from several Puritan colonies subdued the dangerous Pequot Indians, who had attacked a number of settlements.

At least in the early years of English colonization, the Puritan influence on all aspects of life in New England was predominant. In the interior the fact that the land, which was essential for making a living, was available most commonly through towns that could decide to admit or exclude new "members" probably helped maintain a degree of homogeneity in the population unthinkable (but envied by many) in the Old World. Since God seemed to be smiling on their endeavors, even non-Puritans, when they settled in New England, seemed content. Generally such people congregated in port towns such as Boston where commerce with the outside world was centered. Puritans recognized that non-Puritan seamen, merchants and tradesmen who came to New England could not be kept out (at least in towns like Boston) if the area were to prosper; and, at least in the first several decades of settlement, the presence of such outsiders did not threaten Puritan control of the societies they had created.

Exercising complete control over their own society, the Puritans had sought to achieve in the freedom of America what they could not accomplish in England. Their major concern now was to make their communities and their churches as "pure" as fallible humans could. But it was precisely this drive for perfection that produced a serious threat to the continued existence of their churches. As early as 1635 some congregations in Massachusetts had demanded that those seeking membership not only lead decent lives, but also demonstrate that they believed they had received saving grace. However, only children of church members could be baptized. This meant that the new strict membership requirements had the potential to reduce, perhaps even to destroy church membership. If the new requirements proved too stringent for those seeking to join the church, the number of new members would decline, perhaps even disappear. Moreover, if second-generation Puritans, who had been baptized because their parents were already church members, themselves failed to experience conversion, then their children could not receive baptism. This would result in an ever-growing percentage of Puritans that were clearly outside the congregation. Striving for perfection had the potential to reduce church membership drastically.

In fact, that is exactly what happened—by the middle of the century everyone noted that in spite of the religious instruction received by all during Thursday and Sunday services, fewer and fewer Puritans were able to qualify for full membership in the churches. The problem was made more severe because immigration of fellow Puritans from England had dwindled. While some believed that declining membership was a sign that religion and piety were waning in the colony, it is more likely that the problem resulted from the incredible success of Puritanism in America. Puritans had become so scrupulous in their religion that they did not dare to claim having had a conversion experience unless they believed it was genuine. Such scrupulosity and adherence to strictures of perfection was so strong—Puritanism was so successful—that men and women were even able to justify depriving their own children of baptism in order to live up to their religious ideals.

But few Puritans were contented to accept the precipitous decline in church membership or allow masses of children to remain unbaptized. So, in 1662, a synod, or meeting, of Puritan ministers resolved that those children of church members who displayed knowledge of God's laws, lived decently, had received baptism and placed themselves under the guidance of the church might achieve "half-way" membership. Thus they would come under the discipline of the church, which meant that they could be censured or excommunicated, and that their children could be baptized. But this Half-Way Covenant failed to receive unanimous approval in the colony. Under the congregational way of organizing religion, each church was independent of other churches. Even strong pleas from most of the colony's ministers urging adoption of the plan failed to persuade every congregation. Rather, in many churches first-generation Puritans who themselves had not been required to claim a conversion experience in order to join, demanded that their own children meet that requirement, even if the cost was that their grandchildren would remain unbaptized.

Yet just as numerous congregations refused to employ the Half-Hay Covenant after 1662, others adopted even more lenient measures. In some churches, the ministers baptized any who were not clearly degenerate and reserved only the sacrament of the Lord's Supper for those who claimed to have received grace. In Northampton, Massachusetts, the minister, Solomon Stoddard, asserting that his duty was to convert sinners more than to nourish faith in those who were already saved, offered even the Lord's Supper to any whose outward behavior was good. Again, it was the independence enjoyed by individual congregations that permitted such innovations. Even though Puritanism prevailed in New England, that did not mean that every Puritan acted or thought alike.

## Problems in Society

New England's Puritans discovered that in time, as their communities matured, the animating social ideals of the founders were threatened—especially the notion that all men share similar social, political and religious views. For example, Puritans believed that all residents of a town owed the community itself a certain amount of labor every year on projects that would benefit everyone, such as repairing roads or holding minor offices. But some proved more interested in their own personal affairs than in investing time and effort in communal labors. They, therefore, hired substitutes to fulfill the tasks that Puritan communal theory dictated every man take his turn in performing for the good of all. Equally disruptive of older social ideals was the loss through death of those patriarchal leaders who had originally established the various towns—men whose courage, piety and devotion to communal ideals had served as an example few dared oppose while such leaders lived. Those who inherited positions of leadership from the founders could not command a similar degree of respect and deference and could not by mere force of presence influence their communities to hold onto communal values.

The major problem faced by Puritans seeking to preserve tight-knit communities focused on a constantly dwindling land supply in any given area. The goal of early town planners in Puritan New England had been to scatter individual people's holdings within the larger boundaries of a town, while keeping residences near the town center where the church was located, so all could keep watch on each other to ensure conformity to God's laws. As population increased in the towns, however, men required ever more land to support growing families. Ironically, it was the availability of open land, which had allowed the first settlers to fulfill their dreams of creating ideal communities, that eventually led to the dissolution of those communities. Since land near the center was parceled out rapidly, later grants had to be located ever further from it. It made sense for any man to try to consolidate all his land holdings so he would not be forced to spend working hours travelling from one plot to another and, if successful, to move his home there so he could live where he worked. Many did this by trading or selling pieces of property, and in numerous towns this process led to the formation of several distinct residential "centers" within the bounds of a single old town. One, of course, was the original town center, where roads led and the church was located. Massachusetts law dictated that every town of 50 or more families provide a teacher and a school for the children, since Puritans insisted that everyone have the ability to read for him- or herself what the Bible said. Schools, like churches, were usually built in the original town center. However, the newer concentrations of homes were scattered on the fringes, some distance from these buildings, and the existing roads seldom provided the necessary connection between them.

Those living on the fringes of the older town resented having to pay taxes to support a church and school they could not easily access. Residents in the old town center, on the other hand, knew that if those on the outskirts, or "outlivers," broke away and formed a new town with its own roads, church and school; their taxes would be raised in proportion to the decline in the population of the old town. Some argued that the desire of "outlivers" to separate from old towns posed a threat to orthodox religion, because fringe areas located far from the watchful eyes of observant people might become centers of nonconformity. That, of course, might lead to the destruction of the colony itself by an angered God. Puritans attempted to reach a compromise whereby "out-sections," now called "precincts," were permitted to build their own schools and churches but still share civil officials with the old town. In most cases, such arrangements did not last. Precincts usually became new towns, in part because residents knew that opportunities for social and economic advancement were greater if they did not have to compete for business or elected offices with those who had already achieved success in the old town.

This process began with the first Puritan community at Plymouth when, as early as 1628–32 several prominent members of the original community moved north to establish farms over eight miles from the town center, in what would become Duxbury. Though greatly troubled by what they saw, leaders such as Bradford were powerless to prevent settlers from seeking to support their growing families or to profit from the demand for agricultural products created by the growth of new settlements by seeking to amass as much land and livestock as possible, even if in doing so they abandoned their original American homes.

In fact, there were opportunities in new towns, and many who could not achieve economic success as farmers, or who could not amass enough land even to try, sold what they did have and opened small stores, travelled among the new towns as peddlers or gravitated toward large communities such as Boston, where they found jobs as laborers or tradesmen. Massachusetts was maturing, which meant that the colony was being transformed from a place where nearly everyone held the same values, to one where some lived by trade, some by farming, some by hard labor—where some owned property and some did not. Different ways of earning a living implied different attitudes about what was good both for individuals and the society as a whole. But this process of change was slow, especially in New England's countryside. In the seventeenth century, anyone who looked at Puritan New England saw a huge wilderness which had become dotted with communities populated by people who worked hard (usually on the land), loved God and tried very hard to love each other.

## Maryland

One of the nice things about English America, from a colonizer's point of view, was its sheer size. There seemed to be plenty of open space available to be used in a variety of ways by men who wanted to see what their visions of life and society looked like in reality. One such man was George Calvert, Lord Baltimore. Active at the court of James I, Calvert found the idea of supervising colonization intriguing. So he joined the Virginia Company, and later secured membership in the Council for New England. Calvert, however, was not content merely to share control over colonization schemes with others—he had formulated his own ideas about how colonies ought to be planted and organized. Unfortunately, the area in which he first chose to implement those ideas was Newfoundland, where in 1620 he had purchased rights to undertake such a venture. It took only one visit in person to the area to convince Calvert that he must find somewhere with a milder climate in which to plant his colony. He turned to the crown and the king proved generous. Although Calvert died in 1632, his son Cecilius received the charter originally intended for his father. It conferred governmental rights over and title to 10 million acres around Chesapeake Bay. In turn, the Calverts called their colony Maryland after Charles I's Catholic wife.

The Calverts too were Catholics, and they were determined to try something novel in America. From the outset Maryland's settlers were to enjoy a large measure of religious freedom. Catholics and Protestants were to live side by side in harmony, at least according to the Calverts' vision. Lest any claim that as Catholics they favored their coreligionists over all others in Maryland, the colony's proprietors forbade Jesuits to own land in 1641, thereby squashing any rumors that the best lands in Maryland were dispensed according to the prospective owner's church affiliation. In 1649, Maryland displayed a Toleration Act on its statute books, which guaranteed freedom of worship to any Christian who believed in the Trinity. By requiring belief in the Trinity the statute may well have marked a diminution of religious freedom, for prior to 1649 there was no religious legislation in the colony whatsoever.

Maryland was intended by the Calverts to be a feudal paradise. They, as proprietors, were entitled to grant land and collect rent on what they granted. The Calverts granted "manors" to about 60 friends who, they hoped, might fulfill many of the obligations implied in the granting of *seigneuries* in Canada. The terms they offered under the headright system were sufficiently generous to attract common settlers at a rapid rate—Protestants as well as Catholics. The charter stipulated that the proprietor had to gain the consent of the "freemen" (free adult males) to all laws he might wish to enact. Thus, as in Virginia and in Massachusetts Bay, a representative assembly evolved in Maryland. And like that of Virginia, the soil in Maryland proved eminently suitable to the cultivation of tobacco. Economically the two colonies were virtually identical.

With the granting of the Maryland charter the English crown had added a third formula for dispensing its American territory to those who would actually carry out the business of building the colonies. Already some Englishmen lived in corporate colonies such as Massachusetts Bay, where a company and its shareholders or members had been given the right to govern. When he assumed control of Virginia in 1624, the English monarch had created a second type, or royal colony in which the king and his ministers appointed the governor and council. Maryland was a proprietary colony and Lord Baltimore was the proprietor. He was to exercise in his colony all the powers and prerogatives as had the medieval bishop of Durham in England, on whose grant of authority the concept was based. He would own and dispense the land, collect the taxes and appoint the governor.

By the middle of the seventeenth century the English had firmly established their presence in America. They had not done so by annihilating the Spanish (though many Englishmen would have preferred it that way). What they had done was to move into areas largely neglected by the Europeans who had gotten to America first. If those places did not seem quite as glamorous and obviously bountiful as did the areas under Spanish domination, the English found other reasons to stay. All enjoyed a degree of freedom from control by an authoritarian and absolutist home government that would have made no sense to the Spanish or French. But as a way of dealing with the immediate problem of peopling a wilderness, the English solution of making life there attractive through economic, political and religious concessions made a great deal of sense. It worked. No matter how efficient, or loyal, a bureaucracy or homogenous a population, no one was able to say that life there seemed so attractive to potential settlers that they flocked, for instance, to Quebec or Montreal. But the English did flock to Jamestown and to Boston. There was never a Canadian equivalent of the Great Migration to Massachusetts Bay between 1630 and 1640, but, had it occurred, French leaders would have been ecstatic.

Perhaps the major reason English America proved so attractive was that the crown did not impose one single formula for colonization on all its colonies. Several very different enterprises received royal charters to engage in the business of filling America with the English. Such diversity was a great boon when seeking settlers—immigrants were presented with a choice when they considered English America—and thereby gave very different people opportunities to find happiness within the empire. Only when English leaders decided to streamline that empire, to impose order on it, to regulate its trade uniformly and to control each colony in the same way did the diversity guaranteed by charters cause difficulties. But in the era of colonization, what English leaders desired was a stake in America with settlements that might send England raw materials, consume manufactured goods, safeguard English interests in the Americas and provide a place for the discontented and dispossessed to settle and still remain loyal to their mother country. By 1650 the English enterprise in America, measured against those goals, was a stunning success.

## For Further Reading

Bailyn, Bernard, *The Barbarous Years: The Peopling of British North America: The Conflict of Civilizations, 1600–1675* (New York, 2012).
Beers Quinn, David, *Set Fair for Roanoke: Voyages and Colonies, 1584–1606* (Chapel Hill, 1985).
Brown, Kathleen, *Good Wives, Nasty Wenches, and Anxious Patriarchs: Gender, Race, and Power in Colonial Virginia* (Chapel Hill, 1996).
Hulton, P., *America, 1585: The Complete Drawings of John White* (Chapel Hill, 1984).
Jordan, Winthrop D., *White Over Black: American Attitudes Toward the Negro Hill, 1550–1812* (Chapel Hill, 1968).
Kelsey, Harry, *Sir Francis Drake: The Queen's Pirate* (New Haven, 1998).
Klein, Herbert S., *The Atlantic Slave Trade* (Cambridge, 1999).
Kupperman, Karen Ordahl, *Indians and English: Facing Off in Early America* (Ithaca, 2000).
_____, *The Jamestown Project* (Cambridge, MA, 2007).
Lockridge, Kenneth A., *A New England Town The First Hundred Years: Dedham, Massachusetts, 1636–1736* (New York, 1970).
Morgan, Edmund S., *The Puritan Dilemma: The Story of John Winthrop* (Boston, 1958).
_____, *Visible Saints: The History of a Puritan Idea* (Ithaca, 1963).
Smallwood, Stephanie, *Saltwater Slavery: A Middle Passage from Africa to American Diaspora* (Cambridge, MA, 2007).
Townsend, Camilla, *Pocahontas and the Powhatan Dilemma* (New York, 2004).

## Notes

1  Arthur Barlowe, *First Voyage to Virginia* (1584). Available online at http://mith.umd.edu/eada/html/display.php?docs=barlowe_voyage.xml&action=show (accessed March 12, 2013). Original source: "The first voyage made to the coast of Virginia by M. Philip Amadas, and M. Arthur Barlow," in *Old South Leaflets*, vol. 4 (Boston, n.d.).

2  Smith was accused by his enemies of misrepresentation and self-aggrandizement. His account of capture and liberation after intervention on his behalf by Chief Powhatan's daughter first appeared in his *True Relation* (1608) and in more detail in his *Generall Historie of Virginia, New England, and the Summer Isles* (1624). From the fuller account it is unclear if Smith actually was about to be executed or if he misunderstood (or misrepresented) a ritual ceremony intended to signify his death as an Englishman and subject of the English king and rebirth as a member of the tribe and subject of the chief. Here are his words:

> At last they brought him [Smith] to Werowocomoco, where was Powhatan their Emperor. Here more then two hundred of those grim courtiers stood wondering at him, as he had been a monster; till Powhatan and his train had put themselves in their greatest braveries. Before a fire upon a seat like a bedstead, he sat covered with a great robe, made of raccoon skins, and all the tails hanging by. On either hand did sit a young wench of 16 or 18 years,

and along on each side the house, two rows of men, and behind them as many women, with all their heads and shoulders painted red; many of their heads bedecked with the white down of birds; but every one with something: and a great chain of white beads about their necks.

At his entrance before the King, all the people gave a great shout. The Queen of Appamatuck was appointed to bring him water to wash his hands, and another brought him a bunch of feathers, instead of a towel to dry them. Having feasted him after their best barbarous manner they could, a long consultation was held, but the conclusion was, two great stones were brought before Powhatan: then as many as could laid hands on him, dragged him to them, and thereon laid his head, and being ready with their clubs, to beat out his brains, Pocahontas the King's dearest daughter, when no entreaty could prevail, got his head in her arms, and laid her own upon his to save him from death: whereat the Emperor was contented he should live to make him hatchets, and her bells, beads, and copper; for they thought him as well of all occupations as themselves.

John Smith, "The Pocahontas Incident—The Later Version of Powhatan's Treatment of Smith. [From the 'General History of Virginia,' etc. (1624), Lib. III.]," in *Colonial Prose and Poetry*, 3 vols, ed. by William P. Trent and Benjamin W. Wells (New York, 1901), I: 23–4. Available online at http://www.bartleby.com/163/101.html (accessed July 1, 2013).

3  Available online at public.gettysburg.edu/.../hist106web/site18/Personal%20Accounts.ht (accessed June 14, 2013).

4  Winthrop D. Jordan, *White Over Black* (Baltimore, 1968), 17.

5  Note what Winthrop D. Jordan writes in his National Book Award-winning book *White Over Black* (1968): "Negroes had to be dealt with as individuals ... rather than as nations. ... Americans came to impute to the braves of the Indian 'nations' an ungovernable individuality ... and at the same time to impart to Negroes all the qualities of an eminently governable sub-nation, in which African tribal distinctions were assumed to be of no consequence and individuality unaspired to. ... The Indian became for Americans a symbol of their American experience; it was no mere luck of the toss that placed the profile of an American Indian rather than an American Negro on the famous old five-cent piece" (90).

6  Available online at http://www.pilgrimhallmuseum.org/ap_mayflower_compact.htm (accessed March 12, 2013).

7  Available online at http://www.gutenberg.org/files/24950/24950-h/24950-h.htm (accessed March 12, 2013).

8  John Winthrop, "A Model of Christian Charity" (1630). See http://en.wikisource.org/wiki/City_upon_a_Hill

9  Kenneth Lockridge, *A New England Town The First Hundred Years: Dedham, Massachusetts, 1636–1736* (New York, 1970), 4.

10  Ibid.

11  Available online at http://archive.org/stream/earlyrecordstow02hillgoog/earlyrecordstow02 hillgoog_djvu.txt (accessed April 3, 2013).

12  Available online at http://en.wikipedia.org/wiki/Samuel_Danforth (accessed Fall 2012).

13  Winthrop, "A Model of Christian Charity."

14  Ibid.

15  See Perry Miller, *Errand into the Wilderness* (New York, 1956), 60–62.

16  Nathaniel Ward, *The Simple Cobbler of Aggawamm in America* (London, 1647). Available online at http://www.swarthmore.edu/SocSci/bdorsey1/41docs/55-war.html, (accessed March 12, 2013).

# Chapter Six

# THE SEA AND THE LAND: OPEN SPACE, ABUNDANCE, FRONTIER

*[T]o the frontier, the American intellect owes its striking characteristics. That coarseness and strength combined with acuteness and inquisitiveness, that practical, inventive turn of mind, quick to find expedients, that masterful grasp of material things, lacking in the artistic but powerful to effect great ends, that restless, nervous energy, that dominant individualism, working for good and for evil, and withal that buoyancy and exuberance which comes with freedom ...*

—Frederick Jackson Turner, "The Significance of the Frontier in American History" (1893)

## 1400–1650

In 1400, the world's major civilizations lived apart from each other. They maintained virtually no continuous contact. Indeed, some very advanced cultures were completely unknown to others. Probably the most isolated were the Amerindian civilizations since oceans separated their continent from Europe, Asia and Africa, whose own cultures at least had knowledge that the others existed. Europeans had a "feeling" that there were aspects of the world they did not, but ought to know. For years Christians in Europe had believed that a mythical king, Prester John ruled a powerful Christian nation in the heart of Africa. One of Prince Henry the Navigator's aims had been to join forces with him and launch a telling assault against the power of Islam. Generations of Europeans had considered the "islands of the Atlantic" shown on some of their maps to mean that great cultures and perhaps spectacular treasures existed somewhere beyond the known world. Christian lore described voyages to the north and west by Irish monks, most notably that of St. Brendan, in the sixth century, which had led to contact with marvelous people (other Christian monks) and strange places. Closer to their own era were the exploits of the Norsemen, whose adventures had been narrated in sagas with which some Northern Europeans may have been familiar. The Vikings had sailed to Iceland in the latter half of the ninth century (where they encountered at least several hundred Irish monks who had lived there ever since the eighth century). They lived in Greenland a century after that, and at the start of the eleventh century, under Leif Ericson, they attempted to settle a colony in Newfoundland (which they called Vinland). In spite of repeated attempts to secure their foothold in North America, the Vikings failed to leave a lasting legacy, largely because the natives they confronted (whom they called "Skrellings") proved too warlike even for the fierce Norsemen. The Crusades conducted by Europeans in the Middle Ages in an attempt to wrest the Holy Land from the control of Islam had meant that massive numbers of Europeans had experience outside Europe. As a result, some learned to organize and control colonial outposts. Europeans held a colony in Palestine after 1090; a Muslim army under Saladin expelled them in 1187. But such precedents produced no permanent results. Of the world's great civilizations in 1400, only the Muslims had steady contacts with cultures other than their own, through their control of trade with the Far East.

By the middle of the seventeenth century the world was quite different. Largely due to European development of technologies borrowed from Arabs, as well as efforts to devise ways of arming their ships with cannon, the oceans that previously separated the world's peoples now united them. At the forefront was Europe. Through the empires they had established Europeans controlled not only a large percentage of the world's trade, but also exercised power over much of the earth's land and dominion over many of its people.

**The Sea**

In 1650, three major European colonizing powers controlled most of America: the English, the French and the Spanish. The Dutch seemed more interested in controlling American trade than American territory. All relied on the seas to deal with their American possessions, but between them there was one striking difference. French and Spanish leaders had imposed authoritarian rule over their colonies in the New World. They enjoyed systems of imperial administration that permitted them to dictate policies for separate parts of those empires as they saw fit, and to deal with their overseas possessions as a whole. While the Spanish empire in America was divided into a number of administrative units (viceroyalties), the crown controlled all of them; and when it formulated an imperial policy it could impose its decision on the entire empire at once. The French crown, similarly, could decide at will what was to happen in any part of Canada, since after 1663 it directly ruled French America—all Canada was a royal domain. For French and Spanish rulers the seas served as an impediment to enforcing imperial policies. The time it took to cross them caused delayed implementation of their mandates. The distance of the American colonies meant that decision makers in Europe had difficulty supervising the enforcement of their policies. In New Spain, *encomenderos* were able to resist royal attempts to abolish *encomienda*, while in New France *couriers de bois* abandoned life in settled areas as farmers in Canada in favour of life in the woods.

For the English, however, although the seas did separate physically the mother country from her colonies in America, control of trade relations by sea was the only way leaders at home could impose uniform policies on all the colonies at once.

The crown, which originally held mastery over all English America, surrendered much of its authority over the land to individual men and groups of men who agreed in return to assume the burdens and expenses of establishing American colonies. Each colony had its own charter, and each charter provided that its holders were to enjoy prerogatives and privileges in America, which might be exercised independently of the crown. Only in royal colonies such as Virginia did the crown have the authority to name the governor, appoint the council and thereby direct its internal affairs. In Maryland, that authority rested with the proprietors, the Calverts. In Massachusetts, Connecticut and Rhode Island, it resided in the "corporation" which held the charter. Uniform policies for all the colonies at once could be established only in the area of their trade relations with England, through laws governing commerce.

Thus for the leaders of England, the seas divided their empire (as they did for the Spanish and French) and at the same time were the only means for imposing uniformity (as they were not for the Spanish and French). English colonists came to accept this situation. Indeed, it was one of the reasons English America became so attractive, for it allowed different individuals and groups to seek happiness in different ways. As historian Edmund S. Morgan writes, for English Americans:

> the great thing about [the British] empire, aside from the sheer pride of belonging to it, was that it let you alone. The average colonist might go through the year, he might even go through a lifetime, without seeing an officer of the empire. His colony had not been founded under imperial direction but by private enterprise operating under what amounted to a license from the King of England.[1]

As long as the English leaders accepted that way of running an empire everyone was reasonably content. Since each English colony had its own distinctive charter and character, there was but one way the colonists might all come to unite and act as one. That could happen only when the one feature they all shared—the identity of their people as English subjects who were entitled to all the rights of Englishmen living in England—somehow led them to sense that they were being oppressed. Then, common subjugation to a sovereign power which they sensed had come to threaten rather than protect traditional liberties would cement common ties that seemed to have had little meaning before.

In 1400, Europeans who observed the "world situation" had little reason to be optimistic about the future. Some still adhered to the medieval belief that the world did consist of only three continents (Africa, Asia and Europe) with Jerusalem at the center, and that the land mass on which men were known to live was bounded on all sides by impassible seas. Inhabitants of China, India and much of the Muslim world were more wealthy, better educated and more "civilized" than they. Christendom was retreating before its Islamic enemies—in 1453, the Turks would seize Constantinople, once the home of Roman Catholicism. In the middle of the fourteenth century, the population of Europe was devastated as the Black Death swept the continent; plagues continued to reduce European strength for another 50 years. In sum, a European perspective in 1400 offered the dismal view of a world in which Europeans were declining in number, wealth and power in relation to other cultures who, to make matters worse, were also their enemies. And the bounds of that world had been firmly set when God created it—there was no place to escape.

By 1650, however, Europeans who viewed the "world situation" had many reasons to be optimistic about the future. They had established their superiority on the seas and had used it to expand dramatically the bounds of their civilization. New sources of wealth had been found and these now served to enrich Europeans. If travel by land to the Far East was still difficult, it ceased to be a matter of urgency. For Europeans dominated the seas and water routes led everywhere Europeans wished to go. Perhaps most significant in all this was the fact that a European's self-image in 1650 had to be in every respect more positive than in 1400. Europeans had proved that they were capable of purposeful action not only in Europe, Africa and Asia, but that they might actually expand the size of their field of activities. Europeans had, in a sense, come to assume a role parallel to that of the creator Himself. By 1650 Europeans saw themselves as masters of much they encountered.

The actual physical rewards Europeans had gained in the process of revising traditional views of humanity's place in the world reinforced tremendously these psychological rewards. Not only had gold, silver, furs, tobacco, sugar, foodstuffs and timber, been secured but Christianity had been given to (or forced upon) countless heathens. If the Europeans were capable of disproving old and powerful traditions, of mastering the earth's physical barriers, were they not capable of accomplishing anything? This self-image, which they began to construct when the first seamen ventured out into the Atlantic, would ultimately lead humans to strive to break the ties which had held them in Europe, Africa and Asia; indeed, by a slow yet continuous route, to break the bonds which held mankind to earth itself.

Such a confident self-view propelled Europeans to attempt major colonial ventures in the New World. In many cases, the enterprises they initiated proved sufficiently successful to reinforce notions of the immense capabilities of humans, as well as assumptions of European superiority among races and cultures.

### The Land: Open Space, Abundance and the Frontier

Though it presented colonizers with a startling diversity in geography, climate, natural resources and native populations America did display two constants throughout the colonial era. No matter where in the New World Europeans went during this period, they always found open space and virtually everywhere they found some kind of abundance. This was an ideal situation for those Europeans wanting to transform their social or political visions into reality. America presented them with places to erect their "ideal" societies, and in many cases, also provided sufficient abundance to allow those societies to survive and to mature. However, the communities thus begun in the New World did not always resemble the image contained in the master plan devised by their creators once they had matured. While the abundance encountered by the Spanish to the south and the Puritans in Massachusetts Bay allowed them to pursue their goals without much modification to their original ideal master plans, the French in Canada and the early planners of Virginian settlements were not so fortunate. Although the wilderness did offer enough that was exploitable to ensure their survival, what the early settlers found in these places were resources that, if they were to be exploited, required the modification of the original goals, or even for them to be discarded. French leaders found it impossible to create a viable feudal society in Canada because the abundant resources available to them came in the form of furs. Successful exploitation of that resource required men to trap beaver in the woods rather than become common laborers on feudal estates. In Virginia, Englishmen discovered that the soil would provide them with a profitable crop, tobacco, but growing tobacco was an endeavor quite different from subduing natives who would provide the labor needed to mine precious metals or grow crops. In the case of New France, leaders failed to sufficiently alter their plans to make a society based on trapping a great success. Canada's population consistently lagged behind that of the English colonies as relatively few Frenchmen chose to become French Canadians. In the case of Virginia, the leaders and the settlers did manage to change both their aspirations for and organization of their settlement, conforming to the requirements imposed upon them by the specific type of exploitable natural resources they found there.

Based on what actually happened to early European settlers in America, it is possible to argue seemingly contradictory hypotheses about the meaning of America for European community builders. One can claim that the New World was pure opportunity, a place where colonizers were able to create anything they wished, and where what they created could develop without interference. With equal attention to empirical evidence, a student of this period can stress that the frontier wilderness of the New World forced Europeans to modify original plans in order to survive. Evidence exists to support either point of view, and what one concludes depends largely on which part of the New World is being examined.

As discussed in this book's Introduction, historians of the United States have been particularly interested in the way the frontier experience influenced the evolution of the nation's values and its institutions. Frederick Jackson Turner's ideas about the significance of the frontier in shaping the American national character had a powerful impact not only on his audience in Chicago, but also on generations of future historians.[2] His argument struck a responsive chord in a nation that was already well on its way to becoming a world power. It is remarkable the degree to which Americans' sense of their own ideal selves includes aspects of the frontiersman, and how certain characteristics associated with that image continue to exercise a powerful hold.

In almost any field of endeavor, those Americans who most frequently appear on lists of iconic heroes seem to embody traits that we associate with the frontier.

Our image of John D. Rockefeller, Andrew Carnegie, Thomas Edison and Henry Ford, to cite just a few, hardly differs from that of the fictional characters portrayed by Gary Cooper, Jimmy Stewart, Humphrey Bogart, John Wayne or Clint Eastwood. All were self-reliant, independent, practical, impatient. They were doers rather than thinkers. They were active rather than passive. In the American imagination, the traits that define the real-life captains of business and industry are strikingly similar to those that define the characters these legendary actors portray in films that have shaped the American sense of what a hero should be. Indeed, if there is a single film genre that is definitively American, surely it is the Western—whether produced in Hollywood or Italy or Spain.

## Afterword

By the middle of the seventeenth century the American continent was effectively Europe's. Taking a continental perspective, it is clear that Europeans had been remarkably successful in Europeanizing America. Their success meant that in future Americans would tend to assume that any non-European culture was inferior to their own. When, three centuries later, white Americans struggled to admire, much less to comprehend, "Third World" cultures, they would be exhibiting traits that originated in their ancestors' first encounters with Amerindians and Africans unable to prevent Europeans from dominating them. To sense how completely pre-conquest America was altered by its new masters one need only consider that foreign rule in America was ended by Europeans rebelling against their mother countries, and not by natives rebelling against European conquerors. The era of discovery, exploration and colonization was, therefore, crucially important in shaping certain values and attitudes which, in turn, have become part of the intellectual heritage not only of Americans, but of all westerners.

Finally, one can say that by 1650, after two centuries of adventure, certain of the most powerful stimulants to taking on voyages of discovery, exploration and colonization had lost their influence on Europeans. For by 1650 the actual shape of America was fairly well known, and a good part of it had actually been visited by Europeans. Many of the myths about the continent had lost their attractive power. Few still were spurred on by hopes of finding seven golden cities, or a fountain of youth, or a mountain of diamonds. It was not that Europeans had seen every acre of the great continent, only that what they had seen did not give them cause to maintain hopes of finding such legendary treasures. If hopes based on myth, such as finding paradise or absolute riches in the New World, had effectively passed, so had even such "realistic" hopes as the expectation of finding a northwest passage to the Far East. America, by 1650, simply had come to be known too well.

In fact, many Europeans had begun to discuss the New World in highly negative terms. So many exploratory expeditions had returned home, if they returned home at all, with nothing of value and no profit to their sponsors that some could see little to justify continuing such efforts. So many settlers had found not happiness, peace and comfort in America but rather sickness, hunger, cold, conflict and death that some argued against continued colonization. As many of the original sources in this book demonstrate, America was a violent place where Europeans not only inflicted suffering on the native inhabitants, but where they also encountered forms of brutality unknown in the Old World. In fact, what Howard Mumford Jones termed the "anti-image" of America became popular in Europe—a counter to the highly positive image that had driven men to engage in voyages of exploration and expeditions of discovery and conquest.[3] Such an anti-image could only develop after Europeans had experienced certain realities of life in America. By 1650, if they did not yet possess a complete vision of the nature of the New World, Europeans at least had a sense of much of the reality with which they would have to deal in the future.

## Notes

1 Edmund S. Morgan, *The Birth of the Republic* (Chicago, 1956), 8.
2 See Frederick Jackson Turner, "The Significance of the Frontier in American History," *American Historical Association Annual Report for 1893* (Washington, DC, 1894), 199–227.
3 Howard Mumford Jones, "The Anti-Image," *O Strange New World: American Culture: The Formative Years* (New York, 1964), 35–70. See also Henry Steele Commager and Elmo Giordanetti, *Was America a Mistake? An Eighteenth-Century Controversy* (New York, 1967) for a collection of eighteenth-century commentaries emphasizing both the positive and the negative consequences of European colonization of the New World.

# INDEX

Illustrations are indicated by bold page numbers.

Lightning Source UK Ltd.
Milton Keynes UK
UKOW05f0608220114

224994UK00001B/16/P